The
Ethical
Imperative

The
Ethical
Imperative

■

Why Moral Leadership
Is Good Business

JOHN DALLA COSTA

PERSEUS BOOKS

Reading, Massachusetts

Library of Congress Catalog Card Number: 99-61539

ISBN 0-7382-0130-8

Perseus Books is a member of the Perseus Books Group

Cover design by Suzanne Heiser

1 2 3 4 5 6 7 8 9 -MA- 01   00   99   98   97

Visit us on the World Wide Web at
http://www.aw.com/gb

Perseus Books are available at special discounts for bulk purchases in the U.S. by corporations, institutions, and other organizations.
For more information, please contact
the Special Markets Department at HarperCollins Publishers,
10 East 53rd Street, New York, NY 10022, or call 1-212-207-7528

In memory of Dietrich Bonhoeffer
and
With love to Lucinda Vardey

CONTENTS

ACKNOWLEDGMENTS

My thoughts for this book were like a tangle of bramble bush until a spark fell onto the dry and thorny confusion and ignited a flame. The source of that spark was Professor Hans Küng. My first and deepest thanks are to Dr. Küng, for his inspiration, as well as the great courtesy he extended during my visit with him in Tübingen. My original encounter with Dr. Küng was made possible by Dr. Julia Ching. She and her husband, Professor Willard Oxtoby, have since become friends, and to both I offer my heartfelt thanks.

Before this book was an idea, Don Loney of HarperCollins expressed a commitment to publish me in Canada. And from an outline, Nicholas Philipson of Perseus Books bought the U.S. rights. I thank them both, for their confidence, support and suggestions, as well as for practicing the type of collaborative strategic partnership that is the hallmark of smart, trust-building companies. I also want to thank Meg Taylor for an artful edit, reflecting her own insight and belief in this project, and Gerald Rich for perspicacious proofreading.

Bruce Westwood and Hilary Stanley of Westwood Creative Artists managed and supported me throughout this process. I thank them both for getting back to me—so often. Martin Myers and Alan Middleton took time from their busy schedules to read an early draft of the manuscript. I am very grateful for their suggestions and criticisms, not to mention their friendship.

Several people assisted me without necessarily knowing it. An unrelated comment by Professor Jack Costello, SJ, sharpened my conviction and largely set the tone for this writing. Professor Stephen Dunn, OP, helped me move up the very slippery ethics learning curve. And Ric Young, in his enthusiasm for this book, has been nudging me to completion by preselling it for months.

One person has known the why wrapped in the how inside the what I was doing. A very special thank you to my wife, Lucinda Vardey.

DISCLOSURE

Like it or not, the global economy is pushing us all closer together. We may be citizens of a country, members of a specific community, adherents to a particular religion, but we are increasingly joint participants—as workers and consumers of products and information—of a single, interwoven, interdependent economy. Yet, while the structures of this global commerce grow ever deeper roots, the sense of larger human community remains fragile and tentative. This means that the impulse to exploit, profit and selfishly advance is developing much faster than the cohesion and mutuality of the community necessary to temper these excesses of individuality. With the economy affecting the entire globe, the stakes are as high as they can be. The option, therefore, of not attending to the formation of a global community is untenable. A global ethic for the global economy may be difficult to fathom in the context of a world torn and troubled, but it is an inevitability for every nation's now commonly shared future.

Any discussion of ethics deserves to begin with full disclosure. I am first of all a free-marketeer, but one convinced that the free market can and must do better. No other system has spread its benefits as widely as the free market. But this does not mean that it is a perfect system, or that it is optimally and coherently applied. Ten years ago, for example, Chalmers Johnston explained some of the unique attributes of the

Japanese Confucian-based free-market model. More recently, Charles Hampden-Turner wrote about the seven free-market systems in the worldwide economy, each with characteristics reflecting diverse social needs and cultural histories. The market economy is free in part because it is flexible. It can be adapted, and it evolves. My point, and most basic argument, is that the economy is a wonderful invention, *but it must be managed as an instrument of humanity, and never the other way round.*

My second disclosure is that I make my living consulting to some of the largest and most successful companies on the planet. Since 1991, I have worked with Sony, Procter & Gamble, the Canadian Imperial Bank of Commerce, Shell, Hewlett-Packard, Bell Canada, General Mills and Motorola, among others. My bread is buttered by big companies, and during the turbulent years since 1991 I have watched many struggle with issues of strategy, performance, human resource development, as well as the shifting obligations of reputation. In the course of working with CEOs, leading training programs and participating on implementation teams, I have seen first-hand both the most inspiring potential and the most undermining inanity that make such companies so enigmatic.

My third admission is that despite my access to big business, and my affinity for the free market, I am actually a corporate drop-out. In 1991 I left the marketing and advertising company where I served as CEO. Since then, only about a third of my working time has been devoted to consulting. The balance has been divided between writing—with the research and reflection that entails—and the formal study of theology. The latter is what provides me with the greatest satisfaction and joy.

Not surprisingly, these experiences, lessons and beliefs underpin this book. I recognize that achieving a global ethic for the global economy remains a very difficult task, one that is undertaken on the knife edge between audacity and foolhardiness. Nobel Prize–winning economists disagree among themselves about the essential dynamics and shape of the free market. Philosophers and saints have devoted lifetimes of study and debate without resolving the issue of a universal human ethics. And so far, only Harold Innis and Marshall McLuhan have earned any credibility for unraveling the implications of globalization.

A final, if obvious, disclosure is that this project required me to skim lessons from many disciplines without mastering any one of them.

Experts in each of the disciplines from which I borrowed will no doubt cringe at some of the implications, generalizations and conclusions that, despite trepidation, I have nonetheless drawn. Painfully aware of my deficiencies, I continued stone-skipping across this ocean of knowledge because the reality we are confronting is so radically new, and so complex, that it is beyond the scope of any single discipline to fully discern and adequately resolve. Specialization is an incredible contributor to the knowledge and economic wealth of our world, but it also extends and reinforces the compartmentalization that makes so many of our global problems intractable. To move ahead, in ethics as well as in business, we need a new synthesis, a new framework. This book is my contribution to that still rickety but essential construction project.

For this subject matter to be meaningful, disclosures should not end with the author. If this book is to work, I hope that readers too will reflect on their assumptions and beliefs. Too many of us have put too much faith in business books that, like diet bestsellers, promise results that our common sense warns are unachievable. Again, my consulting and research in these last few years has confirmed that many people already hold great, but largely untapped, wisdom within themselves. Often, individuals have grown wise through the great pain of corporate reengineering and social restructuring. Rarely articulated, this wisdom resides not in the mind but in the unease and sorrow of the bones. Indeed, it has been at the bone level that the confidence and context for this book have taken shape. Many people I encountered are bone-tired, working harder and longer, but with less security and much less hope than ever before. The weariness extends to CEOs and senior executives, some of whom feel that they are running flat out on a treadmill that is speeding up even as it is going nowhere. It is in their bones that so many people who retained their jobs feel sadness for those who lost theirs. It is in their bones that they worry about the prospects for their children. And it is in their bones that they regret making business decisions demanded by the bottom line that are at cross purposes with their beliefs about family, community and spirituality.

There will be times when the arguments framed in this book may seem puzzling, unconventional or even far-fetched, for it is a vast and uncharted topic. Your rational judgment in these cases may be absolutely right, but before dismissing what the mind may find uncomfortable or unrealistic, consult your bones. As I had to learn in writing this book, readers too may have to test the evidence and implications at the marrow-level sensibility of their own human wisdom. How does it feel in your gut? What does your intuition tell you? Do not stop at just asking whether the data are correct. Ask whether the flow and conclusion feel right. Any project as all-encompassing as a global ethic is fraught with challenges and contradictions. Rational resistance in these circumstances is rampant. Yet, from my experience, while the quest for a global ethic seems to defy logic, it seems at the same time to align with some of our most deeply held beliefs. The trap we must avoid is seeking or settling for a quick solution. Instead, we must each take greater responsibility for exercising the intuitive sensibility that already knows—or will at least come to recognize—what is right. In being global, the economy now affects us all. In being global, its corresponding ethic requires from all of us the input and creativity to make it work. This leads to a final disclosure, or perhaps more accurately, a revelation. Although it may sound like a tired truism, we are, indeed, all in this together.

INTRODUCTION

W hat are you working on?" For the last few years, I have answered that question knowing that "business ethics" is a concept about which everyone is ready to express an opinion. So visceral is their reaction that most people start explaining their views before I can offer either detail or caveat about my own work. Such intrusiveness is understandable because business intrudes so forcefully into every aspect of modern life. The bottom line is now as much a feature of government, education, the arts and even religion as it is of business. And with that logic comes the pressure to perform, to reengineer, restructure, compete and make a profit. Business thinking has become so pervasive that when something goes wrong in our society—and much does—the clunky footprint of free-market practices is inevitably found at the scene of the crime. The very combination of the two words *business* and *ethics* challenges people's experience and can elicit fear.

The range of response has been surprisingly broad. As people commented on my project, they revealed their passions, beliefs and ideologies. The cynics dismissed the whole topic as an oxymoron. Those to the right of my banker friends explained to me why communism had failed. Many of the people who have worked internationally felt compelled to share nightmare stories of under-the-table arm-twisting in Paris or of corrupt intermediaries in Kuala Lumpur. Bribes, don't you know, are a tax-deductible business expense in Denmark and Germany. Business is business, I was counseled. So why not leave it at that?

I had always understood this issue to be controversial but I had underestimated the emotion it could arouse. While some people attacked me for being naive, others challenged my credentials for undertaking such a mission. A few of my fellow students in theology school proved to be among my toughest critics, turning their despair and antipathy towards business into a judgment that my soul was probably beyond redemption. Much lively debate aside, the vast majority encountering my work were genuinely struck by the possibility of what I was exploring. For the businesspeople among them, including CEOs, there was also an impatience to share their experience, explain their beliefs and often question the strategy and usefulness of what I was doing.

These disparate voices helped enormously because they reinforced to me that business ethics, with its endless questions and messy judgments, is an even more vital issue than I had perceived. More than that, the reactions of these many friends, colleagues, teachers, professionals and businesspeople opened me to the deeper task of including these varied, sometimes contradictory views in the final product. This book has not become a chameleon that appeases all tastes. Rather, by virtue of these many points of view, the book now better reflects that defining challenge of modern ethics to find relevance and practicality across diversity and even discontinuity. In other words, difference of opinion is not an enemy to be conquered but a lesson to be learned. What I had planned to be a thoughtful how-to resource is now a critique and a challenge, as well as a set of models for implementing solutions. And what I had conceived as a business book exploring the application of ethics is now a work about how business mirrors who we are as a society, and the beliefs that we actually live by as individuals.

Nike is one of many companies having a social conscience imposed on it. This organization creates products for the imagination as well as for the feet, but not many remember that it has also overcome enormous odds. A small start-up using a waffle iron to create rubber soles, Nike beat out globally entrenched giants Adidas, Puma, Bata and Converse. Even after its swoosh symbol became ubiquitous, Nike stumbled against Reebok (remember aerobic shoes?) and regained its growth trajectory only after a tough battle of competitive wits. I run, and although I do not wear as many logos as Tiger Woods, I believe that Nike deserves its status as one of the premier global brands and the profits and reputation that go with its marketing smarts and gumption.

Yet for all its momentum, Nike has responded with such insouciance to questions about labor abuses at the off-shore companies to which it contracts manufacturing that it is starting to stink like an overused pair of running shoes. I do not want to oversimplify the issues, and will return to this story in a later chapter. The points I want to make now are that, first, Nike pledged at its 1996 annual meeting to set up a formal audit system to check on its contractors, and, second, this decision was forced on it by its own shareholders. Figuring out how the very people being enriched by Nike turned on it to demand action that could cost them future profits is an exercise in understanding the power of dissonant voices.

The initial, faint clamorings about Nike came in the early 1990s from the human rights extremists who are generally anti-institution and anti-business. These were the tree-huggers in the early days of environmentalism, the fanatic fringe who did not so much challenge as reject the mainstream. But in our wired world, the concerns on the periphery eventually become rumblings in the general media. Under the scrutiny of articles in *Newsweek* and in the glare of special reports by *NBC Nightly News,* the passion of a few became the outrage of many. Local churches throughout the U.S. and Canada started a post-card campaign politely requesting CEO Phil Knight to do more to ensure the fair treatment of workers in Korea and China. Shareholders took turns at the microphone at the annual general meeting to demand action. And Nike finally responded by hiring former U.S. ambassador to the UN Andrew Young to conduct an audit.

For a company so used to being a step ahead of its market, Nike was caught flat-footed. The point is not just that Nike stumbled, but that it took many voices, expressing different beliefs, from across the full range of ideologies, to start the company on its reforms. There are several lessons in this. One is that ethical questions exert themselves even on companies that do not necessarily acknowledge ethics as a dimension of business. This issue is thus neither an oxymoron nor a utopian ideal but a practical pressure requiring a strategic response. Another lesson is that the status quo is never fixed. Not very long ago, the concerns of ecologists were as irrelevant to business planners as those of ethicists are today. "Green" has gone from being a disparagement to becoming a badge that no smart company would risk being without. As Nike learned, and as I will argue further, ethics are similarly en route to becoming a strategic imperative. In this sea change, the companies that do not embrace ethics will be as vulnerable as those that eschewed efficiency or quality or customer service.

The third lesson is that the spreading concern for ethics is not a preoccupation of the left or right. Instead of a constituency, ethics represent a continuity, shared across a wide spectrum of social, economic, managerial and religious positions. It is not that everyone everywhere shares the same definition of right or wrong. It is that everyone everywhere discerns the distinction. Whether you believe ethics are a contrivance of the "selfish gene," an automatic response to an intricate social conditioning or the construct humans have inherited from a divine creator, the orientation to do the right thing is a powerful and defining dimension of human nature.

It took many voices to wear Nike down, and the fourth lesson is that each was both distinct and essential for the others. The radical pricked the conscience; the media painted the picture; the activist mass exerted social and economic pressure; and the shareholders used the power and authority of their holdings to demand action. A very important realization for me was that the final result could not have been realized by any group singly. My history as a businessman has been to get on with solving the problem. And my usual response has been impatience—towards the radical voice for not being pragmatic, toward the middle mass for not being informed and towards the business decision makers for not being visionary. But I now see that the functional benefit of each voice is not to perform the whole story but to act out a specific role.

Recognizing that many voices are needed to move society's consciousness forward caused me to refine the voice of this book. My original formula was to use the learning accumulated in my consulting practice to build the business logic for ethical renewal. I had done this in previous books: describe the problem, posit the solution and provide an overwhelming rationale to validate my conclusions. What is GE doing? Why did IBM screw up? What can we learn from Microsoft or the Japanese? Cut and paste quotes from Tom Peters, Stephen Covey and Jack Welch. Add one or two anecdotes from personal experience. My consulting work involves teaching as well as planning, motivation as well as strategy, so this book about ethics would be a synthesis. I would bring together concepts from disparate disciplines and use my familiarity with strategic language to convince business of the appropriateness of the message.

As I immersed myself in the material, researching the topic, interviewing specialists and enrolling as a part-time student of theology, I realized that the usual business book formula was going to be inadequate. I came to understand that to treat ethics like other business topics was to invite a "flavor of the month" response. Ethics are different because, unlike "total quality," "leadership" or "learning," they are radically essential. They are not a new skill but a profound new sensibility that changes everything. And they are not optional. Emotionally, I could not help getting angry, directing my impatience at those doubting companies and businesspeople who demand to have ethical practices justified to them. Who could survive in an ethical vacuum? Even the hardest of hard-core capitalists need the protection of the law and the mutuality of contracts to exist at all. Rather than convincing business practitioners of the need for greater ethical consciousness, businesspeople resisting an ethical context should be apologizing to society for the mismanagement of the environment, the still widespread inequality of women and minorities, and the inhuman treatment of reengineered individuals and downsized communities. I finally found the voice for this book, and it is more challenging than accommodating, more impatient than evolutionary, and more simple common sense than repetitive case histories.

My impatience does not blind me to the great difficulty of framing a global ethic for the global economy. Clearly, one of the refracted lessons of McLuhan is that we are indeed a global village but not a homogeneous one. If anything, despite the familiarity and instant access made possible by technology, differences between cultures, countries, regions and even neighborhoods seem sharper and increasingly fundamental. However, the imperative we cannot escape is exactly that of resolving the tension between one world and its many parts. The underpinnings of the economy are now inextricably shared, as are the consequences of energy depletion, pollution and resource mismanagement. The presumption of a global ethic is warranted precisely because the problems are so outrageous.

To seek a global norm is not to neglect local or personal ones. The network of principles and behavior that makes up an ethical orientation operates both vertically and horizontally. It is personal, but as philosopher John Macmurray has pointed out, "the personal life is essentially a life of relations between people." Ethics may thus represent the character and choices of the individual, but they are expressed and given dimension only in public behavior. Although ethics flow from deep personal beliefs, the value of an ethical commitment is realized only in its effect on others and on society. This has always been true, but because of the global economy and global sensibility, the gulf between self and society has never been greater. Ours is the paradox of "universal intimacy" in which the ethical construct is no longer limited to "I" and "thou," or "us" and "them," but now must embrace the most comprehensive of "we."

In practice this means that Nike's failings are our failings. When workers are abused in faraway plants it is we—the ones who wear the shoes and buy the imagery and worship the athletes—who are stained by the unfairness. This is the culpability of being informed, the inescapable responsibility of participating while knowing. In the heyday of consumption, buying was a party, and more buying the objective. There were no worries about deforestation or landfills or sweatshops. Now nearly every purchase carries with it some consciousness of consequence. We still buy, but with recognition. We still consume, but with a greater awareness of impending limitation.

The idea for this book came from an unexpected encounter with Swiss theologian Hans Küng. Dr. Küng taught at Massey College at the University of Toronto in the 1980s, and he stopped over for several days in North America on his way to Tübingen from Asia. I contrived my way into a lunch for which my wife, Lucinda Vardey, had received an invitation. Expecting a large venue for the distinguished guest, I was slightly embarrassed to find only a group of twelve. There were two or three teachers, the master and several fellows of the college, a member of the clergy and spiritual writers like my wife. I was the only businessperson, a chicken trying to swim with the ducks. As fate would have it, Lucinda and I were chosen to sit next to Dr. Küng.

In a brief talk, Dr. Küng explained to the group what he had been up to. He, like Picasso, saw his life's work in increments of ten years. First he had plumbed various aspects of modern Christian theology, then devoted himself to comparative studies of the world's great religious traditions, and now, retired from teaching, was focusing on defining and fostering a global ethic. This is a passion as well as an area of study for Dr. Küng. With academic and spiritual leaders from other traditions he had convened the Parliament of the World's Religions, which in 1993 published a declaration on the common values supporting a common ethic. Dr. Küng had also recently founded a center for global ethics from which he would be carrying on his studies, lobbying and writing.

Dr. Küng sees the divisions brought about by spiritual sensibility to be even more dangerous than those of politics and the economy. He argued a very simple formula: There can be no peace in the world without peace among the great religions. There can be no peace among the great religions without deepening understanding of each other. There can be no deepening of understanding until each fully respects the other.

My interpretation was that the business of religion is failing our more compressed world in exactly the same way as unethical business is. Old dogmatic divisions and arbitrary institutional boundaries are defeating the sense of unity and interdependence that this crowded, busy, industrializing world so needs. As Dr. Küng asked us to consider how our own work affected this larger mission, the idea for this book dropped like a rock into the puddle of my creative yearning.

I will explain later how the pressures of the global economy have been diminishing the power and importance of the nation-state. With "missions" and "visions," governments and individuals now approach economics with the same fervor and faith that used to be reserved for religion. Indeed, such critics as Kirkpatrick Sale and Jerry Mander have argued that consumption is fast becoming our only really global religion. I realized, listening to Dr. Küng, that business requires an ethical base not only to fulfill obligations to society but for its own good to offset the confusion and uncertainty of international commerce. Just as one example, the implosion of Barings Bank showed how the ethical impropriety of a single person (compounded by the stupidity of his immediate management group) could bring down a 350-year-old multibillion-dollar institution that handled banking even for the Queen.

As big business gets bigger, as more of the world's economy becomes truly global, the risk of ethical damage grows as well. In his book introducing the Declaration Toward a Global Ethic, Dr. Küng referred to ethics as "a prophylactic against crisis."[1] Business is then both a beneficiary and a potential carrier for a wider ethical consciousness.

This book is constructed to go from thought to action. The early chapters provide an analysis of the current business and social situation, drawing implications that help reconceive the relationship between business and ethics. This involves building an irrefutable business logic for ethics and an inescapable ethics logic for business. Once the rational framework is in place, the middle chapters take the foundational work of Dr. Küng and others and present a new model for a global ethic for the global economy. The focus in this section is on understanding the operational factors that influence the already deep and deepening connection between spiritual and commercial sensibilities. This is not a New Age call to hang crystals in the boardroom but a recognition that the strategic needs for innovation, efficiency and enhanced customer service all depend on the dynamics of relating. The later chapters provide information and support for implementation. Changing company behavior and culture has proven to be very difficult even when the business rationale for transformation is crystal clear. We learned in applying total quality that genuine reinvention happens only when senior management wholeheartedly supports an initiative, when mid-managers and employees are involved, educated and trained, and when the outcome is monitored and measured. The final chapter deals with the obstacles to change and introduces a model that works for both successful transformation and fulfillment of obligations. The progress of this book and the movement from idea to implementation try to fulfill Aristotle's condition that "wisdom is only wisdom if it is of practical use."

Any creative project by definition involves the unexpected. With this idea—mixing business with theology and economics with ethics—I knew the surprises would be even more rapid-fire. Though expecting the unexpected, I was still astonished by some of the forks that appeared on this unmapped road, as well as by some of the turns that I felt compelled to take. The biggest surprise, and most inspiring one, has been my rediscovery of Dietrich Bonhoeffer. A German theologian and Lutheran minister, Bonhoeffer chose to risk his career and life to denounce the antisemitism and idolatry of the Nazi regime. The Aryan clause forbidding Jews to hold jobs in the German civil service was enacted at the beginning of 1933, and by February Bonhoeffer had made a courageous stand on radio, calling the political system corrupt and accusing the state of idolatry.

Persecuted for his words and actions, Bonhoeffer left Germany in the mid-1930s and spent several years visiting America, teaching in England, and even planning a trip to study with Gandhi. With war approaching, he decided to return to his homeland, explaining in a letter to a friend, "I shall have no right to participate in the reconstruction of Christian life in Germany after the war if I do not share the trials of this time with my people." He continued his resistance, not only challenging the Nazis but also painfully questioning the social, religious, learning and artistic institutions within Germany. Bonhoeffer's antiwar activity included "a scheme to help a group of Jews escape to Switzerland in 1941, and a meeting in Sweden in 1942 with the British bishop George Bell at which he tried to secure Allied support for the planned coup against Hitler now known as the Officers' Plot."[2] Arrested in 1943, Bonhoeffer was shuttled between various prisons and concentration camps. He was executed by hanging by special order of Heinrich Himmler, only a few days before the Allies liberated his camp at Flossenburg.

In a brief memoir, G. Leibholz provides a glimpse of the man behind the legend. "In prison and concentration camps, Bonhoeffer greatly inspired by his indomitable courage, his unselfishness and his goodness, all those who came in contact with him. He even inspired the guards with respect, some of whom became so attached to him that they smuggled out of prison his papers and poems written there, and apologized to him for having to lock his door after the round in the courtyard." Bonhoeffer has been lionized for speaking out against a system of evil, yet his letters and poems also reveal him to be fully human, with anguish and doubts simmering just below his convictions and audacity. I had read his *Letters and Papers from Prison,* while still in university. Well after beginning to write this book, I was doing some preparatory reading for one of my theology classes and discovered his *Ethics.*

Immediately, I was struck by the relevance of Bonhoeffer's message and the example of his actions. He had a profound sense of his own Germanness, yet adopted a truly global perspective. He strove in his theology and work for a more ecumenical and holistic response, one that presaged the more recent efforts of scholars to formulate a global ethic. Bonhoeffer also foresaw the dangerous implications of a fanatical adherence to duty, and lashed out at those who assumed that they could divorce their personal morality from their public involvements. He demanded that organizations and institutions—even the most powerful and most sacred—be accountable. Driven by his faith and ideals, Bonhoeffer stressed most of all that ethics must be concrete and practical.

Bonhoeffer's ethics, not to mention his example, are exacting and sometimes troubling, so much so that the German government reversed his conviction for treason only in 1996. My first surprise, then, was finding so much inspiration in his work. The second surprise is that I was so moved by his thinking and example that I decided to use quotes from Bonhoeffer's *Ethics* as epigraphs to each chapter. Bonhoeffer was a Christian. While his work is undoubtably rooted in that tradition, many of his insights are presciently respectful of the cultural diversity that most of us are still trying to accommodate. I have tried to choose passages that neither diminish the centrality of Christ to Bonhoeffer nor proselytize his faith. As you will see, in their most basic values, his ideas contribute to what must be an embracing and multidimensional global ethic.

For businesspeople struggling to keep careers on track and business objectives on target, the wisdom of philosophers and theologians may be interesting but ultimately irrelevant or impractical. How does being ethical make my job easier? Or, more fundamentally, how does being ethical make it easier for me to keep my job? The answer to these questions, like so much else about ethics, is not linear. We must first accept that this is not a topic that will yield any one-minute-manager promises for improving success or guaranteeing results. This ambiguity, however, is not particular to moral weightings; instead it reflects the complexities of business itself. Several generations of formulae and matrices from management gurus and consultants have yet to solve the riddle for effective, and lasting, corporate renewal. We should know by now that there are no instant solutions for deeply entrenched problems. We should also recognize that, because business is now a big part of life, we need the wisdom of human life to manage and give context to the now dominating economic reality. An ethical orientation is of substantial value because it exercises the very skills of discernment and judgment that managers need to unravel the deepening paradox of competition and success. But the real reason for developing this orientation is not just what we gain from being ethical, but in realizing what we lose—in economic, social, natural and personal terms—by succumbing to irresponsibility.

CHAPTER ONE

ORIENTATION

Do dare what is right, not swayed by the whim of the moment.
Bravely take hold of the real, not dallying now with what might be.
Not in the flight of ideas, but only in action is freedom.
Make up your mind and come out into the tempest of living.

Dietrich Bonhoeffer, "Stations on the Way to Freedom"

The global economy holds much greater potential than its critics think, and much more disruption than its advocates admit. By definition, a global economy is as big as it can get. This means that the scale of both the opportunity and the consequences are at an apex. Like a St. Anselm's proof for the existence of God applied to business, the global economy has become the human activity greater than which nothing else can be conceived. But in the advance to this final economic frontier, the global market has also by definition hit its limits. Nothing can be bigger than the global economy, but big is not infinite. So in the midst of our ultimate economic expansion we are also confronting an inevitable narrowing of choice. Most companies and policy makers are still accelerating toward opportunity, not recognizing, or ignoring, the fast-approaching walls that demarkate it as finite.

Granted, this is a great big market. But now all our eggs are in one economic basket. And it is the only basket we have.

The eggs are also quickly adding up. Globally, the economy has been growing approximately 3.5 percent a year for the past several years, and the International Monetary Fund expects it to expand at 4.5 percent a year until at least 2002. Planetary production is now worth more than $21 trillion. Of this antlike industriousness, more than 20 percent now involves global trade. Numbers are inadequate for painting the real picture of such complex interactions, but they do reveal several trends that are giving impetus to the rapid development and turmoil of globalization. As a percentage of the world economy, trade between nations has doubled from 10 percent in 1975. The World Watch Institute, which compiles data on economic development and environmental damage, points out that "trade increased more than twice as fast as world economic output . . . a reflection of the growing integration of the global economy."[1] Beyond garnering dollars, international trade also stimulates aspiration, providing ideas for consumption, information for new products, and standards for quality and productivity that affect the direction and efficiency of any domestic economy.

Industrialized nations worry about being the dumping ground for products made in low-wage countries, but the global economy's momentum is actually going the other way. "Since the mid-eighties, imports into developing nations have grown faster than those into industrial ones," and they are projected "to rise almost twice as much as those of industrial nations."[2] The global interactions of trade and interchange of ideas are also being driven by what the United Nations Conference on Trade and Development (UNCTAD) calls the "complex integration" strategies of multinational enterprises, most of which are based in industrialized countries. These companies "account for a staggering one-third of world private productive assets," and "according to the UNCTAD, sales by [multinationals] outside their country of origin were $5.5 trillion in 1992."[3] Surprisingly, while the value pie of planetary economic output is growing, the job pie is growing considerably more slowly. In another study, the UNCTAD reports that, despite its robust growth, the global economy was not creating "enough jobs to reduce unemployment in industrial countries, or to eliminate poverty in less developed ones."[4] This means that while companies are enjoying larger desserts, more and more workers are going without. Not only are jobs lagging behind output but, as *The Economist* reports, "the differences in income per head between the seven richest and seven poorest countries has nearly doubled from 20 times in 1965 to 39 times in 1995."

The global economy, with its unimaginable volumes and endlessly sticky details, presents us with brand-new paradoxes. The churn of mobile finance and the pressure points of industrial competition are at a level and on a stage far removed from our everyday lives. But the implications are immediate and intimate. The computerized movement of anonymous money affects individual jobs in specific communities. MIT economist Paul Krugman argues that our obsession with global competitiveness is misguided, "that national living standards are overwhelmingly determined by domestic factors."[5] He may be correct in his analysis without being right. The global economy is as much a social condition as a system for trade. It operates not only as a market but as a benchmark, meaning that the productivity, wages and regulations of one region profoundly affect expectations and possibilities in all others. In the experience of the millions of workers in North America, Korea, Australia and increasingly Europe who have been downsized and reengineered, globalization is both the rationale for their displacement and the standard they must produce against. Anthony Giddens, professor of sociology at Cambridge, writes that "globalization is not just an 'out there' phenomenon. It refers not only to the emergence of large scale systems but to transformations in the texture of everyday life. It is an 'in here' phenomenon, affecting even the intimacies of personal identity."[6] By interconnection of cause and effect, the global is indeed local. But more than that, global is now also incredibly particular, specific and private.

The global economy is primarily a free market. I recognize that there are many variations on the free-market theme—China's approach is different from that of the U.S., France's is different from Britain's and Korea's is different from Japan's. They all, however, share some essential features. Markets everywhere are based on competitiveness. But competitiveness, whether based on low wages, high productivity or new technology, means there will be winners and losers. The great advances in living standards throughout the 1970s, '80s and '90s in Japan, Korea, Taiwan, Singapore and other developing countries paralleled a flattening of per capita income growth in North America. Despite an almost 15 percent longer work week, and almost four fewer days' vacation a year, median family income in the U.S. increased only $66 between 1973 and 1993. Such tradeoffs happen not only between countries but within them as well. Those workers who have the skills and context to add the most value to global competitors are reaping the rewards, while those who do not are being left further and further behind. By just one recent measure, CEOs in the U.S. realized a 56 percent increase in compensation in 1996 compared with only 3 percent for the average worker. The total yearly pay of the managerial class is now 207 times that of a typical employee. For Amitai Etzioni, sociology professor at George Washington University, "economic globalization appears to be associated with new kinds of social exclusion."[7]

Hope, apprehension and heartache seem to be the bottom-heavy continuum of the global economy. Yet, although we all have personal stakes in it, none of us has really had any voice in creating the global economy, or in directing its momentum. As Stanford University sociologist Martin Albrow notes, this globalization "has been an outcome rather than a goal."[8] Business opportunity has an inevitable outward thrust. Rapid developments in communications and transportation technology, intersecting with the broad political and ideological changes of the 1990s, made possible the expansion of that thrust to the planetary perimeter. We are therefore global as producers, consumers and managers—as economic units and wealth extractors—but not yet by social design or through conscious desire for any wider human engagement. This is important, and often forgotten. The economy may be global, but people are not—or at least not yet. So whereas the shape and priorities of the global economy may be clear, the form and substance of the larger global community is still an open issue, with largely unasked questions.

Like all human inventions, the global economy represents an imperfect potential. There are downsides to its progress, liabilities that in the short term people have been willing to accept for the benefits of new jobs, better income and a higher standard of living. The most obvious problem is environmental destruction. The global economy preys on the global ecology, and this, it turns out, is where the abrupt halt of limitation is first encountered. Two world wars in this century prompted the creation of the United Nations. The fifty-year track record of such high-level global diplomacy has so far been mixed. In contrast, the first waves of the global environmental crisis in the 1970s prompted a much more grassroots coalition. Greenpeace, the World Wildlife Fund and other groups, outraged at the scale of resource abuse and waste caused by massive industrialization, have created the first spontaneous global social institutions. Even in countries like Japan, where socialization has supported the compact between government and business, the willingness to assume more environmental damage for economic gain has run out. This, then, is yet another duality. The promise of the global economy has united all humans in a fierce competitiveness. But the problems of the global economy are beginning to unite all humans in a tentative cooperation.

The pull and potential of the global economy is immense. For innumerable millions, the opportunity to participate through even menial labor often provides the only way to rise above abject poverty. However, while globe-straddling companies operate to one bottom line—profit—people in different countries have markedly divergent views on the benefits and costs of global economic activity. Populations in highly developed economies see the need for environmental protection; populations in developing countries see the environment as a vehicle for much needed jobs. North Americans and Europeans bemoan globalization for pulling wages lower and taking jobs out of their markets; in China and India even the lowest-paying industrial job is a valued step up. So volatile is this ebb and flow of opportunity and loss that newly developed countries like Korea and Taiwan are already experiencing the displacement of jobs migrating to lower-cost labor markets. Perspectives on the global economy are positive or negative depending on a rather random intermingling of position, location and timing.

This highlights how, for something so unifying, the global economy is also incredibly divisive. Notwithstanding the interconnections of trade, Harvard political science professor Samuel Huntington sees the world becoming more fissured, with cultures and civilizations ¦ each other to retain their distinctiveness in the face of deperso globalization. He writes: "Economic exchange brings people into contact; it does not bring them into agreement. Historically, it has often produced a deeper awareness of the differences between peoples and stimulated fears. Trade between countries produces conflict as well as profit."[9] During the past fifty years, economic tensions were mostly subsumed within the political and ideological conflict between East and West, communism and capitalism. Peace has resulted, less from prosperity than from fear of nuclear war. With the lifting of political worries, economic friction has become more pronounced. Lester Thurow, economics professor at MIT, writes that "global trade is dominated by a fault line, with Japanese trade surpluses on one side, and American trade deficits on the other side. Like real fault lines, this one has long been known—it has existed for more than two decades— and as time passes, the pressures on the fault are building up."[10] Such has been the fractious language between ideological allies and interdependent trading partners. Even more acrimonious and alienating are tensions over trade with China and other developing countries.

The end of the cold war, it was hoped, would pay out in a "peace dividend." With the simultaneous advance of the global economy, people have instead been forced to pay a "productivity penalty." Only since the fall of communism have we experienced in North America and Europe a cycle of economic recovery unrelated to job growth. And only since the fall of communism have we seen corporate restructuring affect the white-collar, highly educated, mid-management ranks. Obviously, the rapid expansion of the workforce, with millions of highly skilled and educated eastern Europeans and former members of the Soviet Union joining the market economy, has resulted in a corresponding dilution in the leverage and value of every other worker in this now integrated system. But the scale of layoffs, with the legions of highly competent and effective workers still being fired during a stretch of record corporate profits, suggests a return to the excesses of the market economy, which gave impetus to communism in the first place. The global economy is thus a flowering of the better ideology, but without any of the institutional competition to pressure intelligent modulation and improvement.

As the momentum of the economy has swung to the global, there has been a corresponding swing in effectiveness and sense of control away from the local. This shift destabilizes systems and culture at the community level. In a report of the United Nations Research Institute for Social Development, research director Cynthia Hewitt de Alcantara writes: "The declining capacity of most national governments to provide social services constitutes an additional element in the progressive disprotection of many groups which could formerly count on certain minimum social benefits."[11] If the global economy is not the direct cause, it is certainly the direct excuse for dismantling social programs. It is not just coincidence that social safety nets were put in place in the U.S., Canada, Europe and Japan in those years when the threat of communism was greatest, when Soviet capacities in cutting-edge ventures like space exploration were strongest and when socialist expansion in Asia and Latin America seemed certain. That social structure—essential during communism, expendable after it—is now argued to be a drag on competitiveness. Governments everywhere, prodded by markets, are reengineering and downsizing the public sector with the same fervor that has already been applied to so many private enterprises.

The scramble to globalize, and the threat of an economy controlled largely from outside national boundaries, has produced paranoia within and between countries. In the consuming drive for competitiveness, people have come to regard social institutions as having the same role as business. It is illogical to assume that the business model of selfish advancement can attend to the people that the economy itself has disadvantaged, yet again and again governments, prodded by markets, have retooled social systems to do less for the most needy and more for the economically productive. The argument, now widely accepted even by populist-championing Democratic, Liberal and Labor governments, is that such social beneficence is no longer affordable. But these cuts affecting the least able are being made exactly when society, particularly in North America, is at its wealthiest. During the last decade, the value of stocks on North American markets has created more than $700 billion in new wealth, and corporations have achieved a string of record profits. The global economy has therefore at the same time raised awareness of the frailty of our local situation and provided the justification for dissociating from any local obligations. Put another way, we who have more goods than ever before also seem to have accepted more reasons to be less generous.

The disconnection from the local to preserve a competitive place in the global is resulting in what Giddens calls detraditionalization. If neighbors are expendable to the cause of global economic advancement, then so too are the ideas, rituals and beliefs that once bound together and defined local communities. Global brands like Sony, Disney, Coke and Mercedes project a set of values and aspirations that engage people and stimulate their imaginations regardless of their culture, country or social class. It is not as simple as saying that people are equally greedy. But in the desire to consume, in their haste to have a share of the modern lifestyle, people everywhere are forsaking who they are for what they can have. Johan Galtung, professor of peace studies at universities in the U.S. and Germany, writes that "globalization means mono culture, less diversity, less symbiosis, less resilience."[12] Peter Senge, business professor and director of the Center for Organizational Learning at MIT, adds: "Just like we are destroying bio-diversity, we are destroying cultural diversity, the 'gene pool' for cultural evolution."[13] The tradeoff between global and local is the tradeoff of comfort for culture. So far, comfort is winning.

This does not mean that people are automatically surrendering cultural affiliation for global citizenship. In many ways, the opposite is happening. The growing fundamentalism around the world, whether Islamic in the Middle East or militia in middle America, represents the reaction of distinct, threatened cultures to this homogenizing onslaught. Huntington quotes sociologist Roland Robertson, who notes that while the world is being shrunk and unified by technology, production and consumption, "there is an exacerbation of civilizational, societal and ethnic self-consciousness."[14] But retreat, no matter how understandable, is never a win. Globalization is moving forward with all the resources and wealth of the market economy. *The Economist* in 1989 projected advertising and marketing spending to total $620 billion, or "$120 for every single person in the world." David Korten, a former Harvard Business School professor now working with aid agencies in developing markets in Asia, puts this spending in perspective: "Overall, corporations are spending well over half as much per capita to create corporation-friendly consumers as the $207 per capita ($33 for Southern countries) the world spends on public education. Furthermore, growth in advertising far outpaces increases in education spending."[15] Proselytizing of this magnitude is hard to resist, particularly when the inducement to consume is directed, as it is by McDonald's, Disney, Star Wars and so many others, at the world's children. Although education may encourage a cultural resistance to globalization, many are often already hooked into the rhythms and patterns of the global economy before they even get to school.

Although menacing, and the fodder isolationists use to support their position, globalization, as Albrow points out, has "no inherent direction or end point," and "we don't know when we will reach it or where it is."[16] Consistent with being a new reality, the global is destructive of the old reality. Not only that, but it is in flux, still evolving, still seeking to find its own equilibrium. Within such great unpredictability, pressures for uniformity and fragmentation are at work. There is no linear sense of what will be. So people experience an upheaval in both their sense of security and their identity. This is obviously dangerous. "It means," explains Ralf Dahrendorf of Oxford University, and a former director of the London School of Economics, "that people have no sense of belonging, no sense of commitment, and therefore no reason to observe the law or the values which support such a sense."[17] The global economy tempest uproots us and renders us isolated and anonymous. It heightens our longing for community and personal context but also allows us an invisibility from which it is easy, and often self-advancing, to avoid obligations and cut corners.

This, then, is the central argument of this chapter: *the global economy, with its momentum, inconsistency and amorality, is developing much more rapidly and substantially than the sense of global community with which to moderate, interpret and ground it.* Put another way, the global economy unleashes all that is selfish about human nature without a global sensibility necessary for the well-being of humans and our natural environment. Developing this sensibility is admittedly a tricky exercise, requiring of people a degree of wisdom commensurate with the scientific and technological expertise that made this global reality a possibility in the first place. It also requires unanimity in a time of great fragmentation, and a belief in community in a time that worships individualism. There are, however, reasons for optimism. "The global interconnectedness of human relations," according to Albrow, "brings awareness of the globe in its train and makes it possible to conceptualize global risks."[18] As in other instances of rapid change in human history, a new situation upsets the status quo but eventually creates its own institutions and framework. The global economy now demands a similar maturation of the global community, and indeed provides it with the technology, expertise and resources for customizing a comprehensive social response.

A second reason for optimism is that business itself is awakening, even if just tentatively, to the need for a wider community structure to contain the burgeoning global economy. Thurow points out that "in tomorrow's global economy, there will be very tough economic competition, but the common environment will require global cooperation. Because, if we are going to mutually prosper, we are going to have to cooperate to create a global economy that works. We will need rules—new systems for managing trade—because the old economic arrangements are not going to work anymore."[19] The chaos of a free-for-all free market is ultimately inefficient, so there is good reason for the business players in the global economy to recognize the need for more intermarket and intercompany cooperation. The scandalous collapse of Barings Bank is but one dramatic case. A centuries-old global institution of solid reputation fell into bankruptcy as the result of ethical improprieties of a single employee, Nick Leeson. Obviously, many more factors contributed to the $1.7-billion trading fraud (some of which will be explored later), but, as business journalist John Plender reports, "many of those involved in investigating and picking up the pieces after the Barings fiasco believe that the competitive nature of the relationship between the Osaka Stock Exchange in Japan and the SIMEX exchange in Singapore prevented a sharing of information about Barings' exposures that would have led to earlier curbs on Leeson's activities."[20] As humans have learned throughout their history, to be singularly selfish is ultimately self-defeating.

Economic institutions, recognizing that corruption undermines not only social stability but the conditions for prosperity, are now bringing pressure to bear on rogue countries and companies. At their 1997 meeting in Hong Kong, officers of the World Bank and the International Monetary Fund announced a crusade against graft. World Bank president James Wolfensohn stated that "a publicly expressed revulsion" in both developing and developed markets demanded "the focus on corruption." The IMF and World Bank have already taken unprecedented action in suspending loans and aid to Kenya and Pakistan because of corruption and human rights abuses there. "What we're finding in the bank," said Wolfensohn, "is that 18 months ago nobody was talking about corruption. Today, it is a subject you can discuss with anybody."[21] In a later chapter we will see that multicountry, multibody initiatives against shady business practices have also been launched by the G7 (now G8) and the Organization for Economic Co-operation and Development (OECD). Ethical considerations are becoming an agenda of mainstream economic institutions. An issue long dismissed as belonging only to a fringe of do-gooders is now being adopted by the heavyweights in suspenders and suits.

While global business is admitting to being hamstrung by unmitigated competition, these agents of the economy are not the ones to lead the global community building. Self-interest, even if it does lead to a cooperative accommodation, is neither the proper nor the authoritative source for a global healing and maturing. Common sense tells us that the entity whose primary objective is profit should not set the rules for group responsibility. Richard von Weizsacker, until 1994 the president of the Federal Republic of Germany, notes: "The market is meant to satisfy our needs; it does that better than any other economic system. But neither [political constitutions nor the market] have any power of integration: constitutions [and the market] cannot provide basic ethical rules for society which are generally respected and desired."[22] Companies changing their business practices have recently discovered the motivating and bonding power of values. Trust, honesty, respect and integrity are some expressions of an ethical orientation, and many companies are trying to incorporate these attributes into their systems and behaviors. Some, like Johnson & Johnson, Hewlett-Packard and Matsushita, have a long and genuine commitment to their values. Nevertheless, these values are not generated by the company but are drawn from the containing community, with its history, culture and beliefs.

Ethics are often presumed to be a rigid set of self-standing rules that, like a business balance sheet, clearly delineate right from wrong, asset from liability. Although they do provide guidance, ethics work more as a living, shifting, dynamic process of reflection for expressing the morality of the community in everyday acts. Professor Joseph L. Badaracco Jr. of the Harvard Business School writes that "the sphere of personal ethical values consists of the duties, commitments and ideals that shape and guide individuals' lives."[23] Duties represent the counterweight to an individual's desires for self-satisfaction. Commitments reflect the ethical reality that although pressures for conformity may be externally imposed, an ethical practice is ultimately a personal choice. And ideals indicate that while we may all generally have a predisposition to discern "right" behavior, we are also dependent on the moral goals of the community for ethical inspiration, context and meaning. Not only are ethics about a personal choice with public consequences, but they also involve a public expectation with personal responsibilities.

Philosopher Thomas Donaldson notes that ethics are both "empirical" and "normative." The first discerns what it *is* that we do. The second instead evaluates what *ought* to be done.[24] In business, it has been much easier to look at and measure the empirical dimension. This is because business has an easier time measuring the concrete, and the inputs for *ought* are necessarily derived from beyond the boundaries of business activity and management decision making. To manage by *ought* implies guidance by a goal other than, or in addition to, basic results. But what is the source of this *ought*? And what is the authority empowering that source? *Ought* represents what social scientist Jonathan Baron calls "moral advice," counsel that "we give to each other about what to do, what choices to make."[25] For such advice to be credible, it must first of all not be self-serving for the advice giver and must be of some envisionable benefit to the advice receiver. For Baron this means that "the effective advice we have reason to give must stem from our interest in seeing the objectives of others satisfied."[26] Ethics basically represent an inextricable blend of "your own interest and your own altruism."

Ethicists have grappled with the issue of *ought* for centuries. Some, among them Thomas Aquinas, have invoked *ought* as divine dictate; others, like Plato, as duty to state or society. Since the Enlightenment, the quest for a rational basis for all movements in nature and human affairs has led to a more scientific *ought,* based on the logical assessment and weighting of utility. With Darwin, *ought* became a biological imperative. Now, with discoveries in genetics, *ought* seems attributable to DNA. The authority and acceptability of *ought* is a conundrum for the global economy and global society. So far, cultural, social and spiritual variances, so pronounced in our fragmented world, have made it virtually impossible to formulate a coherent, unified *ought.* At the same time, for *ought* to be merely relative and subjective risks unleashing chaos. Whether spiritual or genetic, whether both or neither, a common *ought* is constitutive of community. In this case, without a global *ought,* there can be no global ethic.

"Most individuals' ethical beliefs," writes Badaracco, "are firmly embedded in norms and assumptions—some examined and some implicit—that originate with their families, communities, and the cultural and historical traditions that shape their early lives."[27] The reality for North America, and increasingly also for Europe and Japan, is that the sources for an ethical sensibility are in flux. The family unit continues to undergo an historic deconstruction. Still essentially important, the make-up of families is nevertheless much more fluid, often tentative and very stressed. Bedrock values that were once common throughout society are instead varied, differing with each household. In respect for cultural diversity, and to keep church separate from state, schools have also been morally neutered. What may be an inconsistent standard at home is largely a non-standard at school. Companies have often eschewed ethics, downloading responsibility by arguing that moral character is a matter for parents and teachers to inculcate. The reality, though, is that formation of principle is random and irregular because home life and school authority are still largely being redefined.

That leaves community. The traditional source for community mores is a society's religious beliefs—highly problematic in the context of the global economy. There is a sense that religious adherence is widely in retreat before the modernization of industrialization and the rationality of science. But polls show the opposite. More than 90 percent of Americans profess a belief in God. Attendance in traditional churches, synagogues and mosques may have ebbed, but participation in revivalist, Pentecostal and reformed movements has been strong. The return to religion, which started in the 1970s, is a worldwide phenomenon, and not one that is limited to fundamentalists. "The most obvious, most salient and most powerful cause of the global religious resurgence," in Huntington's analysis, "is precisely what was supposed to cause the death of religion: the process of social, economic and cultural modernization that swept across the world in the second half of the twentieth century."[28] The *action* of the global economy has been a "detraditionalization." The *reaction* of people to the global economy has been to seek understanding, rooting and meaning in traditional spiritual belief.

Traditional religions, however, although espousing some common and uplifting beliefs about the sacredness of life, have hardly been a source of human unity. Throughout history, religion has been used as much for exclusion as for community building. This destructive divisiveness persists today. Hans Küng states bluntly: "All over the world, religious convictions are often the cause, not of peace, understanding and reconciliation, but of war, intolerance and fanaticism."[29] This creates an uncomfortable and dangerous sandwich of pressures. People everywhere are being swept up into the unifying, material swirl of global economic activity. Yet at the same time they are being drawn back to beliefs that reinforce personal identity but at the expense of a larger unity.

Unavoidable Demands

The global economy is imposing a unity—the pursuit of material goods and comfort through competitive advantage—but without any of the moral cohesion that is necessary for such a system to survive for long in a limited, shrinking world. The world's religions provide a rich and compelling source for moral judgment but, in their dogmatic factionalism and absolutism, lack the inclusiveness and embraciveness to address the issue constructively on a global basis. This, then, is the crux of the matter, a new need that old systems cannot satisfy, a new problem that old solutions cannot solve. Where do we go from here?

For a first step, let us take stock of the paradoxes. The global economy is the future of humanity, but it arouses heightened, sometimes pathological, connections to the past. The global economy also celebrates and advances individuality and the impulse for selfishness, but leaves society and nature vulnerable to the ego's unchecked aggressiveness. Compellingly, the global economy engages people in a single, deeply held dream of consumer products, comfort and material security but uproots them from the traditions and community that provide meaning, continuity and identity. Through its technology, the global economy compresses distances, and makes even the most exotic experience familiar. Yet, despite the incessant interconnection, it leaves many people isolated and emotionally remote. The global economy satisfies material needs but creates moral ambiguity. Finally, while the global economy has the potential to be a force for human cohesion and justice, it has equally the potential to exacerbate human differences, inflict hurt and inflame a dividing anger.

Tough challenges indeed. But now, as a second step, let us consider the rays of hope encoded in the acknowledgments from a growing number of professionals in a variety of fields. In virtually all disciplines of human activity there is an understanding—often very tentative but still very real—that the implications of the global economy are of such a scale and urgency that some intervention is necessary. Social historian E.J. Hobsbawm writes: "Whatever the most desirable balance between public and private, state and civil society, government and market, nobody seriously doubts that they must be combined."[30] People of varying ideologies will argue about the degree to which these factors should be balanced, but the imbalance of complete inaction is too dire—from a social, individual and environmental perspective—to remain even as a possibility. For economist Robert Heilbroner, the problems threatening capitalism—"the saturation of demand and the degradation of the labor force," "the inability to reach full employment," and "cultural erosion"—arise "from the private sector, not the public." He concludes that solutions must therefore come from the public realm. Heilbroner expects a "spectrum of capitalisms, measured by the all important indicators of social and political contentment, not necessarily by those of economic performance. This is because, in the competitive struggle for survival, economic performance becomes only a means to an end, not an end in itself."[31] Economists themselves recognize that the global economy is causing problems that global economics alone cannot and currently will not fix.

Economists and policy makers from the major economic blocs have weighed in with their own assessment. Robert Lawrence of the John F. Kennedy School of Government, Albert Bressand, managing director of Promethee, and Takatoshi Ito of Hitotsubashi University have written a report about the integration of national economies. They note the gravitational pull of global economic integration, but warn of the "centrifugal forces" that have historically "not only stifled, but reversed movement toward global integration."[32] The authors explore three emerging scenarios: allowing the invisible hand free reign in running its globalizing course; allowing regional and national tensions to brake this advance; or imposing some "imperial harmonization" in which the dominant global economies would impose market order much as the Ministry of International Trade and Industry (MITI) did during the rebuilding of the post-war Japanese economy.

The first scenario, largely advocated by multinational enterprises, is actually producing the tensions creating the second scenario of fragmentation and resistance to any worldwide harmonization. A totally free market raises the question asked by so many who have lost jobs to "delayering," "outsourcing" and "cost cutting": "Would nations and regions engage in a race to the bottom as they compete with ever lower taxes and more lenient regulatory standards?"[33] We know that the invisible hand is remarkably efficient, but communities require more than such utility to hold them together. Competition creates disparity. Unbridled competition creates the conditions for a much more dangerous inequity that finally pushes all parties into separate corners of self-interest. The global community is more than just the global economy. It is a social, cultural and moral complexity that requires conscious intervention and management. Especially for issues like abject, immovable poverty, or the host of looming environmental crises, the invisible hand will take too long, be too insensitive or completely miss the mark. Lawrence, Bressand and Ito conclude: "The invisible hand has many attractive elements but can exist only in carefully defined and limited sectors."[34]

Fragmentation and imperial harmonization are equally unworkable. The first denies our now irreversible interdependence. The second denies the legitimacy of variances in need, style and culture for individual nations and regions. Ultimately, there is only one solution. Rather than have the economy as the basis of community, the solution is to create a global community to be the basis of the global economy. Lawrence, Bressand and Ito write that "the desirable outcome means a world marked by openness, diversity and cohesion." These are essentially ethical conditions. Openness increases competition, but also requires restraint. Diversity encourages experimentation and innovation, but also requires accommodation and mechanisms for fairness. Cohesion provides the opportunity of the whole being greater than the sum of its parts, but also requires what the authors describe as a "community held together by trust, mutual respect, shared basic values, and, where necessary, shared governance and elements of redistribution."[35]

An economy without community is unsustainable. But are humans themselves wired for such an extended community? And can the religions that traditionally provide moral ballast for their respective communities really deliver the unifying and integrating values for the now pressing global reality? Rules and customs obviously vary, as do their underlying traditions and beliefs, but human beings share a universal need and capacity for participation in community. Humans are humans because of each other. And humans are inhuman and immoral when the focus is so fully on self that others are harmed or disadvantaged. A healthy human being mixes self with other, confidence with compassion, desire with accommodation. Hans Küng explains: "Self-assertion and unselfishness need not be mutually exclusive. Identity and solidarity are both required for the formation of a better world."[36] This mix, fundamental to human well-being, is equally important to the economy. The key for the world economy, argue Lawrence, Bressand and Ito, "is a balance in a fashion similar to the ideals of the French Revolution—liberty, equality, and fraternity."[37]

Not a Formula but an Orientation

In the prologue to this chapter, Dietrich Bonhoeffer recognized that to do right is often a "dare"—the following of conviction even when facts are unclear and consequences ambiguous. What is needed is therefore not a rigid following of a prescribed package of behaviors but a deeply held and creatively expressed "orientation" toward the right, the just, the ethical. In opposing Nazism, Bonhoeffer found himself isolated from his culture and at odds with his church. With the institutional source for moral guidance co-opted by a distorted political ideology, Bonhoeffer was forced to create an ethical framework free from any tradition, transcending any national identity and beyond the boundaries of any particular religious dogma. He premised his ethical framework on a radical *otherness*. "Responsibility," he wrote, "is always a relation between persons."[38] When moral rules are unclear or cultures collide, an underlying and ultimately unifying source for ethical deliberation and action is the empathy we have for one another. Act with regard for the other and what is right will eventually emerge and what is wrong will usually be avoided. Put yourself in another's shoes. Imagine yourself as the recipient of the words or actions you are about to impart. The current human reality is less precipitous than it was for Bonhoeffer, yet we too, particularly in the global economy, struggle to define the ethical in the absence of an overarching moral authority.

Orientation is a very important aspect of this book, and of the larger project to practice a global ethic. By this, I mean orientation as commitment as well as a disposition. To be ethical is first and foremost a choice. To be ethically oriented is a dedication to deepen ethical capacities through learning and practice. Orientation is important for three reasons. First, it acknowledges that whatever our motivation, we cannot always be good or right. Ethical character is the result of intent and consistency over time, not just the rightness or wrongness of a specific act. Second, orientation admits that in today's world, ethics must be made up to be applied. New complexities, like those in biotechnology, genetics and nuclear science, pose problems that stretch the relevance and applicability of any current ethical framework. With orientation we promise to use what we know to create anew the ethic we need. Third, orientation implies that the task of ethics is never complete. Not only are the circumstances around us in flux, but we—as individual persons and as institutions—are also changing and growing. Whatever wisdom we achieve, it provides not a capacity for automatically resolving moral problems but only higher tolerance for ambiguity and more integrity in dealing with it.

An ethical orientation works in my model like a spiral staircase. The commitment to ascend accepts that there will be considerable effort and exertion. At first, it will also likely be very frustrating since it involves going in circles and seemingly getting nowhere. But slowly, the spiral-staircase practice of orientation realizes two benefits. As more effort is expended, as we exercise the muscles of ethical sensibility, we eventually become stronger climbers. Orientation is a moral workout, so the first benefit is growing stronger and more confident in our ethical capacities. The second benefit is that, rather than going nowhere, climbing eventually achieves height, revealing a more accurate and insightful overview. In other words, practice makes perspective. While the ambiguity of life means that, Escher-like, we never reach any final top, each step represents a progress that our own personal growth compels us to take.

Küng and other leaders of this process are under no illusions; nor should we be. Seeding this global ethic will be neither fast nor easy. The difficulties of culture, varying stages of development, and moral relativism are significant. So, too, is the resistance from companies committed to their goals, economists to their theories, politicians to their ideologies and consumers to their material goods. Long-established patterns of thinking and habits of behavior will need to be reflected upon and modified. Expectations will need to be reconceptualized. And great courage will need to be summoned up to think that small actions by single individuals can truly affect a global reality.

That said, there are several reasons for proceeding with enthusiasm and confidence. First, it helps to remember that other such world-shaping movements were themselves at first small acts against huge problems. In the beginning the Red Cross, and subsequently the Red Crescent, seemed myopic, insignificant and impractical in confronting the suffering and devastation of modern warfare. What was dismissed as idealistic has instead brought relief to untold millions around the world, including my own father, who while a POW in 1941 received, via the Red Cross, a photo of his one-year-old daughter—my sister—whom he had never before seen. The Geneva Convention took on the even more improbable task of getting warring countries and armies to agree on a humane code of conduct. More recently, the Helsinki Process provided a human rights agreement that bridged the ideologies and nuclear threats of the cold war. Helsinki provided a safety valve for the misunderstanding and distrust during the darkest, most dangerous days of competition between East and West. This at times was the only channel for discourse that, as Martti Ahtisaari, president of Finland notes, played a role in the subsequent rapprochement. All of these have been movements of conscience that have rendered practical, invaluable and large-scale services to humanity.

A second reason for cautious optimism is that multinational business is awakening to the benefits of a global ethic, as well as to the risks of operating without one. Pauline Graham, a management consultant, argues a position that more and more companies are ceding: "A business cannot be abstracted into an economic entity. Its activities are predominantly economic, but they have never been, and can never be, exclusively so. All the other aspects of human behavior—political, psychological, social, moral and so on—enter into the activities of any business and must all be fully recognized."[39] Perhaps the most dramatic example of this is the 1997 decision by Shell to invite representatives from several nongovernment social and environmental organizations to participate in and monitor some of its most sensitive projects. Shell had twice been caught on the losing end of an international controversy. First, it fiercely resisted Greenpeace's opposition to its plans to dispose of a spent oil rig in the North Sea. Second, it maintained operations in Nigeria despite the outcry of European human rights activists. The moves cost Shell dearly in reputation and sales to the point that the company was forced to reevaluate its position.

Reporting on this unprecedented capitulation, the *Financial Times* painted the wider context: "The plan by Royal Dutch/Shell to consult environmental and human rights groups on sensitive projects is a belated recognition of the influence on multinationals of international public opinion."[40] Like other companies, Shell has been adopting the marketing and management tools of customer attentiveness and service. Environmental and human rights issues were, however, regarded as not strategic but more the domain of public relations and corporate complaints departments. Cornelius Herkstroter, senior group managing director of Royal Dutch/Shell, explains that while these groups were listened to, "they were not as important as government, industry organizations and so on. We were somewhat slow in understanding that these groups were tending to acquire authority. Meanwhile those institutions we were used to dealing with were tending to lose authority."[41] All of this bespeaks an acknowledgment of a new accountability infiltrating corporate strategy and global business practice. Performance is no longer simply a function of profit but now also includes global credibility and public access. John Jennings, chairman of Shell Transport and Trading, notes: "It's a CNN world, and that means that it is a show-me world, and not the trust-me world of the past."[42] All of this proves two points. First, it confirms von Weizsacker's view that moral values come from the community and are used only by markets and companies. Second, it just goes to show that the wired world is a trip-wired one.

A third reason for commitment and confidence is actually negative, and it is that the very severity of global pressures demands a new approach and an immediate response. Johan Galtung has developed a revealing construct he calls "spaces," distinct global areas in which global problems are now pressing for a global response. In his analysis, the Nature space is suffering from ecological degradation and the stresses of overpopulation. Human space is beset by poverty, misery, repression and spiritual alienation. The space of Society is struggling with economic underdevelopment and social disintegration. And World space is fraught with massive violence and war. Galtung argues that time is limited, and that the world culture for attending to these world problems is inadequate. "If the world is a society of societies, that society should also be integrated (positive world development), or processes toward disintegration (negative world development) should be reversed."[43]

The muddle and emotion surrounding the risks within the global economy have made most businesspeople and policy makers focus on issues of competitiveness. "How do we get and improve advantage?"

has become the strategic rationale for international joint ventures, process reengineering and wage roll-backs. But, in a wide body of work, MIT economist Paul Krugman goes against the grain of this adversarial assumption. He teaches "that international trade is not about competition, it is about mutually beneficial exchange."[44] Mutuality is a characteristic of maturity, and the global ethic promotes exactly this reorientation from an exclusively competitive economic model to one that also values cooperation and community well-being.

Krugman also points out that the recent obsession with global trade is out of proportion. "It is a little-known but startling fact that world trade as a share of world production did not return to its 1913 level until about 1970; it is even more startling that net international flows of capital (as opposed to complex financial operations that do not finance real investment) were a considerably larger share of world savings in the years preceding World War I than they have been even in the 'emerging market' boom of the last few years."[45] Another way of looking at this is perhaps more sobering than Krugman intends. The world's economy, for all its progress, is still recovering from the world's wars. Despite strong economic interconnections—and in many ways because of them—nations destroyed the common good in pursuit of some protectionism, tribalism or special advantage. More than half a century of development has been lost, and countless lives and creative contributions wasted, by a retreat from global engagement and a surrender to the factors that make us different. In light of the world's environmental problems, the web of connecting technologies and the exponentially greater destructive capacity of war, it is no longer possible to segregate self-interest from common interest. A global ethic is now imperative because we cannot endure the impossibility of living without one.

CHAPTER TWO

LIES

*Rarely perhaps has any generation shown so little interest as ours
does in any kind of theoretical or systematic ethics. The academic
question of a system of ethics seems to be of all
questions the most superfluous. The reason for this is not
to be sought in any supposed ethical indifference on the
part of our period. On the contrary it arises from the
fact that our period, more than any earlier period in
the history of the west, is oppressed by a
superabounding reality of concrete ethical problems.*

Dietrich Bonhoeffer, *"Ethics as Formation," in* Ethics

The need for a global ethic is situated at two intersecting points. The
first is where the material needs of the developing world, the material achievements of the developed world and the exhausted capacity of
the natural world are in near collision. Supply and demand have been the
inputs to our economic model, but in this new tension they are now the
defining factors for a moral one. The second intersection is the timeless
one where the security, freedom and rights of the individual challenge
head-on the stability, accommodation and necessary mutuality of the

community. Inalienable rights make for inescapable responsibilities. Of course, these two intersections are themselves overlapping and inter-connected. World events influence personal values. And individual choices affect a global reality. But this interdependence, although intellectually neat and cogent, remains remote from our experience. Are the global problems really our problems? Put another way, are our individual choices and personal actions really of global significance?

Juliet B. Schor offers a radical suggestion that provides as much a personal test of values as a solution to the push and pull of economy/ecology. Schor, a senior lecturer in Economics and the director of Women's Studies at Harvard, explains that "we are on the horns of a profound dilemma." On the one hand, the priority of growth is driving humanity headlong into an ecological chasm. On the other, "we are facing environmental crisis at a time when a large fraction of the world's population is malnourished, without adequate health care, housing or productive employment." Two sets of moral issues are thus intertwined: the responsibility for managing limitation, and the responsibility for managing inequality. If the environment will no longer accommodate universal, full-throttle economic growth, then Schor's idea is to slow growth where it is not essential and maintain it where it is.

Schor suggests that developed countries "internalize the benefits" of any future gains in productivity, so that gross output remains constant. What this means is that any efficiency realized by managers and employees in modern, industrialized economies would be paid out in more time off rather than in higher wages. The subsequent slowing of developed economies would create opportunities for the underdeveloped to catch up. More would need to be done to bring down energy consumption, clean up toxic waste and protect and manage oceans, forests and arable land. But as a starting point, Schor's construct provides opportunity to those so far left behind, helps those who have the most move toward sustainability and places the economy firmly within the realistic parameters of the natural ecosystem.

People who sit atop the world's wage and consumption pyramid would sacrifice future pay raises but earn more time off. In only three to five years, applying the rates of productivity growth achieved in the 1990s, managers and workers in the industrialized economies would basically be able to go on a four-day work week for the same wage. Within ten years, a three-day work week. Within fifteen . . . you get the picture. Wages stay constant, adjusted only for inflation, and productivity goes into creating quality of life instead of more consumption. A great idea. Or is it? What is your reaction? Would you be willing to tradeoff future wage increases for time off? Would you settle for more personal flexibility but less financial opportunity?

Needless to say, this is an unsettling, if not disturbing prospect for most people. Despite being harried by often inhuman corporate restructuring, despite rating the satisfactions of job as 30 percent lower than in the 1980s, despite working longer hours and having to sacrifice family for career, most North Americans fear the idea of a four-day work week.[1] Work in the global economy may be hard and even unfair, but harder still is having to settle for less. After two hundred years, ideals like the American dream, the Protestant work ethic and creating a better world for our children have become so deeply embedded that, regardless of logic, relevance or personal price, they retain a powerful hold on the collective imagination and individual self-worth.

People are not so much hypocritical as rigidly apprehensive. Uncertain about the global economy, aware of the diminished power of governments to provide any backstop and shell-shocked by the ruthlessness of corporate downsizing, people understandably do not want to risk working less or changing social formulae. However, neither effort nor desire will by themselves yield wisdom. And longer hours will not in themselves resecure job security. Peter Senge observes that people "cope with this by not thinking about the future, by busying themselves with reacting to breakdowns. But they are uneasy. They are fearful. They really do not know what to think. They do not know what to tell their children."[2] The angst is partly that of fear within change. But at a deeper level, people are also distressed by the growing recognition that we are living a lie. We know that unlimited growth is impossible within a limited world. We feel global pressures affect personal lifestyle. And we live uncomfortably with an economy that can turn on us and make us redundant at any moment, or that will inevitably exhaust us and the planet in the not too distant future. Either way we are casualties. Either way we are trapped in the unworkable duplicity of having our cake and eating it too.

John Maynard Keynes recognized that our modern economic practice is based on a moral inversion. He wrote in 1931 "of the pseudo-moral principles which have hag-ridden us for two hundred years, by which we have exalted some of the most distasteful of human qualities into the position of highest virtue."[3] Bald, disrespectful and single-minded aggressiveness that is understood to be destructive in other circumstances has become celebrated in corporate trenches as "competitiveness." Angry, egocentric lust for power that would qualify as tyranny in politics has been elevated to "strategic mastery" and "leadership" in business. And a runaway greed has been sanctioned as "wealth creation," making heroes out of billionaire workaholics. The end seems to make the means irrelevant, so what is bad taste, bad judgment or bad character in life has been made admirable and to be emulated in business.

This suspension of basic moral judgment has been tolerated in the questionable belief that the economy has its own natural law. Now that economics have become the primary and dominant focus of global human activity, this immorality and amorality exact a far greater toll and distort both business practice and the wider culture. Keynes had expected that the eventual wealth of society would allow it one day to be true to its instincts, and address right as right and wrong as wrong. The day of reckoning has happened much before that satiation of wealth has been realized. Unforeseen by Keynes, the rapid expansion of the global economy has run headlong into the rapidly diminishing potential of the natural environment to sustain it. At the same time, the fall of communism and the accelerated globalization of the free market have caused stresses and fissures in the social compact forged over decades to accommodate the economy's moral inversions. These lies about what is right were tolerated because communism was the greater wrong. Now, without the justification of that greater wrong, the cost of these lies—personal stress, community dysfunction and ecological breakdown—warrants reassessment.

In many ways, a global ethic for the global economy is not so much a revolution in values as a return to the genuine human virtues that economic progress has reversed. Exposing such lies will not be easy now that they are institutionalized and carry with them the full authority of academic lineage, government policy and ideological success. However, we know from the wide body of research into and experience with organizational change that any lasting transformation requires as a first step an acknowledgment of the failures and limitations of current beliefs, behaviors and attitudes. To begin that reassessment, I have chosen seven of the most deeply entrenched lies. This is not an exhaustive list; I have not, for example, tackled the lie that business practices and policies are equal for and fair toward women. The stark fact that Jill Barad of Mattel is the only woman CEO of a Fortune 500 company should completely expose this particular fabrication. I will explore some of the related gender issues in Chapter Six, within the context of feminist contributions to a global ethic. For now, my focus is on seven interconnected but distinct inversions (see Table 1 on page 39).

Table 1. Vices in Virtuous Camouflage

Economic Principle	Justifying Implication
1. Business is rational.	Hence, all other human perceptions and perspectives are suspect.
2. Competition is the natural law.	Hence, cooperation and all other relationships are unnatural.
3. "The rising tide lifts all boats."	Hence, those sinking are responsible for their own failures.
4. Business is now "green".	Hence, all other human and social problems are best solved by business.
5. "Let the market decide" is a truism.	Hence, any intervention or non-economic pressure is false.
6. Reward is related to risk.	Hence, stagnant wages are a function of not working hard enough.
7. The economy is central to human well-being.	Hence, everything else is secondary.

1. Business is rational. Hence, all other human perceptions and
   perspectives are suspect.

Why do stock markets go up when unemployment rises? Why do the
values of poorly managed companies, like AT&T and Electrolux,
increase when factory workers who have nothing to do with strategy are
laid off in the thousands? Why has reengineering largely identified
people, rather than waste, to be the opposite of efficiency? Why do
CEOs' salaries grow exponentially faster than their own corporate profits? There are a host of factors, implications and assessments to answer
these questions. But underlying the arguments that justify these contradictions is an ironclad assumption of economic rationality. Business is
rational, while life is messy. Business is objective, while politics, society,
individuals and morality are subjective. Business, like science, is true,
while culture is soft, fuzzy and less valuable for being imprecise.

The badge of rationality is very important to businesspeople because,
against it, there can be no criticism. A decision may be unpopular, like
the persisting cigarette sponsorship of sports events watched by children.
Or it may involve considerable dislocation and pain for people and
communities, as when factories are closed and jobs moved to lower-
wage markets. Or a decision may involve the circumvention of environmental regulations, as when nuclear power plants, such as Pickering
in Canada or Sellarfield in the U.K., flushed contaminated waste into
public waterways. These may be wrong by standard human measures,
but by virtue of their business or situational rationality, they are simply
necessary and therefore above reproach.

There is a conundrum. Although all businesses and businesspeople
claim rationality, not all are successful. This puts a hole in the dogma.
Does failure suggest that rationality, like quality, has gradations? Or
does it mean that, as in science, rationality works only part of the time?
If "gradations" are true, then all decisions taken rationally deserve the
scrutiny of how good, how qualified, how developed each really is.
Rationality is thus subject to the very value judgments it is meant to
have transcended. If the second is true and rationality can be trusted
only occasionally, then, as in science, rationality must share a place with
accident, serendipity, intuition and surprise. Either way, rationality is a

bruised concept that is already losing its aura of invincibility.

In opening this discussion, I made a distinction between rationality and reason. This is not an original differentiation, but one that is frequently forgotten. By not understanding the difference, we end up having rational companies do unreasonable and stupid things, such as in the early 1990s when Archer Daniels Midland colluded with several other global manufacturers to fix prices for citric acid and lysine, used as ingredients in a host of food and consumer products. The rationale clearly was to make more money, but the clumsiness and illegality of the method hardly qualified as reasonable. An important lesson for business, then, is that when rational and reasonable are at odds, executives can go to jail and companies can lose huge amounts of the very profit that provided the motivation. ADM paid a record $100 million in criminal fines to settle fraud and anti-trust suits with the government. And it now faces millions more in losses from such hoodwinked customers as Procter & Gamble, Kraft Foods, Quaker Oats and Schreiber Foods. Common sense indicates that a potent source of competitive advantage is the trust between company and customer, but by the limited rationality of wanting more money faster, ADM has illogically burned some very precious bridges. Amazingly, in yet another bit of rational unreasonableness, ADM fired the executive who blew the whistle on the fraud, while most of the most senior executives who were on watch during the many years of deception and illegality still hold jobs and serve on ADM's board.

Like all rational enterprises, ADM's first reaction to the scandal was to play hardball. It not only denied wrongdoing; it attacked any journalist or critic who questioned it. ADM used all its resources to counter and threaten its foes and capitulated only when one of its Japanese price-fixing partners broke ranks and confessed. Just like the tobacco executives who in 1995, under oath, swore to a congressional committee that cigarette smoking posed no risk to human health, ADM remains more belligerent than penitent. Rationality thus seems to save people from any soul searching or contrition: it is the rationale that was at fault, not the person whose judgment it was or whose purposes were served. The ADM CEO who was at the helm during the deceit and denial is now the chairman of the board. This suggests another characteristic of rationality. Its authority finally rests not so much on reasonableness (its claim) as on power (its objective). Might makes right—by making it look logical.

Some argue that business is rational, but within its own parameters and according to a logic that is unique to the market economy. But it is exactly this part-time application of rationality that creates the almost daily situations of having to lie in order to support the lie, as when senior managers at Daiwa's New York office misled the U.S. Federal Reserve Board to cover up thirty thousand fraudulent trades, and losses exceeding $1.1 billion, by the company's treasury bond chief. Grandiose misjudgments are the price paid by any system that believes its decision processes to be foolproof. Indeed, such "instrumental" or selective rationality inevitably contains the seeds of its own undoing. Sociologist and law professor Philip Selznick explains that selective rationality "depends on definite purposes and clear criteria of cost and achievement, with a natural preference for specialization and for the autonomy of professional or craft decisions. This way of thinking tends to narrow perspectives and limit responsibilities."[4] Specialization creates ethical difficulties because it raises dilemmas for the expert that are far removed from the common experience of the community. Self-regulation is thus often delegated by default to those whose very self-interest is at stake.

Economist Herman E. Daly and theologian John B. Cobb point out: "Economists typically identify pursuit of private gain with rationality, thus implying that other modes of human behavior are not rational. These modes include other-regarding behavior and actions directed to the public good."[5] Rationality in the context of the modern economy has little to do with reasonableness and almost all to do with self-interest. The implication is that the wisdom for protecting the environment, the expectation for a dynamic and rich community of arts and the empathy for those in need are not impulses that are as rational as self-interest. Not only are these less important but they end up warranting concern or investment only in relation to their rationality—in other words, only in proportion to how they contribute to self-advantage. Some argue that greed is already an anachronism, discredited by the dissipation of the 1980s. *The Economist* chides management teacher Charles Handy for wanting "companies to see their workers as vital human beings." This is an old idea, according to the magazine, and "no one disagrees with Mr. Handy that business is about more than profit and loss."[6] The reality, though, is that restraint is random and largely optional. No moral norm is as universally recognized and valued as that principle of self-interest. So while some people may be uncomfortable with the associations of greed, many more play the game with a ruthless disregard for others that is almost Dickensian. Department stores, for example, are to this day struggling with the price versus publicity tradeoff of buying clothes from sweatshops. The point is that the global economy suffers not just from rogue operators but also from a more fundamental rogue principle.

What *The Economist* raises by its objection to Handy's ideas is the even more important issue of outright hypocrisy. Many companies and managers have adopted the vocabulary and cosmetics of more reciprocal practices, but without overhauling the link between self-interest and rationality. In its 1997 report on work and family, *Business Week* writes that "many Americans, caught between the crush of demanding employers and the intensity of their dual income, sandwich generation families, feel abused and angry. They view corporate 'family-friendly' efforts as either empty nods to political correctness, or just shrewd public relations."[7] Some companies have been genuine in their efforts and programs, but even enlightened companies often fall into the trap of having the overwhelming rationality of business undo the tentative reasonableness. TRW Inc. called a meeting for Father's Day. "When a complaint was voiced, the project manager replied, 'You have a problem with that? If you do, we'll find someone who doesn't.' " Another worker set out the most common reality of family-friendly math: "DuPont will take as much as you will give, and it is always implied that if you want to get ahead, you will not broadcast your desire or need to put family before work."[8] Whatever their intentions or policies, companies have so far been better at mastering the more human tautology of a '90s workplace than leaving behind the competitive-only rationality that undermines it.

Our overreliance on rationality finally afflicts individuals as well as institutions. Amitai Etzioni writes of absurdities that we have all encountered: "Multi-millionaires work themselves to a frazzle to increase their income. Executives work 'for their families,' destroying their family life in the process. Societies undermine their fabric in order to accelerate economic growth. This phenomenon has been referred to as irrational rationality, or mad rationality."[9] This trend suggests another destructive, and largely misapplied, rationality of the modern economy. Time has now widely been accepted as money. Of course, time is much more precious than money, even if most of us only discover that when it is too late. By the logic of supply and demand, both time and money can be argued to be scarce. But more money can always be made, whereas time spent depletes a fixed provision. To be fixedly rational is to regard time as a utilitarian commodity. In our bones, we know that this view diminishes and devalues life. Harried people, no matter how successful, are increasingly saddened by the loss of time with family or in other human pursuits and capacities. This shows that while the rationality of business may be extreme, abusive and easy to condemn, we have also—consciously or not—surrendered to it.

2. Competition is the natural law. Hence, cooperation and all other relationships are unnatural.

Many people in business recognize that cooperation is an ever more important factor in success. The "wisdom of teams" has been demonstrated in the highly engaging service strategy of Wal-Mart and in the highly efficient interdisciplinary product development work at Chrysler. Strategic alliances are another strongly advocated management reciprocity, with companies like Toshiba and Corning each using a hundred or so such pacts to spread risk, accelerate development, share efficiencies and capitalize on tangential opportunities. Despite the growing evidence supporting cooperation, the bias to competitiveness remains almost completely entrenched. Economist Lester Thurow explains that "capitalism, the triumph of individuality, however, cannot officially recognize the need for teamwork. Even as capitalism is organizing itself into teams and one might imagine that loyalty to the team and the willingness to work as part of a team have become more important, the ingredients that hold economic teams together (lifetime employment, real wage increases) are disappearing. Just when the need for employing human skills in unselfish teams would seem to call for attaching that skilled work force closer to the company and making it more a part of the company team, real companies are moving in precisely the opposite direction."[10]

Many companies regard competition in Darwinian terms, believing totally that the survival of the fittest is a rigid natural law imposing harsh government on both biological and economic survival. If competition is the natural way, then cooperation, however positive in its outcomes, is merely a deviation that cannot be trusted for the long term. The theories that Darwin developed while observing nature continue to have great scientific and social currency. And the ferocious competitiveness of natural selection is undeniably a harsh dynamic of nature. But there is now a newer understanding that any system as complex as an ecosystem or economy involves a host of interactions, of which competitiveness is but one. Mutuality, reciprocity, altruism, parasitism are as evident and vital in nature as the competitive drama between predator and prey.

According to Edward O. Wilson, professor of science and zoology at Harvard, Darwin captured an essential element of "vertical change" but lacked a "horizontal" understanding of diversity. He saw the valid evolutionary process for a species in isolation, but missed the ecological links and variety that make competition possible. Even now, Wilson argues, "what we understand best about evolution is mostly genetic and what we understand least is mostly ecological. I will go further and suggest that the major remaining questions of evolutionary biology are ecological rather than genetic."[11] In other words, we have focused so much on natural selection that we have so far missed the conditions and interactions upon which it depends. The same is true in our appreciation of market dynamics. With the economy strained by globalization, with society experiencing strife from the economic uncertainty and with individuals stressed by corporate reinvention, the instinct at all levels of interaction is to compete even more. This, though, would be disastrous—exactly the opposite of what is needed. It is the system—

Wilson's ecology—that is in crisis, and the further focus on the individual—the genetic—only further frays and depletes that system.

What does all this mean for businesspeople in the trenches? First, it implies that the trend to strategic alliances and other forms of cooperation is not so much a smart invention of management as the inevitable and only response to crisis. Second, this response is not an aberration of the natural law of competition but the legitimate and essential and enduring complement to competitiveness. Third, there cannot be, in either nature or the economy, a survival of the fittest without a complex and supporting system. Independence is therefore a fallacy, and interdependence, even for the strongest and most competitive, is the only reality. Fourth, what we are learning in nature has already been proven as working in business. Business academics Motoko Yasuda Lee and Charles L. Mulford report: "After an extensive review of past studies on inter-organizational relationships, Galaskiewicz concluded that an overriding reason for a firm to form inter-organizational linkages is resource procurement in order to survive. In addition to resource dependency, Aldrich suggested that socioeconomic environmental uncertainty motivates inter-organizational linkages."[12] When the going gets tough, even for the toughest, it's smart to get together.

3. "The rising tide lifts all boats." Hence, those sinking are responsible for their own failures.

Lies of the magnitude sufficient to engage virtually the whole world work only if there is massive acceptance. The inducement to suspend ethical judgment and turn a blind eye to the abuses of the global economy is that supposedly everyone wins something—perhaps not the big payout, but at least an amelioration of life's hardships and an uplift in hope. This, alas, may be the easiest of the untruths to un-turn, and perhaps the falsehood that most people from their own painful experience already see through. The rising tide of the global economy does indeed lift a few, but for most it has been a tsunami. David Gordon fills in the U.S. data: "In 1972, the average (non-farm and non-supervisory) before-tax wage was $13.11 in 1994 dollars. By 1994 it had declined to $11.13. Take it from the average worker every hour, forty hours every week, and that's enough to reduce the median working family's annual before-tax income by more than $4,200 a year."[13] Wage roll-backs, notes Lester Thurow, have been the case even in union-strong Germany, France and Italy. Highly productive and high-tech-oriented Finns have had salaries cut for the first four of the five years of the 1990s. And even the Japanese have experienced drastic cuts in wealth—because real estate values were more than halved—as well as a disturbing loss in hope as "Japanese companies have built up enormous numbers of idle workers on their payroll."[14]

Whatever advantages have been won through the harder work, productivity initiatives and new technology of the last five years, few of them will accrue to the average worker. Robert Solow, a Nobel laureate in economics, explains: "There may be some measures that are equal to or better than the pre-1973 years. But not the level of well-being. We are not in any sense back."[15] There is no doubt that the global economy has been, and represents for the future, an incredible mechanism for creating wealth. The persistent problem, managed for several decades but now largely left to its own rhythm, is that "the rising tide" is providing only selective elevation. Data compiled by David Gordon from the U.S. Bureau of the Census and other surveys show that during the 1960s and 1970s, income distribution was roughly constant between "the top 5 percent and the bottom fifth" of households. "Between 1978 and 1993, by contrast, the ratio of the income share of the top 5 percent to the bottom 20 percent increased by more than a fifth." In the boom years between 1983 and 1989, "the wealth share of the top one percent of households climbed by fully 15 [percentage points], to a total share of almost 40 percent."[16] Only in the Roaring Twenties has there been a comparable vacuuming up of wealth, a historical parallel with few benefits to draw comfort from.

Although straight-line relationships are impossible to prove in complex situations, the aggrandizement of a few has happened, perhaps coincidentally, but certainly simultaneously, with a stark human dislocation. Thurow reports that, on any given night, there are 600,000 homeless people in the U.S. More than 7 million Americans have been homeless since 1992. Homelessness is also rampant in countries with vaunted social safety nets, like Canada and France; the latter, with its double-digit unemployment, estimates that it too has 600,000 people living on the street.[17] Not surprisingly, the people who are sacrificing so much to make ends meet, who are carrying the burden of their company's higher productivity, are starting to seethe at the injustice. "Few top executives can even imagine the hatred, contempt and fury that has been created," warns management teacher Peter Drucker, "not primarily among blue-collar workers who never had an exalted opinion of the 'bosses'—but among their middle management and professional people. I don't know what form it will take, but the envy developing from their enormous wealth will cause trouble."[18]

If the rising tide is a deeply disappointing fallacy for workers, it is an outrageous deceit for the young. Youth unemployment is up to 60 percent in some European countries, as high as 50 percent among urban American blacks, and in the mid-twenties in Canada and the U.K. To be in a job of limited opportunity may at least induce some compliance to the system. But without any such bribe to secure the next generation's acquiescence, the global economy's lopsided division of gains may be impossible to sustain.

4. Business is now "green." Hence, all other human and social problems are best solved by business.

According to Mike Sutton, director of the U.K.-based World Wide Fund for Nature's Endangered Seas Campaign, we are in the midst of "third wave environmentalism." During the first wave, people developed concern about ecological issues. The second consisted of protest, advocacy and confrontation. Now in the third, environmentalists "are in a mode of co-operation, partnerships, consensus-building, and working out solutions that are acceptable to both environment and business."[19] Many companies have indeed made progress on environmental concerns. The *Index of Corporate Environmental Engagement,* published in 1996, shows that some industrial sectors that were among the most blatant offenders, such as electricity and chemicals, have made the most progress in reforming their practices to respect the environment. More benign industries, among them financial services, have not been under as much scrutiny or regulation and consequently have been much more lackadaisical in greening procedures. In less than a generation, environmentalism has gone from a fringe issue to one of mainstream concern; it has progressed from a nuisance for business to a fully weighted strategic performance measure.

Notwithstanding these developments, the environmental crisis is deepening. The rate of industrialization in the developing world is far outstripping any gains from recycling, reuse and renewal programs. The UN report prepared in 1997 for the seventy heads of state meeting to commemorate the fifth anniversary of the Rio Summit paints a sad picture. About deforestation it says, "Each year an area the size of Nepal is cut or burned. Ocean pollution threatens the health and livelihood of the two-thirds of humanity living near coastlines, and about 60 percent of commercial fisheries are overfished or fully fished and in danger of depletion. Toxic chemicals still pose significant threats."[20] Environmental damage is not just the outcome of China's modernization or Brazil's marching agriculture into the Amazon. Countries with supposedly advanced green credentials are undeniably on the environmental rampage. The World Watch Institute notes: "Public attention has been focused primarily on tropical forest destruction, but timber companies have recently been clear-cutting vast tracts of boreal forest in Canada."[21] The one million hectares slashed in developed, prosperous Canada is equal to half the forest lost in underdeveloped and impoverished Brazil.

The World Watch Institute, in its statistical summary called *Vital Signs 1996–1997*, provides other data that suggest some of the economic causes for some of the ecological effects. In 1995, the latest year for which data are assembled, global oil production rose 1.5 percent, the largest such increase of the 1990s. Carbon emission for the same year broke a record and "is enough to demonstrate that most nations are failing to meet the goal of the Framework Convention on Climate Change (signed at Rio in 1992), which is to limit emissions." All of this is contributing to a continuing warming of planet Earth. The last two years have been the hottest on record, and the last five are among the ten hottest since record keeping began. For the first time in

1995, "a U.N. advisory group of 2,500 scientists" concluded that the "observed warming is 'unlikely to be entirely natural in origin.' "[22]

The negative suggestion of "unlikely . . . natural" is a breakthrough, because scientists are understandably reluctant to overlay the workings of as complex a system as the global economy on the even more complex system of the global ecology. That each system feeds back on itself with innumerable unforeseen stimulae and responses creates chaos upon chaos—not the easiest circumstances from which to deduce iron-clad scientific evidence. But the continuing hedge of policy makers and businesspeople who want more definitive data before reforming laws and practices is a violation of the basic virtue of prudence. The evidence overwhelmingly presents the probability of a problem that cannot be avoided, and therefore must be addressed. Instead, business has spent the years since the Rio Summit reengineering processes, not reintegrating them for environmental sustainability. And governments have focused on fighting the phantasm of national competitiveness, not on the more demanding, essential obligations of preservation and sustainability. Small logos for recycling, however well intentioned, are just not enough. In their 1997 report to the Club of Rome, Ernst von Weizsacker, Amory B. Lovins and L. Hunter Lovins write: "We are more than ten times better at wasting resources than at using them. A study for the U.S. National Academy of Engineering found that about 93 percent of the materials we buy and 'consume' never end up in saleable products at all. Moreover, 80 percent of products are discarded after a single use, and many others are not as durable as they should be."[23] Such profligacy by business is possible only with the complicity of consumers. Waste is thus something done not by the system but by individuals.

More and more companies and their customers speak "green," but their actions so far are more cosmetic than substantial. Increased oil production and higher emissions of carbon have not dented the growing demand for four-wheel-drive sport-utility vehicles. Lincoln, Nissan and Mercedes-Benz have entered the luxury sport-utility market with upscale vehicles that drive more like cars than like trucks. Full-size pickup trucks come equipped with 8- and 10-cylinder engines that break new records for poor fuel efficiency. Not to be undone, GM and Chrysler have their own behemoths in the works, as do BMW and other manufacturers.

This is but one example of supply leading demand, even if both are irresponsible. Auto executives have repeatedly deflected their responsibility for fuel efficiency or safety, citing consumer demands for speed, size or price. These are indeed legitimate market pressures, but to not address the larger context smacks of the rationalizations heard from paparazzi and tabloids for having so relentlessly hounded Princess Diana. For Peter Senge, all of this indicates an "outlaw industrial system" that is functioning "outside the laws of nature." He explains: "No engineer would expect to build an airplane that violated the laws of aerodynamics, that had negative lift, or build a chemical refinery that violated the laws of conservation of matter and energy. Yet we are together running an economic system that violates the basic laws of natural systems, and just hoping that we can keep it going long enough that the problems will have to be solved by someone else."[24]

Perhaps Sutton's conception of the wavelike progress in environmental responsibility is overly optimistic. More realistically, we seem to be still only in the first phase of recognition, which includes a gnawing awareness of the problem but a near-complete denial of its consequences. So strong is this reluctance that we are trying to make tolerable and less catastrophic the antagonism between economy and environment without actually changing the more fundamental terms of the relationship. A real second wave will consist of reconsidering and reconfiguring the economy, its production processes as well as its consumption behaviors, to realize a respectful, mutually enhancing coexistence with nature. This mutuality is central to a global ethic, but in terms more complex than just regarding self-with-nature. Consumption and production create a responsibility to the natural environment, but this interplay also includes self, nature and others. The consumption by one individual of a limited resource not only depletes that commodity but, by virtue of its scarcity, denies it to another. Hence the need for a type of hyper-reciprocity: What I do unto nature, nature not only does back unto me but it also does back unto others.

5. "Let the market decide" is a truism. Hence, any intervention or non-economic pressure is false.

Scratching the surface to reveal institutional deceptions suggests that humans are headstrong aggressors whose gas-guzzling, resource-wasting, garbage-making behavior is rationally sanctioned as an economic asset. My reasons for this harsh assessment are simple. To face the reality of our inverted virtues, we need to understand the full implications of such deception. We also need to work effects back beyond their cause to their motivation. And we must shake the complacency that comes from the supposed progress of business on moral, social and environmental issues. Adam Smith bequeathed the market economy its most potent sound bite when he argued for "the invisible hand." Building on Hobbes's notion that humans are motivated primarily by the fear to survive, Smith saw this selfish instinct as the juice that powers the endless innovation and improvement in a free-market economy. With everyone in it for themselves, the self-interest of competitors would provide a powerful incentive to help keep in check the self-interest of any one individual. Everyone competing against everyone would also keep progress proceeding indefinitely. Smith, like Darwin, was a man of his time who assumed that the civility and social pressures of his community would perform a moderating role in the economy. Indeed, as a moral philosopher, he could not imagine an invisible hand or free market that did not include the guidance of his community's overarching morality.

That the modern global economy is lacking any such moral consensus has supported the spread of the faulty assumption that the free market is by definition free of ethical influence. The only moderating dictum is that the market only does what the market will bear. An already questionable and dangerous concept in the world of business, the free-from-morals free market approach is now being applied to society wholesale. Garbage collection, prison management, social services and even education are not only being restructured but are also being privatized. While efficiency is laudable and fiscal responsibility imperative, the goals and wider needs of these social systems are not those of business. We are bringing to highly stressed social structures the competitive ethos of the market economy that is being discredited, or seen as of diminishing worth. We are turning society itself into a market, just as the depersonalization and waste of the economy are showing the market itself to be inadequate.

To simply let the market decide does two things that more than offset any efficiency and innovation that the market may realize. First, it frees individuals from having to take moral responsibility for their decisions and actions. We know from the recurring tragedies in human history that voluntary self-restraint cannot be relied upon, and that society is always vulnerable when the actions of individuals are free from the accountability for consequences. In business, structures provide a cloak for concealing or dispersing accountability, and for accepting what would be deviation in the external world as an acceptable norm in the internal one. Kenneth Andrews, an emeritus professor of the Harvard Business School and a former editor of the *Harvard Business Review,* writes that "men and women in bureaucracies turn to each other for moral cues for behavior and come to fashion specific situational moralities for specific significant people in their worlds."[25] Such anonymity and suspension of accountability afford a second perversion, allowing individuals to harvest benefits for themselves but leave the downside, however horrific, for others to clean up.

There are daily examples of corporate decisions taken free of any recognition of consequences that result in scandal, penalty and business loss. What is surprising is that among companies thwarting obligation are those that value their reputation for quality, invest in community initiatives and wring every market advantage from complying with legal and environmental codes. For example, U.S. controls on pesticide use are much stricter than for many other countries. There is a cost benefit to some food companies in having U.S. standards diluted and "harmonized" with those of less particular or less developed trading partners. According to economist Mehrene Larudee, "Food industries have avidly lobbied for these changes, [including] corporate executives from Nestlé, Coca Cola, Pepsi, Hershey, CPC International, Ralston Purina and Kraft. Not only do they want harmony, they want to call the tune." Ford and other car companies play a slightly different charade, using the origin of parts to create a fluid mix of import and export cars that meet government fuel efficiency standards for combined company fleets. In some cases, Ford's gas-guzzling Crown Victoria is an import from Mexico. In others, it is tallied as an American domestic.[26] It is not illegal to lobby for reduced standards, or to use the cross-border traffic in parts and finished goods to creatively adjust quotas. What this behavior confirms is that interventions by governments and social agencies, although not ideal and often incurring some inefficiency, are in fact necessary to protect consumers and communities from a free market that would otherwise be responsible only to the lowest common denominator.

Free-market proponents argue that theirs is the only system proven to produce wealth and advance the general well-being of society. This is largely true within the context of the past two hundred years but it does not mean that its historical functioning and current make-up can be or deserve to be projected forward indefinitely. Having provided the economy with an almost free set of resources and having absorbed industry's pollution, the natural environment is close to reaching a threshold where it will be just too frail to sustain *homo economicus*. In contrast to this "outlaw economy," Senge explains that "there is no 'waste' in nature—all outputs or byproducts of one natural system are inputs or nutrients to another. But we run an economic system that truly produces waste, visible and invisible by-products of our industrial processes that can go nowhere—they just 'pile up.' "[27]

Again, the reason for stressing the lack of responsible progress is not that some strategies and practices have not changed. Some have, but the disregard for the natural environment is so entrenched that some, like economist George Reisman, argue that environmentalists are the most severe threat to the free market since communism.[28] This jingoistic simplification is dead wrong for two reasons. First, Reisman forgets that the free market works not just as a sphere of products, services and profits but also as one of ideas. Environmentalism is just like a new competitor in that it forces established companies to invest and renew to remain vital and salient. It also provides real benefits to customers, answers real needs of society and, in demanding efficiency and sustainability, serves shareholders by improving performance and enhancing long-term value. Certainly, for companies accountable only to shareholders, the restrictions of responsible environmental behavior are a threat and a cost. Yet

Reisman would never argue that Microsoft should not have been allowed to sell its ideas because of the cost for software and training to customers, and the threat to IBM and other mainframe computer companies.

A second mistake in Reisman's logic is that environmentalism is really not a constraint at all but a liberation in that it asks companies and consumers to account for the real cost of resource depletion and destructive waste. In their Club of Rome report, Weizsacker, Lovins and Lovins call for "an economic *perestroika* built on economic *glasnost,* for if our prices tell lies, they cannot guide true choices, and if choices are not available, prices hardly matter at all."[29] It is free-market ideologues who are in this sense anti-market, because their resistance to environmental valuing represents exactly the intervention and pricing distortion that they resent as threats to the system. Not only do economists and businesspeople resist the concept of paying full replacement-value prices for energy, they sanction a "corporate socialism" that sees billions in yearly subsidies in the U.S. alone going to the most wasteful and destructive options. Weizsacker, Lovins and Lovins are only advocating a freer market when they suggest that one critical aspect to solving our environmental crisis is to unleash "competition in saving resources, not only in wasting them."[30] We are thus in the precarious position of having our best hope contained within the very instrument that has caused so much despair. The market economy is too productive and creative a human invention to not apply to our most difficult and challenging problems. But it is also too essential and potentially too destructive to operate without the ethical guidance that the community, as a factor in the market, has the right to expect and the necessity to impose.

6. Reward is related to risk. Hence, stagnant wages are a function of not working hard enough.

Risk and reward are assumed to be the defining correlates of the modern economy, but are they? As previously documented, there seems to be no connection between wages of CEOs and the performance of the companies they manage. Not normally a critic of management, *Business Week* commented that "the staggering rise in pay for the good, the bad, and the indifferent has left even some advocates of pay for performance wondering whether the balance between the CEO and shareholder is tilting the wrong way." H.J. Heinz's CEO took home $64.2 million while his company lagged behind its competitors and the stock market as a whole. Disney paid Michael Ovitz $91 million in severance for a not very successful year's work, and CEO Michael Eisner, who hired and then fired Ovitz, was awarded another 8 million options, bringing his total unexercised portfolio of Disney stock to $364.4 million. Rewards here bear no relation to risk; indeed, it seems as if reward were designed to be the opposite, which is risk free. For leadership expert Warren Bennis, "performance criteria are almost like intellectual Silly Putty."[31]

Qualified senior management is a scarce resource. Good people are worth millions. And the pressure to perform is so intense that CEOs are as vulnerable to losing their job as anyone else. That said, the managerial class has become so powerful that it has insulated itself from the very vicissitudes of the free market that are supposed to be its virtue. For these leaders to then impose productivity measures and firings in the name of shareholder value is disingenuous. Freeing decision makers from the consequences of their actions not only promotes expediency but undermines the moral authority for change. Drucker's warning to CEOs about employee anger has to do with unfairness as well as fear, unearned privilege as well as disrespectful heavy-handedness.

Perhaps the most widely known example of reward is Bill Gates, who is America's wealthiest man. Gates works very hard, is very bright, pays himself a modest wage, and expects as much from himself as from his employees. He has devised some smart strategies. He has also been smart enough to admit bone-headed moves and change tack. Since no one really knows where the converging reality of information technology will lead, Gates has vacuumed up all the talent and alliances he can to ensure he has a finger in every recipe for every pie. Gates has been called the most important man in America, and it is all because of a mistake. In 1984, when IBM was desperate to enter the PC market, Gates's fledgling company bought a jumbled operating system for $75,000. After cleaning it up and renaming it MS DOS, Gates offered the program to IBM for $200,000, happy to pocket the profit. In probably the most costly business mistake of all time, IBM turned down the offer to buy MS DOS and licensed it instead. With licensing came clones, with clones came billions, with billions comes clout.

IBM did not see the revolution about to happen. Nor did Bill Gates. This not to disparage Gates, who has shown much leadership in other ways. The point is that reward can be as much of an accident as a design, and that risk in this age of technology and information may not have anything to do with who has the money. John Plender points to "the need to recognize the value in a much wider set of relationships than those acknowledged by the conventional principal–agent model of capitalism, with its heavy emphasis on property rights. Those relationships, whether described in the sociologist's language of social capital or the economist's jargon of implicit contracts, are an important element in the competitive advantage of firms." Risk and reward has a very different meaning in this context. The biggest risk to a company may come not from a competitor but from the loss of an employee or employees who have mastered certain skills and knowledge. Risk may have to do not with money invested but with the trust invested between company and customers, or company and suppliers, or company and employees. Plender argues that companies that primarily reward shareholders and fail to attend to the employees who are responsible for innovation and creating value out of knowledge may "destroy wealth rather than help create it."[32]

Unjust profiteering is pronounced among senior managers and individual stock holders, but not limited to them. Today's equity market is driven more by institutional investors than by individuals. Pension and mutual funds invest hundreds of billions of dollars and wield the incredible clout that goes with those sums. Some institutional agents, like the California Teachers' Federation in the U.S. and Caisse Populaire in Canada, use such sophisticated tools and investment criteria that they can swing entire markets and greatly influence individual managers. Pushing for ever higher returns, these powerful funds have in their own way exacerbated the lemminglike focus on quarterly numbers, and contributed to unceasing restructuring of firms. Many have already noted the irony of these widely held funds pushing for efficiency and job reductions that in effect compromise or displace their own holders. My point is that such mutual funds represent a distortion of risk/reward, just like the non-performing but highly paid CEO. By definition, mutual funds spread risk. But by expectation, these funds seek maximum reward. The whole system is thus squeezing out costs and employees to an often unreasonable and destructive degree to satisfy the inflated prospects of a group actually taking only the most nominal risk. Wanting something for almost nothing may be illogical, selfish and irresponsible, but it is also an ethos that is now widely shared. Once again, the problem is not just the "them," but the "us."

7. The economy is central to human well-being. Hence, everything else is secondary.

The value of human life is an enigma for the ages, but it is also one that we must all finally resolve in the choices we make during the course of our lives. Increasingly, our choices revolve around an axis that is exclusively economic. Not very long ago, business was news only to businesspeople, but today the issues of business are of news to everyone. Politicians run mostly on economic promises. Interest rates and inflation are given the attention that used to be focused on superpower summits. And it is now a given that social institutions and systems are to be reengineered to achieve the efficiency and fiscal accountability of companies. Society has become infected by economics, and every aspect of human life (and nature) has been reduced to a weighting on some balance sheet. The world knows as much about Michael Jordan's multimillion-dollar sponsorship deals with Nike and Gatorade as it does about his remarkable feats on the basketball court. Movies are made or broken less by the opinion of critics than by the publicized tallies of opening-weekend box-office receipts. And annual university ratings now list the starting salary of graduates.

The intense interest in economic matters is understandable. The biggest threat to most people in industrialized countries is no longer war or ideological invasion, but reduced job security, wages and standard of living. Seeing highly qualified, highly committed fellow workers dumped from payrolls has been very sobering. Lost jobs once rebounded after a recession or restructuring, but in this chilling modern marketplace, jobs are cut and pay scaled back even in companies that are realizing record profits. The focus that used to go into planning careers or the next advance up the earning ladder is now devoted to keeping what we have and keeping from falling behind. Although it is right to worry about jobs, to seek political policies that expand opportunity and to refashion social structures to be more responsive to the needs of our time, it is also fair to say something very precious has been lost in this reduction to bottom-line valuing.

In the dominant calculus of the global economy, human beings have been rendered merely units for producing, consuming, earning, saving and spending. Marketers call this lifetime value—affixing dollar values to customers that represent a life's worth of deodorant, detergent or credit card usage. We know this to be too simplistic a reduction. We also know from our growing fatigue and frustration that work alone is unsatisfying or at least not fully fulfilling. And we know that even the attainment of great wealth and material pleasure does not automatically bring happiness. Wise though we may be about the deeper value of love and friendship, modern behavior tilts away from family and community to work, career and consumption. Somehow, the fear of economic loss, the worry of not getting the share we believe we deserve, keeps us locked into a system that our instincts understand is not fulfilling. Herman Daly and John B. Cobb Jr. explain some of the dangers of this contradiction: "On the basis of massive borrowing and massive sales of national assets, Americans have been squandering their heritage and impoverishing their children. They have done so for the sake of present consumption, the enjoyment of shopping that accompanies it, and most of all as a way to postpone questioning the efficacy of free trade and continuous growth."[33] With governments focused on competitiveness, and with society fixated on budgets, growth assumes greater importance than quality of life, a situation that management consultant Charles Handy warns "can lead to an economy of 'useless things.' "[34]

Perhaps the deepest irony in this growing attachment to consumption is that people are sacrificing more of themselves to the values of working, earning and obtaining at a time when there has been a marked turning away from secularization and toward the spiritual. Huntington writes that "the renewal of religion throughout the world far transcends the activities of fundamental extremists. In society after society it manifests itself in the daily lives and work of people and in the concerns and projects of governments."[35] It makes sense in the face of great social and economic precariousness to seek solace in the certitudes of religion. But whatever the lessons of higher human purpose and fuller meaning derived from such spiritual reorientation, people for the most part seem to separate this inner moral conviction from the dogged pursuit of commercial advantage and material possession.

There are several lessons in this. When we workers accuse senior managers of making business decisions free of any moral reference point, we are pointing out not an anomaly in their position but something we share with them. Another lesson, one more difficult to learn, is that the already great and growing investment in the economic dimensions of human life are in many ways abnegating the very meaning derived from spirituality. The compounding worries about protecting jobs and surviving economic upheaval have only intensified the selfishness that most religions castigate and all spirituality opposes. We draw much of our meaning and spiritual awe from nature, yet unrelenting economic expediency is devastating the natural environment. We draw identity, duty and moral worth from social interaction, yet accelerating economic competitiveness causes us to tolerate more and more poverty, inequality and injustice. Johan Galtung describes the culture of *homo economicus* as a "syndrome" that "not only detaches the individuals from each other by making the single individual the supreme decision-maker (egocentrism), but also detaches the satisfiers (goods/services) from each other as objects to be possessed and consumed one by one."[36] Though we seek God, we settle for mammon. Though we long for "family values," we will not devote the time to them. Though we crave for belonging, we opt for the radical individuality of "cocooning." The lesson is that our obsession for the economic is not something that can be managed apart from or in parallel with our spiritual sensibilities. If they are not integrated, then they are inevitably at odds. If they do not work as complements, then the economic inevitably erodes the spiritual.

The accumulated wisdom of history across all cultures confirms that people realize fulfillment in life experiences beyond commerce, work and consumerism. Philip Selznick writes: "Equality of opportunity alone cannot fashion a moral order. The principle must be embedded in a larger context of social justice. A society committed to moral equality needs to offer something more than the opportunity to seek reward through merit. It must find ways of upholding the ultimate worth of persons without regard to differences of talent, effort or character."[37] The unfolding of identity, the integration of personal character, the realization of belonging, the opportunity to experience love, and the sense of legacy are what we know make life complete. From these we also derive our sense of what is possible. And from these we also draw our convictions about what is right and ethical.

There are really only two ways to deal with lies. The first is to come clean, own up to the falsehood, and then work through the consequences. The second is to deny the lie and confront its implications from the disadvantage of its inevitable implosion. After its crumbling and quick dismemberment, it became obvious that the Soviet Union was in large part undone by its own lies. Five-year plans were a sham. Comradeship was a charade. And the system's heroes, like Stalin, were mass murderers on a scale greater than any external enemy in history. When the lies were out, there could be no turning back. Gorbachev may have envisioned a new Russian communism that combined *glasnost* with a China-style market economy, but his system's lies denied him the moral authority for proceeding with the reforms.

Although the deception is of an entirely different scale, the global market economy is as vulnerable to being undone by its moral inversions as communism was by its deceptions. Capitalism has vanquished communism, but its leaders and practitioners seem to have already forgotten that the threat of communism emerged only in opposition to the excesses of capitalism. The free market's original proclivity to excess and abuse is evident again. Indeed, the behavior of the economy in the years since the fall of communism suggests that much of the moderation and commitment to justice that companies and society adopted at the height of communism's power are being discarded. How ironic that in the great historic unity of a single global economic system, we face the paradox of every individual being left on their own to sink or swim.

The work of a global ethic is to address the lies of the modern world and its economy before the world and its economy are undermined by the lies. If the deception is that the economy and its corporate parts have the authority of rationality, then we must involve the deeper capacities of our wisdom and demand judgments from our fullest sensibility as humans. If the deception is that competition has the incontestable legitimacy of natural law, then we must go back and study nature to see how it so magnificently masters diversity. If the deception is that the economy is more important than either people or nature, then individually, corporately and institutionally we must convert to a perspective and behavior that subordinates commerce to serve what is essential for life. Hard though this may seem, as Hans Küng writes, "The answer is that human beings must become more than they are; they must become more human."[38]

Table 2. Lies and Other Business Truisms

Perception	Reality
The competitiveness of the economy is compromised by environmentalism. "It's either trees or jobs."	Despite record economic growth, North Americans—already the world's greatest polluters—have failed to meet promises made at the Rio Summit in 1992. Canada has the dubious distinction of announcing a balanced federal budget on the same day that it confirmed a 13 percent growth in green-house gas emissions since its Rio commitment.[39]
Business used to be a man's world, but it is getting to be a lot better for women.	Most corporate practices since reengineering have so stressed productivity and output that family preoccupations are made secondary. Resigning from her job as president and CEO of Pepsico's North American division, Brenda Barnes noted: "I am not leaving because my children need more of me; I'm leaving because I need more of them."[40]
"No pain, no gain." The steps taken by companies have indeed been painful, but stronger companies create better jobs.	Few benefits from these years of record-breaking profits have cascaded to the average worker. Corporate layoffs in the economic expansion of 1993–95 exceeded those of the recession of 1990–92. Later cuts hit hard at the most educated segment of the population. Most found jobs, but in one study, the new work paid wages averaging only 47 percent of previous pay.[41]

Many of the process changes of the last five years have been made to improve service to customers.	Systems like automated answering machines have created quagmires for most customers, requiring listening to endlessly droning messages to self-choose the self-service that self-satisfies (if you are lucky) the need. Not surprisingly, customer loyalty has been in precipitous decline in most industries, and most "customer first" mission statements have been rendered rather hollow.
Technology is the key to competitiveness.	Numerous studies show that the productivity gains from new technology have been elusive if not nonexistent. More disconcertingly, much of the new technology exacerbates the gap between rich and poor. According to physicist Freeman Dyson, "The failure of science to produce benefits for the poor in recent decades is due to two factors . . . Pure scientists have become more detached from the mundane needs of humanity and applied scientists have become more attached to immediate profitability."[42]

CHAPTER THREE

COSTS

*With the loss of past and future, life fluctuates between the
most bestial enjoyment of the moment and an adventurous
game of chance. An abrupt end is put to any kind of inner self-
development and to any gradual attainment of personal or
vocational maturity. There is no personal destiny, and
consequently there is no personal dignity.*

Dietrich Bonhoeffer, *"Inheritance and Decay," in* Ethics

White-collar crime is conservatively estimated to cost North American businesses more than $100 billion a year. This is "conservative" because in 1992 the U.S. General Accounting Office projected fraud in health care services alone to be between $20 and $75 billion.[1] These are staggering losses. For comparison, this is equal to the profits of the top forty corporations in North America. Imagine all the activity, capital, people, projects and hard work at General Motors, Ford, Exxon, Wal-Mart, General Electric, IBM, AT&T, Mobil, Chrysler, Philip Morris, Texaco, State Farm Insurance, Prudential Insurance, E.I. Du Pont, Chevron, Hewlett-Packard, Sears, Procter & Gamble, Amoco, Citicorp, Pepsico, Kmart, American International,

Motorola, Chase Manhattan, Lockheed Martin, Dayton Hudson, Kroger, Fannie Mae, Merrill Lynch, Conagra, Allstate, JC Penney, United Technologies, Metropolitan Life, Boeing, UPS, BankAmerica, Johnson & Johnson and the Travelers Group. Cancel out the profit contributions of these companies in 1997 and you have an amount that corresponds to what is lost in illegal or unethical behavior. Put another way, if we assume that salary and benefits cost an employer $80,000 per year per employee—this time a liberal estimate—the loss to corruption in North America equates to 12.5 million jobs. Imagine the workplace of today had companies spent the last decade reengineering to eliminate fraud, crime and unethical waste rather than disposing of people and jobs.

Two studies—one reported by B.R. Crossen in the *Journal of Business and Psychology* in 1993[2] and another by Amitai Etzioni—show that "in the last ten years, roughly two-thirds of America's largest corporations have been involved, in varying degrees, in some form of illegal behavior."[3] It is unfair to extrapolate too wide an indictment based on single infractions, but the missteps of many of the top forty support these findings. GM lost a class action suit from drivers hurt or killed in pickup trucks that were designed with a vulnerable side-saddle gas tank. It was also the victim of shady ethics when NBC's *Dateline* newsmagazine staged an impact of the truck but used explosive charges to ignite the ruptured fuel tank. Ford carries the stigma of knowingly selling the faulty and lethal Pinto; Exxon has the stain of the *Valdez* disaster in Alaska; Wal-Mart bruised its reputation by procuring clothes for its Kathie Lee Gifford label from sweatshops; General Electric repeatedly paid fines for fraudulent billing practices and bribery scandals in its jet engine division, and in 1993 was fined $350 million for fraud in its (since sold) Kidder Peabody unit; and AT&T's chairman, Robert Allen, became the poster-boy for reaping millions of dollars in wealth from stock appreciation related to firing forty thousand workers— many of whom lost their jobs for strategic failures for which Allen was responsible. The point of this litany is not to impugn the companies but to stress again that moral issues are pervasive, and that neglecting to prepare any organization for exercising ethical judgment risks huge costs and failures.

This is a global problem. As noted earlier, the world's economy is developing faster than the world community's social, legal and moral norms for guiding and containing it. As a result, the disorganized economy of a disorganized world is not just prone to gray behavior. Increasingly, and disturbingly, the mainstream economy of the world has also been infiltrated and manipulated by organized crime. Japan's three largest securities brokerage firms, France's largest bank and several of Italy's former prime ministers have all been tainted by involvement with gangsters. In Korea, Hong Kong, South Africa, Mexico and Russia, ruinous bribes, scams and insider trading have linked politicians, bankers and stock exchanges with violent criminals and mobsters. A cover story in *Maclean's* magazine in July 1997 concludes that "to law enforcement agencies in North America and abroad, Canada is now better known as a global leader in commercial or white collar crime. And, increasingly, it is becoming the land where the Mounties do *not* get their man—or woman." And in the U.S., "a three month investigation by *Business Week* reveals that substantial elements of the small-cap market have been turned into a veritable Mob franchise, under the very nose of regulators and law enforcement."[4]

Scandals that seemed only possible in the Third World and among dictators are now everywhere in the industrialized world and are even contaminating democracies. So pervasive is this intrusion of the underworld into the mainstream economy that both conservative President Jacques Chirac of France and communist leader Jiang Zemin of China have decried corruption as the major impediment of competitiveness, development and social well-being in their countries. For a communist and capitalist to agree on an economic issue is remarkable, but the real lesson is that the line between amorality and immorality is very fine indeed.

Executives pressured to achieve results at any cost will have the tendency to place the end before the means, just like any criminal. And companies single-mindedly locked in a survival of the fittest competitiveness are subscribing to the same law of the jungle as gangs on the street. Greed may wear different clothes and employ different tactics, but it is still characteristically damaging to many for the benefit of a few. Not all elements of the economy are criminal or immoral. And most people who are competitive in business would not break the law to win. The point is that in the absence of clearly defined laws, the proclivity to self-interest can overwhelm common sense. Peter Senge puts it this way: "The more stress we put on our organizations the more their tendency will be to revert to their most primitive behaviors."[5] In the moral vacuum advocated by those who see the market economy as self-regulating, the price fixing of profit-driven executives at such companies as ADM and Bausch & Lomb is in the final analysis as usurious as loan sharking by a neighborhood thug. Criminality may not be affecting a reverse takeover of the global economy. But it remains an inescapable irony that criminals, along with a handful of some senior business executives, are the early beneficiaries of the gap between the profit aims of global business and the still-forming moral standards and legal regulations of the global community.

This is not the first time that the excesses of capitalism and the penetration of criminal elements into the mainstream economy have occurred in parallel. During the 1920s, unregulated speculators made a killing on Wall Street while mobsters made millions supplying booze despite Prohibition. In an environment of business profiteering, the attitude that trickled down to law enforcers, law makers and the public was that ambition had more value than morals. Corruption was everywhere, involving the courts, the police and companies as well as gangs. It took one generation, and the false economic expansion of a world war, to undo the structural damage of unfettered speculation and unchecked business greed. It took two generations to rebuild the middle class and rebalance the distribution of wealth to create a more stable society. And it took three generations for the laws to finally come into play that gave enforcement officials the upper hand against organized crime. Is it now just coincidence that legitimate business and the criminal class are again profiting disproportionately while average workers are left behind and losing ground?

Financial institutions are the heart of the world's economy, providing the cross-border capital flows and the international exchange of debt and equity upon which global commerce depends. It is this most essential sector that, in country after country, organized crime has penetrated. In France, one of the biggest financial scandals of the 1990s was the looting of Paris-based Credit Lyonnais. Two Italians with criminal records bribed bankers for a $2-billion loan with which they bought the MGM film studio. In an indicative snapshot, the head of Credit Lyonnais's Dutch office, who participated in the decision, had received a Picasso drawing as a gift from the two. It turned out to be a fake. This would be farcical, except that Credit Lyonnais has so far lost more than $5 billion in its failed Hollywood ventures and is sitting on a catastrophic total of $35 billion in bad loans. *Fortune* reports that "investigators in France, Italy and the U.S.—a sort of bicontinental legion of financial geologists—are drilling deeper in the mountain of fraud" and "there are dark indications that the corruption reaches high into the French and Italian political systems." A former Italian prime minister and a former Italian foreign minister were allegedly bribed to pressure bank officials to make the loans.[6]

In Japan, Kuniji Miyazaki, former chairman of the Dai-Ichi Kangyo Bank, one of the country's top ten banks, committed suicide after officials questioned him about approving $250 million in "uncollectable loans" to racketeer Ryuichi Koike. Nomura Securities, Japan's largest brokerage, had already been implicated in loaning money and trading for Koike, and its president, Hideo Sakamaki, was jailed. Three other of the country's largest stock trading companies—Daiwa Securities, Nikko Securities, and Yamaichi Securities—fell victim to the same scandal. The *International Herald Tribune* writes: "What we're talking about is Japan's three largest securities companies caught seemingly red-handed, now with a confession, breaking the law in an open and defiant way."[7] Organized crime has been the bane of Japanese business for generations. And for many of these companies, this is not the first time that such scandal has befallen them.

In 1991, Nomura suffered disgrace when it was revealed that the company sheltered criminals and politicians from stock market losses. While millions of Japanese citizens lost much of their life savings in the stock and real estate crash of the late 1980s and early 1990s, up to one thousand "special accounts" at Nomura were protected from the fall. (Yet another distortion of reward being commensurate with risk.) The president resigned, and new policies and practices were introduced. However, in byzantine fashion, the discredited president was soon returned to the board, and the old ways of doing business persisted. When the new scandals broke in 1997, *The Economist* called them "Familiar Sins" and reported that "Nomura response to the suggestion of wrongdoing smacks of previous practice too—deny everything. It has released only the sparsest details."[8] Nomura's new president, Junichi Ujiie, wrote a contrite memo to his staff explaining that "the line between right and wrong has been a bit blurred at Nomura."[9] But it remains to be seen whether acknowledging this "bit" represents coming to terms with the company's entrenched illegal and immoral business practices.

A similar labyrinth of bribes has embroiled business executives, bankers and politicians in South Korea. Chief Judge Son Ji Yol in 1997 sentenced Chung Tae Soo, the chairman of Hanbo Steel and Construction, to fifteen years in jail. In his judgment, he stated: "Your wrong doing has caused a great shock to the Korean people, harm to the country's economy, and chaos to society." Hanbo is one of South Korea's top *chaebol*—the twenty or so conglomerates that control virtually the entire output of the country's economy. "Mr. Chung had made payoffs totaling millions of dollars to bankers and to senior lawmakers of both parties in exchange for loans to the over-extended steel company."[10] The trail of bribes and favors subsequently led to the arrest of President Kim Young Sam's son and several of the president's closest advisers. All of this is happening within a reform-minded administration that had already sent to jail the previous president, Roh Tae Woo, for accepting millions in bribes.

In Italy, a former prime minister, Giulio Andreotti, has gone into self-imposed exile to escape the prison term for his conviction for malfeasance that included accepting bribes from the Mafia. Silvio Berlusconi, head of the Finivest conglomerate and the previous prime minister, has been convicted of fraud. And the current prime minister, Romano Prodi, may soon go on trial for conflict of interest charges from his days as chairman of IRI, the giant holding company. In South Africa, securities enforcement officials are investigating seventy-nine cases of insider trading, a 50 percent increase from 1996. In Canada, police and regulators are trying to unravel the Bre-X scam that involved tampering with ore samples from an already discredited gold mine in scandal-plagued Indonesia. In Hong Kong, the new communist administration "has also made considerable efforts to *gao guanxi,* or 'create a network of relationships' between its security ministries and Hong Kong's crime rings and secret societies."[11] As many as fifty triads may be involved in this state-sanctioned co-opting of criminal elements toward achieving a new post-colonial Chinese-centered equilibrium.

Beyond mere coincidence, these expanding and recurring scandals suggest that the countries and economies at the very apex of development and globalization are struggling with a pervasive corruption that uncomfortably mixes politics, business and crime. This epidemic of high-level impropriety raises several questions. First, what are the lessons of this corruption? Second, why are business and politics so prone to criminal interpolation? And, third, what are the costs of this illegality and immorality?

What are the lessons?

Ethics are the norms that a community defines and institutionalizes to prevent individuals from pursuing self-interest at the expense of others. An assumption of ethics is that persons will not usually self-regulate—that without the opprobrium of society, and threatened punishment for non-conformance, people will slip into behavior that maximizes personal advantage. The high-level improbity, in different cultures and in societies reflecting a variety of religious traditions, confirms that human beings are essentially similar. People will yield to temptation, particularly when the payout is rich. Illegal deals and bribes are negotiated in the shadows, in the gaps where public scrutiny does not readily penetrate. Big business casts big shadows, and international business is even more opaque, in that the morality of transactions is easily masked by distance and indigenous customs. The global economy, like the human individual, cannot create a customized morality but must draw upon the morals and beliefs of the larger community. Self-discipline is possible, but the terms of that discipline are derived from society.

Another lesson is that these crimes are recurring. Nomura and the Japanese securities industry are in the second wave of scandal that repudiates any of the reform realized since the first transgressions were revealed only five short years ago. Credit Lyonnais has gone well beyond the MGM debacle. That it has so far squandered a staggering $35 billion in bad loans suggests that incompetence and profligacy have been the rule rather than the exception. Five years and three governments after the original investigations caught politicians, businesspeople and the Mafia in corrupting interaction, the so-called reformers in Italy now seem entangled in their own web of abuse and conflict of interest. In the U.S., the Supreme Court in 1997 reversed the acquittal of James O'Hagan, a Minneapolis lawyer who used insider information during Grand Met's take-over of Pillsbury to realize a profit in options trading of $4.3 million. The decision caught many by surprise not because of the illegal trading but the court's decision to assign guilt and mete out punishment. On yet another scale, the Bre-X scandal is amazing, less for the billions lost than for the fact that the same mine was used by the same lead geologist in the 1980s to attract Australian investors. Despite hundreds of millions of dollars in losses, and without even bothering to change the name of the mine, a second, even more damaging and preposterous duping was perpetrated. Getting caught is thus an incon-venience more than cause for penitence. Just as criminals tend to be repeat offenders, flagrant companies, executives and political leaders rarely reform or genuinely mean the "utmost apologies" that companies like Nomura issue after being caught out.

Not only are the same companies repeatedly embroiled in scandal, but a third lesson is that illegal business activity runs both deep and wide. To escape paying the bribes and payoffs demanded by Japan's yakuza and to prevent gangsters from disrupting proceedings, 2,355 Japanese corpora-tions held their annual general meetings simultaneously. So far, more than five thousand senior executives in Italy, including CEOs of Fiat and Olivetti, have been convicted of bribing politicians. France lobbied hard in the early 1990s to prevent Italy from joining the European Common Currency on grounds that its economy was rife with corruption. Now the French have their own corruption mess on their hands. *The Econo-mist* notes that "the bosses of almost a quarter of the companies in the CAC40 stock market index have been formally investigated for one infringement or another."[12] In 1996, Loik Le Foch-Prigent, chairman of France's national railroad, SNCF, was jailed for corruption tracing back to his tenure running Elf Aquitaine, France's biggest industrial holding. The *crème de la crème* have also been implicated in Korea. Of the four *chaebol* that control 84 percent of the country's economy, senior executives of three have been jailed for illicit payments to senior government officials. And in Hong Kong, five traders were arrested, and the premier equities company, Jardine Fleming Investment Management, paid out $19.3 million to cover bilked clients, "repaying money that might have been lost as a result of its own transgressions."[13]

And this is only what sees the light of day. Employees in North America, Europe and Asia have suffered the severe dislocation of reengineering and downsizing in the name of enhancing corporate competitiveness. But in some cases, senior managers have only squandered much of that hard-won efficiency in unscrupulous—often illegal, often immoral—payouts, perks and practices. While it would be grossly unfair to paint all businesspeople as crooks, it would be equally unwise to deny that business is sometimes itself crooked. Even well-intentioned people may on occasion, by virtue of having to compete within a corrupt global system, resort to evading the law or suppressing personal morals. Some argue that business is best left to the market to regulate. But this is just not working. Indeed, rather than self-regulate, many enterprises seek the corners and shadows of the global economy to obscure behavior and accountability. For example, lax disclosure laws have attracted 200,000 corporations to register in the British Virgin Islands, a corporate population ten times greater than the human one. If these companies earn their revenue in the global market, then does the global market not have the right to see and judge their practices, profits, taxes and behavior?

Why are business and politics prone to criminal interference?

From afar, the corruption in Italy or Korea, with political reformers transforming into the next generation of suspects, looks almost like the Keystone Kops. Although the scandals in the U.S. and Canada involve a lower order of personalities, the scale of wrongdoing in North America is still sobering. Hundreds of billions were lost in the S&L debacle of the 1980s, much of it in shady circumstances that resulted in a few people going to jail. More recently, several billion investor dollars evaporated in the demise of Bre-X. *Business Week*'s investigation of organized crime's foray into Wall Street included stories of violent beatings and death threats. First the Italian and now the Russian gangs were using "kids with clean records" in the brokerage houses to launder money. *Business Week* made two stark conclusions: the first is that "Wall Street has become so lucrative for the Mob that it is allegedly a major source of income for high-level members of organized crime"; the second is that "what all this adds up to is a shocking tale of criminal infiltration abetted by widespread fear and silence—and official inaction."[14]

In some ways, Canada has become a safer market than the U.S. for criminals to practice their business. In 1996, after a generation of successfully fighting cigarette smoking as public policy, the federal government was forced into an embarrassing retreat. Higher taxes had resulted in such higher prices for cigarettes that demand was being hampered. Suddenly, Canadian cigarettes being exported into the U.S. at untaxed prices were streaming back via the black market. Just as with Prohibition, organized crime was ready to supply product even if the demand was illegal. But in an ironic reversal, rather than being the source and beneficiary, Canada had become the market and victim. As the deluge displaced Canadian product and Canadian taxes, the government was impelled to lower the price in the originating market. Although not necessarily an explicit union, that big business and mobsters found a common advantage is, to say the least, a source of discomfort.

With laxer laws and more dispersed securities regulation, Canada has also become a magnet for unsavory boiler room operators and stock manipulators. In her book *Greed: Investment Fraud in Canada and Around the Globe,* Deborah Thompson investigates numerous situations in which fraudsters came to Canada to set up shop. In one telemarketing scheme, mostly American customers were defrauded of millions through sales of supposedly investment-quality gems. The U.S. Postal Service and the Royal Canadian Mounted Police collaborated to indict the perpetrators. But while the fraudsters extradited to the U.S. were forced to pay million-dollar fines of restitution and serve prison terms, those criminals who fought to stay in Canada remained free and were documented emptying their Canadian holdings into Swiss bank accounts.[15] Similarly, penny stock manipulators found guilty by the Vancouver exchange were reprimanded without fine and were prohibited from future trading. That such crimes are low priorities for overstretched courts invites those who fear stiffer prison sentences in the U.S. to simply move north.

There are many reasons why scandals, bribes and frauds have become so frequent in business. The growing complexity of technology increases the access to information and contacts, creating opportunities for misuse and at the same time a shield against being exposed. Another characteristic of technology is its depersonalization. This abstracts the victim of any abuse or crime and provides a cloak of anonymity for the perpetrator. Some people have argued that people who bought gems or Bre-X stock to "get rich quick" essentially only got what they deserved. But this is another distortion of sensibility that creates such fecund conditions for business excess and crime. That the greed of the victim is somehow justification for the greed of the crook absolves people of responsibility for their actions. Thompson notes wryly that "society's drift away from morality, having moved more swiftly in recent years, is another factor in fraud's rise."[16]

Morality has been undermined by a variety of factors. In business, downsizing has made people feel disposable. Since the loyalty employees invested in their companies has been so rudely cut, the sense of obligation and propriety to the company has also been severed. Fewer people doing more work creates the build-up of pressure that sometimes results in cutting corners. Fewer people doing more work also means that there is less supervision, learning and constructive interaction at exactly the time corners are most prone to being cut. The tone of discretionary morality has been set by the objectives emphasized by business itself. Companies have in the past decade greatly increased the expectation for results, particularly for higher profits and greater efficiency, without making parallel demands for respect for the law and the community. Such single-mindedness over time inflates the importance of effect and deflates that of means. Behavior as well as words have been adding to the ambiguity. That senior corporate officers take more and more compensation out of companies, including those that are struggling and firing workers, reinforces the perception that the system is based on power and exploitation rather than on fairness.

Declining moral sensibility unleashes the more negative aspects of human nature that morality by definition works to contain. "At its core," writes Thompson, "fraud involves some of our most basic human characteristics: fear, ego and greed."[17] Back to Keynes and business making a virtue out of vice. Fear, ego and greed, properly channeled and focused, are assets in business because they provide the motivation, urgency and means of self-sacrifice for working hard, taking risks and creating real value. What is rarely admitted, though, is that these powerful forces of human nature require enormous self-discipline and maturity. Few people know themselves well enough to honestly acknowledge and wisely manage these deep emotions and needs. In most cases, greed is suppressed or ignored or downplayed. Everyone has some degree of greed, but not everyone has the wisdom for managing it. Ethics, in part, serve as the wisdom of the community, providing guidance and stricture to those without the maturity, self-discipline or responsibility for moderating their own greed. For the global economy, the issue is that while everyone's greed is being encouraged, there is not yet in place an overarching framework for bringing to bear the global community's wisdom for moderating it.

One surprise that emerges in Thompson's profile of fraudsters is how closely these deviants resemble the corporate worker we usually admire. "In addition to the money they steal, fraudsters also enjoy basking in the power they hold over people and relish passing themselves off as kind, capable, diligent people. In a corporate setting, they're the employees who regularly work late, or start their days unusually early. They prefer not to take vacations, and even boast about it. The reality is that the fraudster can't afford to stay away from their scams too long—they are their lifeblood. Ironically, their 'devotion' to work can make distinguishing the fraudster from the honest employee a real challenge for management."[18]

The greedy and the driven who are in business are in a sense the easy part of the problem. There always have been—and always will be—those for whom objectives and advantage are paramount, so much so that legality and morality are irrelevant. Laws, punishment and constant vigilance are the only remedies for those who not only straddle but flout ethical convention. Much more difficult is dealing with the many generally law-abiding and morally responsible people who nevertheless succumb to criminal or unethical behavior. John M. Darley of Princeton University reviewed a variety of high-profile criminal business cases for his paper, "How Organizations Socialize Individuals into Evil-doing," presented to the conference Behavioral Research and Business Ethics convened at Northwestern University in 1994. Darley identified the dynamics that contributed to sensible people, in generally reputable companies, doing illegal and immoral things. Among the situations he dissected were the "Ford Pinto, sold for years by a company in which many executives were aware that it had a gas tank likely to rupture in low-speed rear-end crashes"; the Robins Company, which continued "marketing a contraceptive product that it knew caused disastrous medical consequences to many who used it"; and Morton Thiokol, whose executives remained silent despite being "aware of the dangers to the space shuttle of O-rings at low launch temperatures."[19]

One lesson from Darley's analysis is that these companies, and the individuals who knowingly went along, not only did wrong but did harm, causing death, injury and untold suffering. More than stealing or making money was at stake, meaning that motivations had less to do with greed than with "belonging," "going along" and "fitting in." It does not take a sinister person with sinister aims to achieve sinister results. So a second lesson is that "the potential for incubation of harm is high" in virtually any organization, even those, like "universities, manufacturing firms, research organizations and government organizations," that are usually considered benign. Wherever people gather in groups to undertake a project, a tendency emerges in which social norms and ethical rules get subordinated to the pressures of that group's objectives. "Crimes are committed," Darley notes, simply "because they fulfill an organization's goals."[20]

Darley established four basic constructs that induce or facilitate corporate "evildoing." The first, already noted briefly in relation to technology, is the "diffusion and fragmentation of information and responsibility." In the case of the Dalkon Shield, a quality control supervisor, on his own initiative, found a design flaw that he believed could cause infection. But that information, in the manufacturing "compartment" of the company, never made it to the "compartment" of Robins medical people and decision makers who had to respond to complaints and worries from doctors and customers. Similarly, the growing specialization of workers contributes to a distancing from responsibility for the whole. NASA and Morton Thiokol engineers both knew of the risks of launching in a cold climate. Everyone had expertise to do with only part of the operation, and although one engineer bravely spoke up to object, the pressure to perform from the decision makers effectively silenced all the other specialists.

A second cause of evildoing is what Darley terms "commitment to a course of action." Once strategic decisions have been cast, and, more important, once investments have been expended, the momentum of a project can easily overtake the good judgment of those responsible for it. This again reflects the belief in the infallibility of business rationality. If something has been approved, then its logic alone warrants compliance. This also points to the fundamental importance of strong, clear and effective leadership and management. Harvard business professor Francis J. Aguilar, in his study of business ethics, writes, "Among companies observed, those with the most favorable ethical climate also enjoyed strong business leadership. Poor operating performance invites cutting close to the line of acceptable behavior—even crossing it—to avoid the consequences of failure."[21] Ineffective planning or mistaken management puts people into the uncomfortable position of always being behind, always having to catch up. In frustration, judgment gets short-circuited. In desperation, people do desperate, even illegal and harmful, things.

Darley's third socialization factor is "abstract harm and tangible gain." Companies work to objectives. The organizational structure plans and manages projects. Workers have defined tasks and roles to fulfill that project. And performance measures quantify results, be it delivery against a deadline, sales figures or company profit. While the internal interest of the project is always clear and present, the repercussions beyond the company's focus and measurement are hazy. Pressure to perform at work further distracts people from assessing the fuller consequences of their decisions. For Ford workers, the Pinto was a project of great competitive urgency. The deadline was fixed and fast approaching. The performance criteria were also very specific: "two thousand, two thousand," which stipulated both maximum body weight for the car and maximum price to the consumer. To accelerate development, tooling for the car was carried out simultaneously with engineering. Engineers and managers "discovered prior to production but after tooling was under way that rear-end collisions in crash tests would easily rupture the Pinto's fuel system."[22] To not confront the costs, delay, weight penalty and management opprobrium, this ultimately fatal flaw was intentionally overlooked.

Two lessons can be derived from this abstraction of harm. The first is that the concrete reality of efficiency and work takes priority over any eventual, distant and possible outcome. Companies may depend on the customer for their sales and livelihood, but that customer is rarely present in the process and thus remains a disembodied unit of economic value. Darley notes that "a good many of the forces that cause people to avoid doing harm to others rely on the salient presence of specific or specifically imagined victims; if such victims are not present then restraining forces are considerably weakened."[23] If there is no connection to the victim, then the rights of, and obligations to, that victim are diminished. The second lesson is that even with the knowledge of a great potential for harm, moral questioning, discussion and intervention are rarely part of business. Frederick B. Bird and James A. Waters, who have written extensively about business ethics, call this moral muteness. Morals are awkward and seemingly subjective, and therefore counterproductive to the efficiency and objective-orientation of business. They write: "Managers shun moral talk because such talk seems to result in burdening business decisions with considerations that are not only extraneous, but at times antagonistic to responsible management."[24]

So deeply are businesspeople convinced of the inherent rationality of business that the morality of the community, created over thousands of years, is considered an impediment or a constraint to operations. What is dangerous about this arrogance is that people fail to learn from even the most tragic mistakes. As noted, in the 1990s, General Motors largely repeated the Pinto debacle, releasing pickup trucks with side-saddle gas tanks that were suspected, and then proven, to be prone to bursting on side impacts. GM denied wrongdoing, although it finally redesigned the trucks to place the tanks in a more protected position, and was found guilty of negligence in a class action suit. The repetition of potentially harmful decision making points to a process flaw in business itself. As Darley notes, "Information about product dangers, as opposed to information about products sales, markets, and profits, is generally 'abnormal' information, and the mechanisms for its analysis are not well developed."[25] Companies, like emperors, do not like being told they have no clothes.

The fourth contributor to individual evildoing within companies is "employee self-interest and job survival." This seems to be the obvious motivation for wrongdoing: sacrificing an obligation or duty for personal gain or advantage. But like everything else, employee self-interest and job security have been vastly transformed by the globalization of the economy and the reengineering of work processes. The impunity with which companies cut employees in the past decade will likely have implications for generations. In so harshly and inhumanly severing any reciprocity between company and employee, reengineering has unwittingly lowered the motivation for moral behavior and eased the consequences of ethical transgressions. Economist William Wolman and business writer Anne Colamosca compare the savagery of corporate reengineering to China's disastrous Cultural Revolution of the 1960s. "Mao's reengineering was not very different. Both revolutions put the responsibility on workers—professional workers—to reexamine and reshape themselves so that institutions could thrive and move into the future. Implicit was the understanding that if failure occurred, the worker was to blame."[26] The disregard toward individuals by companies cannot but invite a correlative disregard by individuals of company rules, norms and standards. Since the company is only looking after itself, employees had better only look after themselves.

Even employees who risk doing the right thing, who rise above the disdain companies often show for their own people, will not necessarily be acknowledged or applauded. Darley reports what happened to the quality control supervisor who raised concern over the design flaw in the Dalkon Shield. After presenting the results of experiments to his superiors, Mr. Crowder was told that this issue was not his responsibility. When Crowder persisted, saying that "he could not, in good conscience, keep quiet about something that he felt could cause infection in the women who wore the Shield," he was told by his boss: "Your conscience does not pay your salary." Crowder was accused of being insubordinate and was told "if he valued his job he would do as he was told."[27] In an often repeated perversion, someone seeking to be moral is seen as a threat or a nuisance, even though the moral course would clearly have been the most beneficial to the company, let alone to those it intentionally harmed. Mr. Crowder did not let himself be derailed by the threats. He took his concerns higher into the organization, only to be rebuffed and was laid off in a corporate reorganization several years later. As Darley notes, "He is a genuine hero, and his heroism cost him his job."

A caution to all managers is that even good companies do bad things. General Electric is one of the most imitated companies in North America, and its CEO, Jack Welch, is widely acknowledged to be one of the premier managers in the world. Admired for its provocative strategies and incredible growth in shareholder value, GE has nevertheless been tarnished by repeated scandals. Johnson & Johnson has long been a case study for its inspiring corporate Credo. When the company encountered the unprecedented situation of product tampering, it demonstrated the perspicacity of its Credo, winning the respect of consumers and businesspeople everywhere, when it responded with its now famous recall of Tylenol. The Credo is critically important and deserves emulation, but it is not foolproof. In 1985, a disgruntled chemist at 3M stole samples of an experimental fiberglass cast material used to mend broken bones. These were sent to 3M's competitors, including J&J, with an offer to sell the secret technology. According to 3M, J&J used these samples to develop its own technology, and after a long, drawn-out trial, the court agreed and fined J&J $116 million. (The misdirected employee was convicted of mail fraud and transporting in stolen property.) Business is very complex as well as competitive, very ambiguous as well as intensely aggressive. In such a maelstrom, usually good people, in usually good companies, will sometimes forsake training, ignore codes and even suppress their own better judgment to gain advantage.

From this perspective, the "them" who perpetrate such gross violations of social law and morality can all too easily be the "us." There are truly sinister businesspeople with sinister intentions, but, for the most part, ethical and legal lapses are the stuff of average people who know better. Much of the behavior research into organizations has struggled with exactly this conundrum. Kellogg Graduate School of Management professor David M. Messick and University of Notre Dame assistant professor of management Ann E. Tenbrunsel write that social psychologists homed in on this issue "following the Second World War, when scholars were puzzled by the apparent ease with which citizens of one of the world's most civilized nations, Germany, acted brutally towards citizens of other nations and to many of their own citizens as well." What numerous studies since the 1960s show is that people acquiesce to authority, even in matters that violate personal values and beliefs, much more readily than most of us are comfortable acknowledging. As Messick and Tenbrunsel note: "Much of the evil that was done by the fascist state was done 'institutionally'—that is, within the context of organizations in which people, influenced by the prevailing organizational cultures, followed or gave orders, doing what they thought others wanted and expected of them."

Dietrich Bonhoeffer wrote most of his *Ethics* while imprisoned by precisely that institutionalized evil. Needless to say, there is an especially poignant connection between his moral scholarship and the almost universal surrender of judgment by his society as it went to war and mechanistically implemented the Holocaust. Bonhoeffer did not mince his words, arguing that judgment premised on achievement is ultimately morally vacuous. He writes: "When a successful figure becomes especially prominent and conspicuous, the majority give way to idolization of success. They become blind to right and wrong, truth and untruth, fair play and foul play. They have eyes only for the deed, for the successful result. The moral and intellectual critical faculty is blunted. It is dazzled by the brilliance of the successful man and by the longing in some way to share in his success."[28] This is a sobering warning for the global economy. Too often, success functions as an ideal rather than as a desired outcome. As an ideal it is normative—creating not only expectations but justifications for its achievement. Pressured by the fierce competitiveness of the world's business, every company is understandably struggling to win. But as success becomes more equated to survival, by implication it assumes a transcending importance over any other value. "Whatever it takes" is thus the latest business Credo, valued by managers as an attitude as well as a behavior.

Whatever it takes, however, means that the goal overrides the means. Indeed, the yardstick for acceptable behavior in pursuit of success has been shifting rather markedly. Ten years ago, the infamous line uttered by Gordon Gekko in the movie *Wall Street*—"Greed is good"—genuinely shocked people, and was meant as an indictment of the excesses of the 1980s. Now the sensibility that greed is good is essentially operating in the mainstream of North American society. The accordance of gospel validity to success is evident in the widespread resignation with which employees and communities have accepted company cuts at a time of high and growing profitability. The shift to the center by Democrats in the U.S., Liberals in Canada and Labour in the U.K. also means that the larger social debate is now not whether greed (extreme success) is good or bad, but how much greed (concentrated success) is politically palatable.

What are the costs of this illegality and immorality?

Starting in the global context, business practiced without regard for law, community or morality is heinously damaging the already precarious natural environment frustrating even the limited ways in which countries, companies and consumers have tried to address the problem. One so far successful global pact has been the Montreal Protocol, which, in response to the dangerous deterioration of the earth's ozone layer, called for the halt of CFC production in industrialized countries by 1996 and in developing countries by 2010. While production has dropped, *Business Week* reports that a black market for CFCs has boomed in Europe and North America. "Worldwide, the U.N. estimates that some 30,000 metric tons of CFCs were smuggled into industrialized countries in 1996, one-fifth of the total production. The U.S. Justice department estimates that the CFC-smuggling racket is larger in value than the trade in illegal guns."[29] Just another example of supply and demand, except that in this case the supply kills, and the demand is fueled by already well off consumers who want to save some more money. One report cited in the *Business Week* story "estimates that up to 1.5 million cases of skin cancer could be averted each year if the CFC ban is enforced." Even on the black market, CFCs are considerably cheaper than their ozone-friendly substitute. But the primary use of CFCs is for car air-conditioning, so it is average people who already have the means to spend for a car that are breaking the law and distancing themselves from any moral obligation.

Hardly the exception, environmental abuse is often murderous. Taipower, the company that runs nuclear power stations in Taiwan, has been storing 98,000 barrels of radioactive waste on a small island that is home to Yami aboriginals. The company and the dump have lately drawn attention because of Taipower's plan to export the waste, for a payment of $230 million, to the highly unpredictable state of North Korea. The deal is in limbo because of the protests it has raised, but only now, in part through the efforts of Greenpeace, are people coming to terms with the tragic costs of the dump itself. As reported in *The Economist,* the storage silos are starting to leak and are blamed by the Yami for causing increases in cancer and birth defects.[30] Taipower, in the good corporate tradition of ADM, Nomura and GM, denied until recently that anything but low-level waste "such as used gloves" were at the site. Taipower is not alone in playing this lethal shell game. Darley tells of how "the Allied Chemical company, manufacturer of Kepone, a substance known to be toxic, set up a dummy corporation as an 'independent contractor' to continue the manufacture of it."[31] Allied failed to take similar precautions for the environment, and over time a hundred miles of fisheries on the James River had to be closed.

As disturbing as this behavior is, more pressing is the pattern that it represents. First, those with the weakest voice, often aboriginals and those most dependent on nature, are the ones saddled to deal with the waste, and attendant toxicity, of the affluent. More and more, part of the trade of the global economy will involve the rich exporting their malignant problems to the poor. Second, companies mask the threat and usually deny the problem until the evidence of harm becomes incontestable. Such spin doctoring not only is highly cynical but further distances the culprit from the victim, and further immunizes individual managers from the consequences of their decisions. Third, the costs for waste, in terms of suffering, penalties and payouts, are growing exorbitantly but have yet to arouse an intense program of conservation and prevention. As noted by von Weizsacker, Lovins and Lovins, what are missing are "rewards for saving resources, not for wasting them . . . and competition in saving resources, not only in wasting them."[32]

While companies circumvent laws to gain an advantage, as often as not they lose more than they gain. Bausch & Lomb, famous for its contact lenses and Ray-Ban sunglasses, is a case in point. Driven like many other corporations to achieve double-digit annual growth, B&L's managers, according to *Business Week,* "by the early 1990s increasingly resorted to what was expedient—often at the expense of what consti- tuted sound business practice or ethical behavior." In Hong Kong, North America and Latin America, managers overshipped products to meet sales targets and then dumped contact lenses and Ray-Bans on distributors, creating a huge image and inventory problem for B&L. It also seems the company ignored Latin American practices that may have indirectly involved money laundering.[33] This is a company that Wall Street lionized during the 1980s and early 1990s. But, in an often repeated—and just as often forgotten—lesson, the years of strong revenues at Bausch & Lomb were not an indication of a strong company. High profits hid the pressure points and unethical tactics that finally resulted in an implosion of sales and revenues.

Subsumed in the mess was one transgression with perhaps the most pointed ethical implications. For years, Bausch & Lomb sold consumers two brands of contact lenses that were identical. One, however, cost only $7.50 per pair while the second sold for $70 per pair. Outraged consumers who found themselves paying ten times more for the same product launched a class action suit. B&L managers initially dismissed the pricing discrepancy as an issue of "volume discounts," but the court did not agree and charged the company with a $350-million settlement. In the final tally, the company lost far more than the revenue it made from the pricing duplicity. The hard way, Bausch & Lomb learned two truisms. Results have a cost, a realization few senior managers heed until crisis imposes it. And lies will be found out, an eventuality in this information-leaking world that no company or person can ever presume to escape.

Nomura, caught out yet again for providing preferential payouts to criminals, has lost more than face and precious reputation. Institutional clients Sony and Nippon Telegraph & Telephone have pulled all their securities and equities transactions, costing Nomura hundreds of millions of dollars in revenue. Nomura also lost the experience and contacts of its past and present chairman, its current president and twenty other company directors who were forced to resign as a result of the scandal. In an industry in which success depends on knowledge and relationships, this self-inflicted brain-drain is destructive to both Nomura's business prospects and the confidence of its investors. And as the premier trading house in Japan, the consequences of Nomura's repeated criminality ripple across the Japanese financial services sector. *The Economist* comments: "Bad enough for Nomura, but far worse was the damage done to an already tarnished industry. The Nomura affair confirmed that crooks, the rich and the powerful (and often a combination of all three) make money from the stock market."[34] In Japan, as in virtually every other market, the small investor and average worker increasingly regard the benefits of business as beyond their reach, available only to a small cadre of powerful and unscrupulous managers and mandarins.

The gap between manager and worker, rich and poor, wasteful and deprived holds many other not yet tabulated costs. Employees who have sacrificed so much in restructuring are now seeing that they will not in any way be beneficiaries of now strengthened, more competitive, more profitable companies. "The reengineering movement," write Wolman and Colamosca, "and the series of changes made in the way in which work is organized have, quite simply, led to the degradation of work—workplaces that are populated by psychologically withdrawn workers with low expectations about their own economic security and that of their children."[35] Desperation is hardly conducive to cooperation, so companies lose the very precious commitment and creativity that, along with profitability, are essential for competitiveness.

Desperation also erodes the social fabric. In their 1996 survey of Canadian psychographic trends, Toronto-based Environics Research uncovered a disturbing pattern that they coined civil disobedience. Cutbacks by companies and now cutbacks by government have set the terms for social participation as everyone for themselves. This reverse reciprocity usually leads to small infractions. Bullied by the self-interest of their managers and companies, individuals are now more likely to feel that "stealing" time on the company Internet is only their due. So too with inflating expense reports. Companies have taken more from their workers, and now workers are taking it upon themselves to take more from their companies. Since workers feel disposable, their behavior toward the firm is not that of commitment for the long term. Since rewards and cuts have in many cases been so unfair, average people are making pilfering and self-aggrandizement the leveling behavior.

The recent mess at Texaco is an example of this increasing rogue individuality. The company had been embroiled for more than a year in a class action suit by black employees who felt victimized by an institutionalized prejudice. After at first denying the charge and fighting the suit, Texaco was embarrassed into settlement by tapes, made public in 1996, in which senior executives uttered racial barbs while plotting to destroy incriminating documents relating to the suit. With apologies and promises of new training and promotional policies, Texaco promptly paid out $115 million. Ironically, the infamous tapes were made by a white manager, not out of concern about inequality toward fellow employees but as a negotiating lever to protect his job in a forthcoming reengineering. There is no doubt that this manager, arrested and prosecuted for his role in destroying evidence, did something illegal, something grossly self-serving and cynical. But it must also be acknowledged that he was behaving not unlike the way Texaco itself was behaving toward its own employees.

In microcosm, the scandal at Texaco suggests many of the costs we all bear, and contribute to, in this now global market economy. This is a huge, global company that profits by extracting and selling a critical but limited natural resource. It is an organization that, despite policies of equal opportunity, remained hostile and prejudicial to a large number of its employees. The privileged few in the executive ranks protected their turf in ways that broke federal law and violated common decency. Despite being successful and profitable, Texaco also planned another round of job cuts, creating fear, dislocation and a profound sense of unfairness among employees who were loyal, long-tenured and competent. That fear led one person to plant a tape-recorder in an executive meeting and seek his own inverted justice.

Evidence of this broad social unsettling is showing up along a whole spectrum of economic study and analysis. Harvard economist Dani Rodrik concludes in a recent book that he and his economist colleagues "underestimate the effect of freer trade and capital flows on the established power between employers and employees," and that "globalization will undermine social norms such as worker's rights."[36] What is perhaps most remarkable about these conclusions is that they are published by a pro-market and pro-globalization think tank, the Institute for International Economics, based in Washington, D.C. Representing more passionately the plight of workers, David Gordon explores the connections between the larger economy and the decline in values—particularly family values—so lamented by neo-conservatives. A very dark picture emerges, in which stagnant wages and growing insecurity contribute to the pressures that feed family violence, teen pregnancy, crime and violence on the street.[37] This is obviously a cauldron blending many ingredients; it is moot whether the growing immorality of business contributes to social breakdown or whether social breakdown contributes to the growing immorality of business. The point is that corporations and businesspeople hold an immense power that makes them the initiators of the norm that their employees will respond to. When the power is exercised negatively—what Gordon calls the Stick Strategy—people are disenfranchised, demeaned and often left cynical.

For good or for bad, acknowledged or not, human beings have an innate sense of justice. When odds are stacked against a person or a team, we recoil intuitively against the unfairness. No one would argue that not everyone deserves the same chance. Or that not everyone deserves equal treatment. Or that not everyone be subject to the same rules. People seem to have a barometer for fairness. Professor Joseph W.

Weiss of Bentley College explains this "Equity Theory," which was formulated by social scientist J. Stacey Adams. He writes: "People compare their efforts (inputs) and rewards (outcomes) with others to determine the fairness of outcomes. Inequity is based on perception as well as situation-specific, objective observations. Perceived inequalities can motivate individuals to take action to remedy the felt inequality."[38]

Equity and inequity are issues of justice, and this is why business and ethics can no longer be segregated. Weiss writes: "The question of justice is a big one—one that society will grapple with for some time. A major issue is the unfair distribution of burdens and benefits: benefits to multinationals, burden to nations' taxpayers, and burdens to workers who lose their jobs."[39] The people of the world need the global economy to survive, but the people of the world can also survive only if the global economy reorients to include a host of performance criteria. In addition to profit, the economy must sustain and renew nature. In addition to productivity, the economy must generate equity and opportunity. In addition to heeding the needs of inanimate capital, the economy must respect the needs of the human family. Philosopher Mary Midgley explains that "moral judgment is not a luxury, not a perverse indulgence of the self-righteous. It is a necessity . . . Morally as well as physically, there is only one world, and we all have to live in it."[40] The economy has always been a moral agent. Only now, because of its breadth, we can no longer pretend that it is not.

Table 3. The Global Economy Costs Index

Lost Security	The largest employer in North America is Manpower Inc., renting out 767,000 workers each year. This is not exactly the participation in the new economy that most people welcome.
Lost Endurance	The average life expectancy for a corporation is about forty years. One-third of the *Fortune 500* companies in 1970 had vanished by 1983. Obviously, short-termism is self-fulfilling.
Lost Creative Capital	Only 10.6 percent of board seats at big companies are held by women. Clearly, after thirty years of feminist progress, big companies have a lot to (eat) crow about.
Lost Profits	Accused of false lab and health care billings, SmithKline Beecham Clinical Laboratories agreed to a $350-million settlement with the U.S. Justice Department. So much for giving shareholders priority over stakeholders.
Lost Public, Private and Political Support	The most successful single branded product in the world is Marlboro. After regulators reversed themselves and *did not* allow the tobacco companies to write off payments to states' attorney generals as a tax deduction, executives jacked up prices on each pack of cigarettes. This way, the people who smoke will not only generate the tobacco corporations' profits but also fund the payments smokers will be entitled to when they get sick or die.

Lost Sustainability	The global free market is taking a free ride on the planet's ecology. Ecological economist Robert Costanza of the University of Maryland estimates that the services provided by the natural ecosystem are worth $33 trillion per year—almost twice the annual production of human-made goods and services.[41] Purists who argue that government subsidies distort the efficiency of markets have yet to answer for the far more comprehensive distortion of assuming nature's bounty to be worth nothing. This is changing by necessity. After decimating bee stocks with chemical fertilizers, North American farmers now spend over $100 million each year to hire colonies for pollinating.
Lost Credibility	Top executive pay has skyrocketed without any real relation to company share growth, performance or revenues. Surprisingly, among the people who think this is wrong are CEOs. Almost half thought CEO pay in 1996 was too high, and almost three-quarters thought CEO performance was not penalized for poor results.[42] No CEO, however, has yet to volunteer to be the first to go should more job cuts be required at their company.
Lost at Great Cost	Swiss banks have seen their bottom lines bashed, as well as their reputations, over their decades-long resistance to make available Holocaust-era accounts. In just one week it was revealed that both the City of New York and the State of California suspended their business with Swiss banks. These defections, along with the loss of already outraged private banking customers, indicate that lost profits may eventually amount to tens of millions. An institution historically renowned for secrecy has learned those awful lessons of the information age: knowledge leaks, and the reckoning for impropriety may be delayed but never avoided.

CHAPTER FOUR

CONTRARIETIES

Radicalism hates time, and compromise hates eternity.
Radicalism hates patience, and compromise hates decision.
Radicalism hates wisdom, and compromise hates simplicity.
Radicalism hates moderation and measure,
and compromise hates the immeasurable.
Radicalism hates the real, and compromise hates the word.

Dietrich Bonhoeffer, "The Penultimate," in Ethics

Appreciating the benefits to be had from an ethical orientation does not mean that progress toward a more responsible business model is imminent. Institutional resistance is high. When Texaco's management capitulated to the lawsuit filed by its minority employees, it paid out $115 million to settle the class action and provided the affected workers with a one-time 11 percent salary increase. But, like most companies caught in the glare of an infraction, Texaco promised even more. Chairman and CEO Peter I. Bijur pronounced that "Texaco is committed to developing and instituting specific, effective policies that will ensure that discrimination is wiped out wherever it may be, and that will expand the positive economic impact we can have in the minority community."[1] Included in this sweeping promise were the formation of an independent Equity and Tolerance Task Force that would oversee Texaco's progress and report twice yearly to the company's board, plus commitments for "diversity and sensitivity training," an ombudsman program for complaints, and a formal monitoring program. Total cost—in hard dollars and not counting the loss in reputation and the likely permanent disenfranchisement of some customers—was $176 million.

The path Texaco trod is well worn. Companies first deny any wrongdoing and fight righteously. Following an unofficial but often used crisis-control script, they then wage a public relations war externally while attempting to destroy incriminating documents and cover up the mess internally. Eventually, the wrongdoing and cover-up are exposed by the media, which happened with Texaco, or targeted by law enforcement officials, which happened with ADM and SmithKline Beecham. When caught red-handed, companies finally admit they were mistaken. All this, however, is only phase one. Once exposed, the public soul searching begins. This is usually kicked off with a public confession, preferably on CNN. There is remorse for the crime, and an apology to all constituents whose trust was violated. To prove the genuineness of the contrition, restitution is paid. And to reestablish goodwill, new programs and monitoring initiatives are announced to rid the company of whatever blight tainted its image. Bijur provided a paradigmatic promise when he said, "With this litigation behind us, we can now move forward on our broader, urgent message to make Texaco a model of workplace opportunity for all men and women."

Either implicitly or explicitly, either sincerely or out of strategic posturing, companies attempting to reform and achieve at least partial public relations rehabilitation adopt some program of ethics learning, training and monitoring. Edward Petry, a professor of philosophy at Bentley College and executive director of the National Ethics Officers Association, estimates that "90 percent of the top U.S. companies have formal, written codes of ethics."[2] The degree of commitment varies, but some companies, learning the lessons of the total quality movement, have gone so far as to institutionalize a formal ethics function. More than 250 of the top North American corporations now have an

Ethics Officer, many of whom, like Total Quality Officers, report directly to the CEO. Altruism may be incidental to the founding motivation, and the reason for momentum may be the sad one of expanding crime, but nevertheless, ethics are now getting more attention among businesspeople and economic policy makers. Suggesting a genealogy of lawbreaking, Petry notes that this trend of anointing an Ethics Officer "started with the defense industry in the 1980s, spread to telecommunications businesses, and now we see the financial services industry signing up."

Is this then proof of the market's self-regulation? Does the fact that companies are setting ethical standards, for whatever reasons, mitigate the imposition of an external norm? Are businesses proving the infallibility of the invisible hand by once again using competition to solve problems and create opportunity out of need? While it is tempting to believe that business is slowly converting to an ethics orientation, the progress relative to the scale of the problem is minuscule. More than that, the prevailing entrenched and still-defining attitude of the market economy that most businesspeople subscribe to with their souls is anti-ethical. Petry estimates that of the thousands of companies with formal standards for ethics, only "about one-third have made theirs a living document."[3] Commitments to ethics made in the heat of scandal often wither in the chill of competition, or die in the toxic cultures that provided the conditions for the original infraction. Many companies are repeat offenders *precisely* because ethics are applied as a cosmetic solution to a much deeper organizational problem. "Much of the bad conduct," explains Gary Edwards, "results from people taking decisions they know absolutely are wrong. They act in the belief that certain actions are expected by supervisors or senior management even if the actions violate stated policy."[4] Those beliefs linger, and are often explicitly reinforced in the push for better results, even while ethics get preached, trained and encoded in mission statements.

Edwards is director of the non-profit Ethics Resource Center in Washington, D.C. Not surprisingly, with "some two-thirds of clients coming off the front page as a result of serious wrongdoing," the business of ethics advice is booming. That companies seek out an ethical framework in response to crisis is not, however, a confirmation of conversion. As Edwards notes, "Virtually every company has become a client with a view to the sentencing problems that might arise in court cases." The U.S. Federal Corporate Sentencing Guidelines set in 1991 mitigates the penalties substantially for convicted companies that "are not only against sin, but have taken steps to prevent sinning and catch sinners." As much as 60 percent of a fine may be absolved—$10-million assessments have been reduced to $4 million—so ethics programs now have a hard cash value, and serve as an insurance policy to minimize the hard costs of any future iniquity. Other countries are slowly adopting similar views and laws. So, while not denying the progress, it is still important to understand that ethical commitment in the economy is so far more the result of pragmatism and public relations than of any real, spreading sense of remorse or responsibility.

Ethics are up against the entrenched philosophy of self-interest. The rewards of exploitation continue to be too tantalizing. And the moral intervention by managers and the larger community is still too tentative. Writing in the *Harvard Business Review* in the early 1980s, management professor Kenneth Goodpaster offered this: "It is hard to look at the record of the past decade, including as it does insider trading, industrial espionage, falsifying labor figures on government contracts, ignoring plant safety, deceptive marketing and insensitivity to employee rights, without a growing recognition that the bracketing of moral reflection, both at the level of the individual and at the level of the organized group, is a key part of the explanation."[5] Not only have the problems remained eerily unchanged, but in the harsh restructuring in the decade or more since Goodpaster's insight, the "bracketing" has only become that much more pronounced. At Texas Instruments, vice-president and ethics director Carl Skoogland admits encountering the moral suspension before people even start working at his firm. "New hires have often stated that they couldn't see that their day-to-day work had any ethical content at all." In a National Business Ethics Survey commissioned by the Ethics Resource Center of Washington, D.C., nearly a third of employees "reported that they had 'often' or 'occasionally' observed conduct that they thought violated company policy or the law." Amazingly, even when ethics hotlines or ombudsman's offices were available, less than half bothered to report transgressions.

There are several lessons in this. First, piecemeal ethics programs, like the piecemeal quality programs of the 1980s, are doomed to failure. Endemic problems require endemic solutions. Second, ethical behavior can be achieved only by ethical intent. As long as the objectives of business are hostile to people and the environment, the behavior may be modified to be more politically correct, but the outcome will inevitably be self-interested and exploitive. In the fury over its most recent settlement, people forgot that Texaco had lost several similar cases, suggesting a history of discrimination. As well, as recently as 1995, the Office of Federal Contract Compliance Programs reprimanded Texaco for unfair employment practices at its facilities in Houston. And only four months before the racially charged executive conversations were made public, prompting its public *mea culpa,* an investigation by the Equal Employment Opportunity Commission warned that "there was reasonable cause to believe that Texaco discriminates against blacks in certain salary categories 'because of their race.' "[6] The flat-footedness of senior management's response can be explained only by a near-total moral "bracketing," and can only cause us to question the effectiveness of its latest compliance monitoring programs.

A third lesson is that society itself contributes to the improprieties of business. It does so by now almost completely accepting the market-economy doctrine that lightly regulated self-interest best serves the needs of the common good, and by expecting so little, if any at all, moral virtuousness from business. Summarizing the results of a survey among Harvard Business School students, Sharon Daloz Parks found that "when asked whether they think our economic system should remain the same or be changed, these students tended to respond in the conventional code language of 'capitalism versus socialism,' 'trickle-down economics' and 'market forces.' They responded at a mythic level, without further analytical nuance."[7] Even before entering the managerial workplace, many people largely subsume personal right and wrong within the black and white ideology of the market. Already, the choices involving great ambiguity—involving serious ethical consequences—are made with the overriding certitude that the market knows best.

What all this means is that, although unethical, immoral and illegal actions are growing in number, scale and consequence, the commitment to ethical, moral and legal behavior remains tentative. Only a minority of companies, and especially only a minority of infractors, have adopted ethics as a genuine strategic dimension of doing business. For the majority, ethics are tangential and warrant consideration only as an optic in response to a short-term crisis. Even though companies and shareholders suffer financial costs for criminal acts, and even though an ethics infrastructure of consultants and think tanks is now blossoming, ethical reform from within the system is largely cosmetic. As with the other lies and costs attending the market economy, the prospect for ethical reorientation will not be persuaded by facts or won over by logic. Such intransigence is neither rational nor emotional, but ultimately only fatalistic. And this may well be the psychological root of the problem. *The global market economy and the companies operating within it desperately need an overarching ethical framework, not because businesspeople are primarily liars but because they are primarily pessimists.*

Many will recoil at this, particularly because a positive attitude is revered as one of the mythic qualities of corporate success. Attitude and belief, though, are not the same thing. I regard as an optimist a person who is open to new thinking, solutions and approaches, while a pessimist basically believes they are stuck with only one, unchangeable course of action. Many businesspeople have very positive attitudes, and great confidence in their ability to move the mountains of commerce, but they are essentially pessimists for believing that the market alone is the best judge for value, and by implication, values. Open to new ways of managing, most are still closed to any new way of doing business. Hence, programs of human respect, like empowerment, have had only superficial success, while programs of exploitation, like reengineering, have been so thoroughly implemented as to be exhausted. To reiterate an earlier analogy, pessimists believe that the bottom line is the only line, while optimists recognize that there can be no bottom line without a balance sheet.

The institutional pessimism of business is evident in many ways. Its continued focus on the short-term result, even when managers acknowledge a mortgaging of future potential, is hopelessly pessimistic. Cutting workers, even when it is obvious to all that future competitiveness depends on better service and more innovation, bespeaks an inherently negative frame of mind. Uncoupling effect from cause, exploiting non-renewable resources, polluting and risking the planet for future generations are as much reflections of despondency as of expediency. And as the power of the economic factor in human affairs has grown, so has the general hopelessness and cynicism of people. The pessimism of now economically inspired governments is so deep that they fail to take the steps essential for human health and survival for fear of upsetting some market-growth-job symmetry. How else to explain the failure of most rich, industrialized countries—including the U.S. and Canada—to meet the reduction in greenhouses gases that all had pledged to at the Rio Summit? The evidence is mounting that the continued atmospheric warming caused by burning carbon-based fuels may contribute to flooding, to a disruption of harvest patterns and the food supply, and to the extinction of still more species. Costs need to be sensibly managed, but when costs take precedence over health, it can only be a sign of either terribly bad judgment or unmovable despair. Profits are essential, but when profits are maximized at the expense and exclusion of all else, this becomes not so much a sensible value creation as a desperate hoarding.

Pessimism is usually a product of fear. All the upheaval in the economy brought on by globalization, new technology and competition has exposed a host of fears: fear of profit loss, fear of job loss, fear of being overtaken by competitors and fear of being left behind. Displaced by events we cannot control, we fear for our children's prospects, the fragmentation of our communities, the crime on the street, and now, with the ozone hole, we even fear exposure to the sun. This is a scary time that good economic news alone has not made people any more positive or hopeful. Beyond this very visible type of fear there is another layer of anxiety in business, a trepidation that has much deeper roots and is much more pessimism-inducing. This is the fear of making mistakes, of trying something new, of seeming in any way to challenge the orthodoxy of management. One common thread in John Darley's analysis of corporate evildoing was that people usually kept silent, or went along with obviously harmful outcomes, out of fear. In such circumstances, critical, ethical judgment gets distorted, disengaged or suppressed altogether.

Disturbingly, this fear operates before any crisis, and even before people get jobs. Daloz Parks, again drawing on a study of MBA students, writes that "another feature of these students' prevailing ethos is presumed success and a masking of failure." Already, these students know that making mistakes, questioning wrong turns and admitting not knowing something is career retarding. The danger in this is that "their understanding of the 'good' may be shaped in significant measure by what will ensure a positive flow of events, success and security—and thwart at least the appearance of failure. The risk is that these young adults may develop a sort of 'armor,' an inextricably vested interest in being a success despite what that may mean for others."[8] Success and fear are not unfamiliar bedfellows, but what is not usually acknowledged is that success imbued with such fear is also likely to sabotage ethical judgment. This was Bonhoeffer's point when he observed: "The proposition that success is good is followed by another which aims to establish the conditions for the continuance of success. This is the proposition that only good is successful."[9] Rarely explicit, modern management operates with the thesis that fear motivates success, success is "good," so the fear motivating success is "good" and warranted.

Any system of ethics is simply the bare minimum accommodation needed for self-preservation in a world in which all human beings are out for themselves. John Costello S.J., professor of philosophy at the University of Toronto, comments, "We reach across our radical individuality in either contract or lust."[10] Business offers both. Laws and social norms as a result need to protect individuals from being blatantly abused but should not interfere with the realization of personal, short-term benefit.

The notion of radical self-interest has spread hand-in-glove throughout the global market economy. Charles Handy provides a graphic description of this transplanted capitalism. He writes: "We recently went on a visit to South China and Guangdong province next to Hong Kong, where the growth rate is 12 percent per annum. And in Shenzhen City, a New Economic Zone, it's 21 percent per annum. When something is growing at that rate, people don't walk, they run, with their mobile phones to their ears, and you can see this happening everywhere there. It's called the 'wild east of capitalism' by some people, and rightly so. But they are causing a tremendous amount of destruction. The red earth is razed, everywhere, to a uniform base for new buildings or highways. The pollution is horrible. People fall off buildings and get killed every day because there are no laws or rules of industrial safety. There are few effective laws at all, in fact. It is truly like the old gold rush."[11] Acute though they be, the dangers of sanctioned self-interest are not just in out-of-control Third World development. Any society preoccupied with consumption, production, jobs, income, success, winning and having more and more and more is locked in its own dance of fear.

This also reminds us that fear is a social phenomenon, not just a personal one. Fear is generated in relation to another person, or other people. And fear is ultimately calmed or resolved together. In the darkest days of the Great Depression, Franklin Roosevelt made the fear collective, and therefore manageable. In the darkest days of the Battle of Britain, Winston Churchill made the fear public, and therefore beatable. And in the darkest days of the cold war, while still in the shadow of the Cuban missile crisis, Lyndon Johnson made the fear social and, with his programs for civil rights, hopeful. In each of these situations, fear, if it had been left to itself, would have undermined and destroyed the very reality that was valued and at risk of being lost. As if we did not already know, fear is self-fulfilling. In the context of the global economy, the fear aroused by the churn of restructuring, and the imbalance of rewards, is similarly a threat to the entire structure. In these dark days of environmental devastation and growing exclusion, a global ethic gives expression to the growing and shared fear and provides an embracive and equitable framework for responding to it.

Again, however, this is not entirely about logic or common sense. Pessimism assumes a fixed outcome, so alternatives are untenable or ineffective or more negative that the current reality. For pessimists, not only is the glass half empty, but it is the only glass. Ethics are beginning to earn consideration in the strategic framework and pragmatic rationality of business, but the notion of moral value guiding business decisions is still basically repellent to its pessimism. At least five core fallacies ground this antipathy and warrant correction.

First, pessimists believe that the application of moral thinking in business decision making is an abrogation of fiduciary responsibility, even when it is obvious that unethical behavior costs shareholders money, value and opportunity. Turn-around CEO Albert Dunlop states that "the responsibility of the CEO is to deliver shareholder value. Period. It's the shareholders who own the corporation. They take all the risk. How does a CEO maximize value? He does that by focusing on profit."[12] Dunlop, though, creates value the new way which, in a reversal of Joseph Schumpeter's famous dictum, represents a destructive creativity. During his two years at Scott Paper, he fired eleven thousand workers and sold the company to its biggest competitor. Although he is called "Chainsaw," the term is actually one of endearment. Shareholders realized a 225 percent increase in the value of Scott, and the shares of a company inevitably rise when Dunlop is appointed to effect another restructuring. Dunlop personally made $100 million from the Scott episode. He has been criticized as the paragon of self-centered CEOs, but he has turned notoriety into celebrity, writing books and touring the media with his message. "Let the market decide" is thus a code for "Let individuals seek every advantage they can."

Dunlop's view is overly simplistic for several reasons. What if all CEOs took Dunlop's drastic approach? What if all companies simultaneously sought outright maximization of profit? Society, drowning in the unemployed, and riven by the vast gulf between rich and poor, would plunge into crisis. As it is, the balance has already been tipped and the cohesion of society is more precarious as a result. Edward Luttwak, a fellow at the Center for Strategic and International Studies in Washington, D.C., comments: "This country [the U.S.] is much richer than it is stable. It is half West Palm Beach and half Burundi."[13] A similar teetering of more wealth to the rich and tottering of less security to the poor is occurring in Canada. Instability is a threat as much to shareholders as to the community, so it is impossible to focus on the latter without also respecting the needs of the former. Another hole in the fiduciary argument is that companies that forsake any moral obligation can harm themselves and their equity, as well as the community. This is clear in cases like Barings Bank and Bausch & Lomb, in which shareholders paid a steep price in value for managerial transgressions. Texaco's shareholders lost $3 a share in the first few days after its race-bias scandal broke—a neglect or omission of fiduciary obligation on the scale of $1 billion.

Although they do not always show up on the balance sheet, the disloyalty of disgruntled employees, legal and public relations expenses to cover impropriety, and the general executive profligacy that tends to go in tandem with a self-serving corporate culture create millions of dollars in drag on potential earnings. Robert B. Cialdini of the University of Arizona has created a model called "The Triple Tumor Structure of Organizational Dishonesty" that identifies some of the most damaging of these revenue leaks. One that Nomura and Credit Lyonnais and ADM are now paying for is "the costs of poor reputation." Another that is acutely familiar to Texaco is "the costs of bad fit between employee values and corporate values." Poor morale hampers many aspects of corporate performance, including customer service, product and service innovation and the willingness to participate in the more open, trust-dependent boiler-rooms of high-performance teams. This costs companies and shareholders, not only in employee turnover and lost opportunities but in the hard costs of crisis recovery, training new employees in an environment of churn, and legal protection. Finally, the third tumor involves "the costs of surveillance on work climate." Companies that should not be trusted, not surprisingly, in turn do not trust anyone else, most especially their own employees. As only one small example of this cost, Cialdini reports that seventy thousand companies spent $500 million in only two years (1991 and 1992) on surveillance software for the workplace.[14]

Business is complex and confusing, as I keep saying, but what is clear is that seemingly straight-line relationships between self-interest and profit involve many other factors that often impede, diminish and sometimes destroy shareholder value. Rather than harming value, an ethical orientation often creates the conditions necessary for enhancing and preserving it. Fiduciary responsibility and ethical responsibility are thus symbiotic. Lynn Sharp Paine, professor at the Harvard Business School, reminds us that "assuming an obligation to one party does not automatically extinguish a person's existing obligations to other parties. This principle of continuity applies with special force to obligations flowing from membership in the human community. If, as a human being, a person is obligated to respect the rights of others, to refrain from fraud, to avoid imposing unconsented-to harm on innocent people, she does not escape those duties by assuming the obligation to promote the interests of a third party. A straightforward case involving theft illustrates the point. If it is wrong to steal to enrich oneself, it does not become right to steal to enrich someone else."[15] A tragic case of the reverse point is the fires started by plantation owners in Indonesia with the tacit support of government. During the summer of 1997, this conflagration created a blanket of smoke that shrouded much of Southeast Asia for weeks. Thousands died, many older and younger people were hospitalized, schools and businesses were forced to close, and the dense smoke contributed to the crash of a Korean Airlines jet and to the collision of two ships. Even high-tech Singapore was partially incapacitated by the ecologically catastrophic wood burning. The lesson, again, is that economic activity is situated within the human community and natural ecosystem, not the other way round. The values of the economy are thus subordinate and never superordinate.

The single-mindedness of pessimists—that fiduciary responsibilities have precedence over the ethical—is supported by that belief in a single motivation, self-interest. The second fallacy of pessimism is that the application of moral thinking will run contrary to the self-interest upon which the free market is based, even though it is obvious that business cannot function without cooperation. But ethics are not an "either-or" between self and other. Nor is the ethical goal impediment and constraint. Ethics essentially provide a framework for fairness that benefits both the individual pursuing self-interest and the community that must manage to stay functional. In Küng's words, "Self-assertion and unselfishness need not be mutually exclusive. Identity and solidarity are both required for the formation of a better world."[16] Economists focus on transactions. Competition delineates between winners and losers. But human interchange is far wider, deeper and more complex than just financial. We as individuals are not the opposite of our community, but its members, contributors and beneficiaries. Self and other, economy and community, competition and cooperation are not therefore antonyms but continuities of interdependent ebb and flow.

Philosopher John Macmurray provided this framework: "The development of civilization depends on the interplay of two factors, individual initiative and social cohesion. If the forces which maintain social cohesion manage to overcome individual initiative civilization stagnates and deteriorates. If the forces making for individual independence and initiative—for individualism in fact—become overmastering, they disrupt social unity and produce a catastrophe."[17] An ethic constructively weaves together the capabilities, priorities and obligations of self and group. It is not an abnegation of individuality but instead a context for mutuality—for fairness—upon which human exchange, particularly economic exchange, is predicated. In economic terms, Amitai Etzioni calls this heightened understanding of mutuality the I & We paradigm. Economics are not just "me" versus "they," nor are companies always in an "us" versus "them" competition. Instead, self-interest and the "we" often have a logical, if often forgotten, complementarity. A company that emits toxic waste is polluting the air and water; that also affects its own managers, workers and shareholders. The smaller the world gets, the more immediate and intimate is the I & We. Etzioni explains that "the term highlights the assumption that individuals act within a social context, that this context is not reducible to individual acts, and, most significantly, that the social context is not necessarily wholly imposed. Instead, social context is, to a significant extent, perceived as a legitimate and integral part of one's existence, a We, a whole of which the individuals are constituent elements."[18]

Texaco suffered from exactly this endemic "us" versus "them." When one of the privileged insiders was threatened with exclusion, the "us" became the "them." The distorted loyalty of bigotry became the distorted hostility of self-destruction. Pessimists regard mutuality as some wasteful, unrealizable ideal. But that people need each other, that we acknowledge that no self can exist or thrive independently of the larger community, is only pragmatism of the most essential type. An ethic simply creates the conditions for self-interest and group interest to proceed in some workable, sustainable harmony. In the cartoonish oversimplification of ideologues, unfettered self-interest seems more efficient because any ethical factors, with their messy assessment and possible restraint over implications, are ignored. But in reality, it is the ethical that affords the greater pragmatism, because what is practical for the individual ultimately cannot be divorced from what is practical for the community.

Managers stuck in a self-interest model end up risking more than the costly and destructive exposure of ethical abuses and crimes. The focus on internal advantage also creates a myopia regarding new ideas and opportunities for corporate regeneration. Dr. Paine writes that "moral thinking brings a distinctive point of view to the management enterprise, a point of view not fully captured by the traditional business disciplines. It places management decisions squarely within a social and normative context, thus highlighting important factors that might otherwise be overlooked in the search for opportunities, the identification of problems, the analysis of decisions, and the implementation of action."[19] Self-interest, self-rights and self-preservation involve and are even advanced by self-sacrifice, self-discipline and self-giving. This should be obvious, but so deeply ingrained is the pessimism that mogul and financier George Soros fell out of favor with peers for stating "that cooperation is as much a part of the system as competition, and the slogan 'survival of the fittest' distorts this fact."[20]

The third fallacy of pessimists is that laws should suffice to protect against criminality, even though the laws have already proven insufficient to deter business villainy from growing almost out of control. Texaco knew the law, proclaimed adherence to it in corporate literature and fought tooth and nail against any suggestion that it was not complying with equal opportunity strictures. Only when the incontrovertible evidence was made public did the company admit to wrongdoing. Tobacco executives also knew the law, and for several generations used every leverage to protect the industry from liability suits launched by sick or dying smokers. Despite such legal savvy, these same executives lied, while under oath, to the Congress of the United States, denying the addictive nature of nicotine, when subsequently released documents show that the properties of this drug were long understood and covered up. Some executives and companies are even more brazen in their contempt for the law. Carlo di Benedetti, former chairman of Olivetti, went so far as to state publicly that had he to do it over again, he would just as quickly, without reservation, break the law and make bribes to secure competitive advantage. Thousands of senior executives and politicians have been convicted in the seven years of Italian attacks against corruption, but di Benedetti's comment underscores the reality that bribery and disregard for the law, as they became less and less exceptional, became the norm. The law is important, but inadequate, because its spirit is missing and its letter is too often merely a pylon to maneuver around.

Lawlessness has been made easier by the porousness of globalization. Companies that do not like the laws in one country move facilities or practices to those that are less stringent or poorly policed. In his doctoral dissertation, Hector Saez of the University of Massachusetts reports that "even firms that comply with environmental standards in their countries of origin take advantage of the leniency or lack of environmental legislation or enforcement in their host countries, even when comparable legislation is in place."[21] GM notoriously exported thousands of cars with defective catalytic converters to the Middle East, avoiding compliance in Canada by passing the pollution problem on to less developed jurisdictions. Saez adds the example of U.S. firms that "have shifted the production of trioxides to Peru, the chemical intermediate furfural to the Dominican Republic, and pesticides to Mexico, Brazil and Colombia."[22] In the global economy, laws are only as strong as their weakest expression.

The inadequacy of laws is perhaps most vivid in the now rampant practice of outsourcing. Companies constrained by laws pass on to "strategic partners" the option of transgression. Many executives doing business in China and other developing Asian countries admit to handling the widespread pressure to bribe through third parties. The rationale is clear: if they don't do it, someone else will, and that someone else will then walk away with the sale, contract or other competitive advantage. Since such lawlessness is seen as business as usual, lawlessness slowly *becomes* business as usual. Outsourcing not only allows companies to camouflage illegal practices, it also inevitably puts pressure on employees eager to protect their position from outsourcing to also play loose with regulations. In the previously cited National Business Ethics Survey, about a third of employees reported frequent or occasional transgressions. Only half of these employees reported what they saw, and of those, "55% were dissatisfied with their companies' responses. In fact, 35% of those who reported misconduct were very dissatisfied." The reason for the dissatisfaction emerges in another finding of the study. Almost as many employees who observe impropriety—29 percent—also feel "pressure from co-workers or management to compromise ethical standards."[23]

Governments are banding together to close loopholes and standardize laws. In 1997, the OECD began drafting a law to deal with bribery and corruption. The OECD represents twenty-nine of the richest countries in the global economy. So far, only the U.S. has imposed such laws—as the result of which "one government study estimated that American firms lost some 100 deals worth $45 billion over the past two years to less principled rivals."[24] Why this consensus now, more than twenty years after the U.S. initiative, and in the face of such insouciance that Denmark allows bribes to be tax-deductible? The reason is that deregulation in many markets, including the privatization of critical assets like telecommunications and financial services, is creating gaps in the rules and authority structure just as global competitiveness is intensifying further. The *Financial Times* reported that "Australia, Belgium, Japan and Norway have recently said they plan to criminalize corporate bribery, and the European Commission proposed recently that all EU member states should do like-wise."[25] Non-OECD members such as Chile, Argentina and Brazil have suggested subscribing to at least parts of this norm. This is progress. But is it enough? Will international legal agreements pre-empt the need for a global ethic?

The answer is no. For thousands of years, as long as there have been laws, there has also been a set of ethics guiding the community's behavior. The two are complementary but not redundant. Laws emerge largely by precedent, whereas ethics derive from moral belief. Laws create authority by the threat of punishment, whereas ethics are usually an expression of principle that engages individuals at the deeper level of identity and belonging. The focus of laws is compliance, while the focus of ethics is human character and community development. History provides ample examples of widely followed, strictly enforced laws that clearly have been unethical: the laws enshrining slavery in the U.S. states; Nazi laws depriving Jewish citizens of their property; apartheid in South Africa. Neither the law nor ethics are ever perfect, since the examples just listed also involved a moral (immoral) complicity on the part of the majority. The point, however, is that justice may be served without satisfying moral right.

Many companies love the law and hate any moral intrusion for several reasons. First is resources. Corporations have the financial wherewithal to engage teams of the brightest lawyers to fight and delay and discombobulate any threat to their operations or practices. The sheer heft of these resources often intimidates even counties and countries, whose public resources may not match those of the private sector. In one case, McDonald's spent $93 million in legal fees to fight two British environmentalists who besmirched the corporate name in pamphlets detailing supposed nutrition and environmental problems. (Goliath won the legal battle, but the two Davids are still slinging rocks.) Companies also prefer the law to the ethical because of the often very minor punishment that goes with lawbreaking. No one from Ford went to jail over the Pinto. No one from Texaco has yet to serve any time in prison for its legal infractions. Even huge environmental disasters like the *Exxon Valdez* spill carried only a fine. Surprisingly, at least from an ethical perspective, many of the senior managers get away with criminal infractions. John Darley asks: "What happens to the executives who commit the harm-doing actions in the first place and then engage in the cover-up?" His answer: "Since organizations are generally involved in denying the existence of the harm or of the cover-up, they are in an awkward position. If they punish the executives, they will be admitting to their corporate misrepresentations. Also, the wiser executives, as a price for participation in the cover-up, may extract guarantees of no retaliation."[26] As Darley found, whistle-blowers get fired or harassed. Meanwhile, executives, like Lee Iacocca, who was in charge of the Pinto project, tend to get promoted, write books, make money and get honored for excellence in any business competency other than taking an ethical stand.

A final reason that pessimists prefer law to morality is that both deploy "artificial reason." Philip Selznick explains: "A scientific assessment or moral judgment may draw on whatever ideas are helpful in reaching conclusions justified by fact and logic. A judicial conclusion must demonstrate continuity with what is already received and established."[27] The legal world and the business world are very similar in that both have their own distinct vocabularies, decisions, procedures and precedents. Both eschew emotion for rationality and construct models that emphasize efficiency over humanity. Constantly harking back to Adam Smith, many economists and businesspeople are simply trying to invest the commercial world with the historical authority, tradition and apparent objectivity of law. Business, like justice, would like to be blind, only for different reasons.

Legal and even business rationality perform important functions, but neither truly encompasses the fullness of human reality. We live not merely in contract with one another but in a more profound relation, seeking place, identity, freedom, growth and love, among other human fulfillments. Selznick distinguishes between a legal "contract," with its "terms and conditions" and "nonperformance calculations," and a "covenant," which "suggests an indefeasible commitment and a continuing relationship.[28] Macmurray goes further, explaining that it is in "relationship with one another in which we can be our whole selves and have complete freedom to express everything who we are."[29] Seemingly a paradox, we are not free alone but are free only in how we think, speak and act in interaction with others, and in how we are received by the larger community. To have a thought is naturally human. To express that thought to others is freedom. Law provides one important but narrow forum for this human freedom and engagement. Ultimately, however, to live only by contract is to be constrained, since humans are more than just rational units. To relate only in rational terms, if it were even possible, deprives us of the emotional and spiritual experiences that are with rationality parts of the rich, creative, questing human complexity. Selznick provides a telling definition, explaining that "covenant presumes an act of faith and resolve, a self-defining commitment. It is a decision to embrace the pregnant promises of moral ordering."

The law is only an imposed community restriction, while a covenant reflects the human freedom to accept a constraint for the principle, philosophy or meaning it holds for the individual. Attempting to codify its ethical practices, Levi Strauss & Co. first adopted a "compliance-based program." Robert Haas, chairman and CEO, explains the legal antecedents of this approach. "These ethics programs are most often designed by corporate counsel. They are based on rules and regulations, with the goal of preventing, detecting and punishing legal violations." Eminently rational, this approach is widely used across business and involves formulating detailed rules for "hiring practices, travel and entertainment expenses, political contributions, compliance with local laws, improper payments, gifts and favors." An exhaustive, legally vetted and legally clear list of do's and don'ts covered every imagined conflict or ambiguity. However clear and comprehensive, the list did not work. Haas explains: "First, rules beget rules. And regulations beget regulations. We became buried in paperwork, and any time we faced a unique ethical issue, another rule or regulation was born. Second, our compliance-based program sent a disturbing message to our people—*'We don't respect your intelligence or trust you!'* Finally, and one of the most compelling reasons for shedding this approach, was that it didn't keep managers or employees from exercising poor judgment and making questionable decisions."[30] The inadequacy of law is that, in most cases, because it is imposed, it has neither the free consent nor the moral commitment of the individual. It is a dictate rather than participation. It demands obedience but without engaging free choice. Laws thus remain someone else's priority.

A fourth fallacy of pessimism, related closely to the third, is that personal conscience should be enough to guide the propriety of business decisions, even when centuries of evidence prove that personal conscience by itself is vulnerable to group pressures or personal ambition. The regimen of business is such that people speak openly of "parking their conscience at the door." Surveys and cases already cited have indicated that people often feel pressure to bend moral or legal rules in order to deliver a result or achieve an objective. Conscience may stir, but, as with the 50 percent who saw but did not report transgressions, the stirring for many may not be sufficient to act. What is so haunting about the Texaco situation is that the whistle blower who taped the racial slurs did so for reasons of personal protection. Unfairness toward black employees, although illegal and immoral, did not move him. Indeed, because he subsequently lost his job he now regrets ever having gone public with the tape. Some people thus not only park their consciences but seemingly lock them up in dark and distant underground parking garages.

Fundamentally, conscience alone is not an effective guide for moral decision making. Without the reference point of community moral values, personal conscience can all too easily slip into a relativism or subjectivity. Already, in the creeping consciousness of political correctness, "I'm OK, you're OK" has become "I'm right, you're right." Bonhoeffer regarded conscience as only one, incomplete dimension of ethical judgment. He wrote: "Conscience is satisfied when the prohibition is not disobeyed. Whatever is not forbidden is permitted. For conscience life falls into two parts: what is permitted and what is forbidden. There is no positive commandment. For conscience permitted is identical with good."[31] Conscience is therefore primarily a capacity for judging what decision or action to take, without necessarily providing reflection, understanding or illumination about why.

In the widespread imposition of reengineering, and the growing investment in employee surveillance software, it is obvious that companies have a hard time trusting workers to do their job, let alone decide for themselves on ethical and moral issues. After studying the business practices and decisions of middle managers, Professor Joseph Badaracco of Harvard and Allen Webb, a consultant at McKinsey, reported that "the ethical climate of an organization is extremely fragile."[32] As with Darley's investigation of corporate evildoing, Badaracco and Webb discovered that the intense pressure to perform, and the dreaded consequences of failure, overwhelm ethical considerations. Indeed, the expectation to put business first was well grounded, so much so that "sleazy but successful managers seemed to be granted 'immunity' from ethical strictures." What this shows is, first, that the restraint of conscience requires the reinforcement and bearings that are provided by relation to other people. To generalize, society provides the coordinates and personal conscience provides the navigation.

Second, it shows that conscience alone is less than effective in moral decisions, not only for tending to egocentric misjudgment but because of an all-too-frequent nonjudgment. In other words, individuals may have the right moral values informing their conscience, but that does not mean that their conscience is always in session. This, for Bonhoeffer, is one of "the great naivetés, or more exactly, one of the great follies, of the moralists that they deliberately overlook this fact and start out from the fiction that at every moment of his life man has to make a final and infinite choice, the fiction that every moment of life involves a conscious decision between good and evil. They seem to imagine that every human action has a clearly lettered notice attached to it by some divine police authority, a notice which reads either 'permitted' or 'forbidden.' "[33] Relying only on conscience in a corporate setting is another great folly, because it is usually accorded no or low priority, and is invoked most often to redirect blame from the offending organization to the implicated individual.

The fifth fallacy relating to ethics, and expressing the inherent pessimism of business, is that ethics cost too much and are a burden on competitiveness, even though the cost and burden of unethical corporate behavior is already clearly too much for nature and humanity to continue to countenance. Ethics do indeed have a cost, but so do computers. And ethics do indeed require commitments of time, training and measurement, but so does any other organizational learning. The point is that although ethics are not free, they are nevertheless valuable. Like any other capital or training investment, ethics pay out over time, and not only in soft, intangible ways. NYNEX reported more than three thousand calls to its ethics hot-line in 1995. Presumably, many of the issues were inconsequential, but some may very well have prevented the costly embarrassment of scandal and criminal fines. For Texaco, the cost of an inadequate ethics program is clear—the $176 million in total that covered class action settlements as well as training and corrective initiatives, plus the millions more in sales lost in the consumer boycott led by such organizations as the National Association for the Advancement of Colored People.

Some of the people studying business and ethics are increasingly making the argument that good ethics are good business. Many issues, including the prosaic ones of product quality, employee productivity, product innovation and customer service, are latent with ethical expectations and implications. Decision making itself is one such business practice. Lynn Sharp Paine writes: "In a fast-paced business environment characterized by rapid technological change, managers often face conflicts between competing responsibilities or novel moral claims which cannot be resolved by appeal to familiar general level-one principles. Such problems are often complicated by factual ambiguities. Hence, the need for moral thinking at the critical level."[34] Strategic plans are now generally understood to be too removed and too fixed from the highly chaotic and uncertain business reality to provide much more than superficial guidance. The capability of implications-thinking that inheres in ethical reflection is exactly the knowledge skill managers need to imagine and construct new solutions to the entire range of business problems. Ethics are not an antidote to ambiguity; they are an aptitude that, with practice and conscientiousness, develops the individual's confidence and flexibility for creatively dealing with uncertainty. Just as the mastery of quality brought with it the wider skills of employee motivation and customer satisfaction, so the genuine commitment to ethics has the potential to revitalize the entire managerial skill-set.

Some believe that this is a weak argument to make in support of business ethics. If companies adopt moral rectitude to be more successful, then the motivation for correctness is contaminated with the very self-interest that ethics are supposed to mitigate. There is some validity to this, but the very premise of ethical orientation is that it is a work in progress. Not all companies or individuals can ever be in a similar stage of moral sensibility. Like all other human growth, ethics involves stages of development, and some people or companies will indeed be less altruistic and more self-focused than others. But like environmentalism, the movement of the whole social consciousness, pioneered by a few, pulls everyone forward. Sincerity of motivation is obviously an issue. We do not need the cynicism and ethical spin doctoring of companies using ethics only as a positioning tool or advertising claim. However, there is also no denying that an ethical framework, particularly in an economy of information transparency and intellectual capital, has practical benefits. For example, psychologist Howard Gardner has shown in his study of genius that trust and group support are critical ingredients to creative breakthroughs.[35] A relation of trust assumes the mutuality of values and obligation that are the core of ethics.

Regardless of their importance, ethics are not a replacement for management. Ethics are a competency, and in many companies are as important as the one that developed for quality in the 1980s. "The well-being of the corporation as a whole depends on both the technical and moral excellence of its employees," write Kenneth Goodpaster and Joanne Ciulla. And it is the fusion that is ultimately constructive because "technical excellence without moral excellence can lead to serious problems (e.g., a government contractor may be brilliant at solving problems but have fraudulent business practices). On the other hand, moral excellence without technical excellence can lead to bankruptcy or business failure."[36] Costly though they may be, ethics are not an expenditure but an investment. What's more, the human community and natural environment affected by the global economy are increasingly restless for an accounting. Transgressors, like Texaco and the tobacco companies, will eventually pay the price of ethical standards, whether they want to or not.

One lesson in all these biases and refutations is that, while pessimists accuse optimists of idealism, they fail to recognize their own fatalism. Pessimism is not easily changed in individuals, and it is proving to be even more recalcitrant in its institutional manifestation. Whatever the facts about the mutually beneficial relationship between ethics and fiduciary responsibility, the majority of businesspeople remain either skeptical or under too much pressure to keep their job to believe that a fairer, more honest alternative is possible. It is this hopelessness that is fueling the so-called race to the bottom, the nearly exhausted strategy of increasing profits by cutting costs, people and investments in the future. "A pessimistic attitude," writes Nicholas Rescher, a professor of philosophy at the University of Pittsburgh, "tends to immobilize." His point is that if you expect the worst, all you have left is insurance. With the elaborate "platinum parachutes" now common among senior executives, those who have secured the most insurance have thus revealed themselves to also be the most pessimistic.

Pessimism denies hope for anything better, inviting, as Rescher notes, "inaction and, even worse, a despair that brings no benefits at all."[37] Businesspeople are the epitome of action, but their ultimate despair is that this action is concentrated within the limited sphere of only what is assumed to be possible and viable. There is little experimentation to see how the systems of profit can be enmeshed with those of responsibility. There is little hope that fiscal and moral realities are compatible, let alone mutually enhancing. Optimism can never really convert pessimism, except in action, when it can prove the hopeful to be possible. A global ethic represents just this type of hopeful action. It asks businesspeople to try to think and act with the optimism that, as Rescher writes, "presses beyond fact to the impetus of value—not by failing to see things as they are but by looking also toward what they might and should be. As the optimist sees it, the good outweighs the bad not in the balance of actuality but in the balance of importance."[38]

Many of the people I have worked with—even those sympathetic to responsible business practice—doubt whether the far-reaching institutional change required for a global ethic can ever be achieved. Although the evidence overthrowing this fatalistic view is overwhelming, businesspeople still perceive the ethical to be an ideal while the amoral is regarded as the much more realistic practicality. This pessimism, however, is now too costly for even business to afford. With the greater scrutiny of customers, regulators and the media, it is now clear that the costs of impropriety are potentially much higher than any gain. For example, the A.H. Robins corporation realized about $500,000 in profits from its Dalkon Shield but spent more than $500 million in liability settlements with injured women before finally filing for bankruptcy. Unethical practices that seem to advance careers also increasingly boomerang and bring down perpetrators. This, for example, seems to be the fate of Michael Andreas, heir apparent at ADM, who was forced to take a leave of absence and awaits trial for the company's 1995 price-fixing scandal. Corporate self-interest, practiced to the extreme of greed, has in a big way also alienated workers and customers. This in turn has created a host of new costs for companies, to "buy" the loyalty that used to be offered in affinity, and for the surveillance to guard against employees and customers who increasingly treat the property of companies with the same impunity that companies have treated their people. Political reforms to stamp out corruption in China, Mexico and France, and the management reforms to undo the price fixing at Bausch & Lomb, the yakuza-infiltration of the Dai-Ichi Kangyo Bank and the repeated leaks of contaminants by Ontario Hydro, show at least by default that businesspeople understand that they can no longer afford the high price of ethical insouciance.

Table 4. An Imbalance Sheet for the Global Economy

Assets	Liabilities
Growth in production, consumption and revenues.	Growth in waste, environmental destruction and disparity between rich and poor.
Accelerating development of a global economic infrastructure.	Stunted development of global human community.
Economic development premised on creating more consumption.	Infinite capacity for instant gratification cannot be sustained by limited environment.
Corporate competitiveness linked to higher productivity.	Fewer jobs, and less personal time for those who have them.
Corporate reengineering has created unprecedented efficiency and wealth.	Unprecedented homelessness in all the richest, most developed countries.
Budget deficits for companies and governments are being eliminated.	Opportunity deficits for middle managers and the unemployed youth are growing.
Those with the skills to excel in the knowledge economy are getting ahead.	Unable to produce in this new economy, many resort to small acts of civil disobedience.
More perks and toys.	More surveillance and jails.
Social status is increasingly determined by the possessions of achievement.	Personal self-esteem is rendered subsidiary to the image of brands.
The free market works because it rewards individual initiative.	Not measuring up to the efficiency of the private sector means that the community warrants less and less investment.

CHAPTER FIVE

IMPETUS

In responsibility both obedience and freedom are realized.
Responsibility implies tension between obedience and freedom.
There would be no more responsibility if either were made
independent of the other.

Dietrich Bonhoeffer, *"Freedom," in* Ethics

The world of business, like life itself, is dynamic and imperfect. In the constant change, and in the ever-present shadows, there will always be a messy intermingling of human hope with despair and generosity with greed. Flashes of opportunity, breakthroughs in potentiality, will likely always be tainted by tendencies for exploitation and by a hunger for personal advantage. A global ethic, like any moral framework, is necessary in part to manage the flaws of the human psyche. As technology and science have greatly expanded the reach of the human family, they have also greatly increased the stakes of wrongdoing. But other than reacting to crisis, what is the basis for a global ethic? In a world that is in many ways polarizing in beliefs while integrating in economics, from where can any such global ethic hope to derive its authority?

Among many revolutions, the information age has included an equalization between institution and individual. In what is a rather sudden development within the scope of human history, people now have access to data and knowledge that used to be so costly that it was assembled, controlled and used only by governments, churches, universities and big companies. One characteristic of this newly empowered world is that any topic can be downloaded from anywhere, drawing from resources in any country, from any discipline, at any time. Such ubiquity and flow of information have been noted as contributors to the fall of communism in Eastern Europe. These also are a major reason why entrepreneurs with a PC can launch titan-threatening new products, as happened several years ago when Netscape rode the crest of the Internet wave to challenge (for a time) Microsoft's dominance.

Historians, anthropologists and sociologists of the future will have to unravel the cause and effects of this still-emerging information society, but one implication that we cannot escape dealing with has been the fairly radical disintegration of a cohesive moral framework. The swing in power to the individual has engendered a mostly positive focus on individual rights. This in turn has given greater legitimacy to the relative, making social consensus harder and harder to achieve. Governments, churches and other social institutions have in many ways lost the trust of constituents because their monolithic beliefs do not engage or respect these new values of diversity. In their extreme, this dispersal from centralized to individual creates a heightened focus on personality, celebrity and subjectivity while diminishing the validity of the group. Nonetheless at this time, all group-based structures—including communist China as it reintegrates with Hong Kong—are struggling to renew their social charter by mastering issues of diversity.

This oversimplifies a very complex human and social transition, but there are three points to be made in relation to a global ethic for business. First, a global ethic will work only if it applies to everyone, and it will apply to all only if everyone recognizes its validity and subscribes to it. Second, a global ethic works only if all are united in expecting conformity from each other, and this expectation is realistic only if the ethical orientation is in harmony with human growth and development. Third, a global ethic works only if it provides both the imaginative pull of an ideal and the common-sense push of pragmatic value.

Moral judgment is a defining capacity of human nature. Indeed, those persons without any moral sense are regarded not as exceptions but as pathological. John Kekes, a professor of philosophy at the State University of New York, explains that "most people have some moral wisdom, since most people act wisely at least some of the time in matters affecting the goodness of their lives."[1] Darwin regarded the social instincts of humans as one of the behaviors favored by evolution, and although he saw evidence of socialization in other species, he believed that the word *moral* should be reserved for humans. George Williams, an evolutionary biologist, gave more specific dimension to Darwin's argument about human morality in 1966, when he wrote that "an individual who maximizes his friendships and minimizes his antagonisms will have an evolutionary advantage, and selection should favor those characters that promote the optimization of personal relationships."[2] The self-survival of such reciprocal altruism is compelling, and although it contributes to the universality of human moral impulses, the argument of "calculating self-interest" does not fully explain it. As Mary Midgley points out, "People who do make an effort to behave decently plainly are often moved by a quite different set of motives, arising directly out of consideration for the claims of others. They act from a sense of judgment, from friendship, loyalty, compassion, gratitude, generosity, sympathy, family affection and the like—qualities that are recognized and honored in most human societies."[3]

Point one, then, is that even as we grow more aware of and accepting of diversity, humans of all cultures are united in sharing a capacity for altruism and a predisposition for morality. We may not always practice this beneficence, but that does not deny that it is a personal capacity. The possibility of formulating a global ethic thus starts because of its relevance as a personal ethic. Instead of an abstract superstructure imposed on all, a global ethic works by engaging the principles already defined as common, and already understood and practiced by people everywhere for the practical benefits to their lives, families and communities. It is not a replacement for any cultural or religious code, but represents what Professor Leonard Swidler of Temple University calls the ethical minimum that all share and to which all can agree. A global ethic will have validity to apply to everyone, not because it is global but because it is essential, foundational and common to all humans. And all humans already subscribe to it, again not because it is global but because their own societies and local communities could not function without it. We increasingly live in a global reality, so the task is to bring what we already value as individuals into norms for this interdependent worldwide community. "This one world society," writes Küng, "certainly does not need a unitary religion and a unitary ideology, but it does need some norms, values, ideals and goals to bring it together and be binding on it."[4]

A global ethic is possible only because more and more people from around the world are pushing for it to be defined and implemented. Like-minded individuals from around the world have created globe-straddling organizations for advocating environmentalism and human rights. Countries are coming together, slowly and with sometimes antagonistic agendas, to try to deal with shared development problems. Consumers are looking beyond traditional valuations of product and price, demanding that companies protect the world's environment, honor the human rights of its Third World workers and not exploit the smoke screen of outsourcing. And companies are themselves pressuring for initiatives like that of the OECD to eliminate the legal gaps between nations that foster corruption. These activities substantiate Martin Albrow's observation that "the global is not simply a culmination of transnational relations, but the intrusion of a new level of organization."[5] Such sensibilities are still tentative, of course, but point two is that the desire for a planetary norm is already there and growing.

The movement to this norm aligns with that even more inevitable progress—that of human growth toward maturity. We have more than 100,000 years of experience with territoriality. Cultures have met and traded for at least the last 5,000 years, and although some ideas and values were exchanged with goods, most people lived their entire existence in almost complete seclusion from the influence of other communities. Only in the last two generations, as the capabilities of new technology have come onstream, have we as a species lived life in our particular communities while concurrently exposed to and influenced by ideas and happenings everywhere else. The jarring experience of this intertwined global reality is completely new, and we are, as individuals, institutions and distinct cultures, only adolescents in dealing with it. Attempts to regulate CFC and greenhouse gas emissions, to ban land mines, protect endangered species, and link human rights to trade express a maturing brought on by the inescapable and shared crises within our new global reality.

In 1986, citing these problems that in no way respect political or geographical boundaries, Ulrich Beck suggested that the still-forming global cohesion is resulting from our being a global "community of risk."[6] The ascent to wisdom is not, however, simply a response to crisis. Problems may force us to confront inadequacies and formulate more mature responses, but human growth also involves the joy of participating with others in projects that contribute to the common good. In relationships with others, we receive both identity and meaning, often far beyond what we may give as individuals. In interactions with friends and colleagues, we also often strive for more than just a utilitarian mutuality, and we thrive by giving generously and serving more than we necessarily expect to get back. Philip Selznick, writing as a sociologist and law professor, argues that "moral well-being has its roots in the mundane facts of dependency and connectedness," but that it ultimately involves much more than just sympathy and concern. "Moral competence is the capacity to be an effective moral actor. This requires reflection as well as feeling, responsibility as well as love."[7] As individuals, we grow by sharing, by making choices to include others in our attention and affection. In this way, the pull of maturity toward wisdom is an analog for the movement of the global community toward a shared ethic. In other words, we are starting to expect of the global community the conformance to moral norms that we would of any individual emerging from the raucousness of adolescence into the responsibility of maturity. This means that a global ethic is an imperative at this time, not just because of the crises it resolves but as the naturally occurring and fully expected realization of our maturing as an integrated world community.

In the prologue to this chapter, Dietrich Bonhoeffer points out that human life, as well as the creative expression of our moral values, occurs within the tension between obligation and freedom. That tension implies also that with the ethical we are compelled to strive for the ideal yet at the same time accommodate reality. The prototype is that which is preached. The practice is our imperfect application of that prototype. We can grow and progress only by striving for both: seeking the inspiration of what can never be fully attained in order to realize in day-to-day life the most that is possible. John Kekes writes: "Moral wisdom is not merely disinterested knowledge of what is true or right: it also requires that the knowledge be used for making good lives for ourselves. Moral wisdom, however, is not purely practical either, since what it aims at is not just a good life pure and simple, but one that is pursued through choices of both means and ends, informed by knowledge of what is true and right."[8] The question remains, however, of how to define "true and right." Pluralism by definition gives validity to variety, to different perspectives and interpretations of truth. Diversity by definition does the same thing for what is right. Any ideal broad enough to encompass all this relativity risks being so general as to be meaningless. And any ideal specific enough to be relevant risks excluding other points of view. How in a time of such fragmented relativity can an ethic or ideal have meaning without it too becoming only relative?

Some philosophers and theologians have struggled in the rubble of deconstruction to build a basis of morality that begins with the most essential similarities that are shared by persons in all cultures. Called constructionists, this group or theory posits that humans are by nature relational. No person can be a human being by themselves. Ethics in this context are not so much a set of fixed norms as the attitudes and behaviors that from the reality of our own individuality give attention and honor to another person. In its most reduced form, to be ethical is to be compassionately aware of the other. Compassion, which is our ability to empathize and experience the reality of another person, orients us to make choices and behave in ways that honor the physical, emotional and spiritual reality of the other person. Only compassion can finally provide a cohesive ideal and the structure for ethical guidance.

There are several implications to this that are relevant to business. First, compassion is natural. We may need to learn to better heed it. We may also need to develop more in making our institutions and organizations respond to it. But compassion, and its ethical sensibility, do not need to be grafted onto corporate behaviors. These need only to be activated, to be permitted, nurtured and reinforced as legitimate factors in strategy and implementation. Second, compassion is least effective and most likely to be subverted when it is abstracted. Thinking in terms of the public good is not as compelling as recognizing the effects of a decision on a living, intelligent and sentient person. For example, releasing toxic waste into a body of water is unjustifiable in any circumstance, but Ontario Hydro and others have done so routinely for many years. Whatever the science or business reasons, such action is possible only by abstracting the harm it may cause, much as fighter pilots are removed by their height and speed from having to confront the destruction of the weapons they deliver. To be ethical requires encountering and reacting to the real situation and real repercussions for a real person. A third implication is that compassion is basic not only to individuals but also to the religious organizations that have for the ages provided moral guidance and community identity. The ethical sensibility is our spiritual sensibility.

Companies have dealt with this spiritual yearning primarily in the stealth language of "values." These are increasingly understood to be the vital source of identity and guidance that help employees manage the blank spaces that no strategy or structure can fully fill in. But values are not the same as ethics. As implied by the word, values represent qualities that are held in worth or appreciation. At Microsoft, values would include intelligence, aggressive competitiveness and composure under interrogation from Bill. At Wal-Mart, friendliness, loyalty and competitiveness would be some of the qualities considered distinctive and inspiring. Values provide glue between people, and shared values create the conditions for trust. Good things can come from values, but not all values are necessarily good. Competitiveness taken to the extreme can lead to charges like those leveled at Microsoft for burning out its own people, or at Wal-Mart for sucking up the livelihood of local merchants, thereby decimating smaller communities. Ethics, on the other hand, may be held in worth, but they represent not just what is appreciated but what is right. The ethical indeed may not be popular or esteemed; however, its legitimacy is that it is "right." The distinctions and respective roles are shown below as a continuum.

Table 5. Distinctions and Attributes

	Values	Ethics	Morals
Sphere	Attitude	Action	Belief
Relation	Belonging	Practice	Aspiration
Quality	Worthy	Right	Good
Attribute	Appreciation	Judgment	Wisdom
Benefit	Cohesion	Obligation	Meaning

Compassion is a vital starting point for bringing an ethical orientation to our corporate values. However, to provide more functional guidance requires giving dimension to this concept. Throughout history, up to the present day, and across every culture, societies derive their moral ideals about compassion from their religious structures. We may indeed be moral animals, but the primary structure for encoding and expressing morality is still religion. Despite modern discomfort in melding personal spirituality with public institutions, the global religious resurgence referred to earlier by Samuel Huntington proves this as a continuing force. Religion is so deeply embedded in the experience of all cultures exactly because human beings are inherently sociable. Sociologist Emile Durkheim observed that "religion is something eminently social. Religious representations are collective representations which express collective realities."[9] John Macmurray went a step further, explaining that "religion is essentially concerned with society—with the expression and creation of community. Indeed, the development of religion to maturity is the story of the groping efforts of men to realize the social nature of their own being."[10]

This is not to say religion is a panacea. Macmurray and others have railed against the irony that such institutions of compassion have so often been responsible for great, horrific harm. Religion has too often provided justification for tribalism, exclusion and the deepest of hatreds. In moments of social crisis like the Holocaust, religions have been damningly silent and by this passivity complicit. These failures require considerable reflection and vigilance, but again, that we have been inept in spirituality does not negate the need for it, nor its latent possibilities. I do not mean to attempt an apologia, but religion remains a vital component in our global ethical sensibility for several reasons. The reality in which the global community must find its common ethical structure remains one in which religion and religious questing remain central to the vast majority of human beings. Any ethic that does not reflect that centrality, that does not engage the authority of religious belief, would be largely non-credible to large parts of the world's people. Religion has often failed humanity, but so have economics, politics, science, technology and virtually every other ideology. Like these other human endeavors, religious experience and practice are a work in progress—incomplete, imperfect, but still evolving. In a sense, participating in forming a global ethic allows religion and the religious an opportunity to redeem themselves and help construct a reality more in keeping with their own ideals. This, however, is another book. For the purposes of this chapter, religion and religious sensibility are the factories that manufacture the morality that society and business both need to function.

Herman Daley and John Cobb suggest that the economy consumes moral capital. In other words, the activity of commerce, in seeking the fulfillment of self-interest, in seeking profit and advantage, draws from but does not replenish the reservoir of social beliefs and goodwill. Some trust, some mutuality, are essential for any exchange. In competitive jostling, with clear winners and clear losers, that trust and mutuality inevitably get eroded. Contracts of ever greater complexity and provisions for protection are the legal tools business uses to compensate for this erosion of moral capital. But, as noted in Chapter Four, the law is not enough. The self-interest and quest for advantage behind economic activity requires that the community through its spiritual resources recreate the moral threads that keep the whole system functioning. Religious exploration and expression supply the conditions and expectations for trust and decency and fairness that the economy and community demand as consumers. Companies interplay assets and liabilities to generate profit. Religions too use a balance sheet, in this instance one of rights and wrongs, derived from their transcendental precepts and the accumulated wisdom of tradition. This spiritual accounting is essential because, as Küng notes, "rights without morality cannot long endure, and . . . there will be no better global order without a global ethic."[11]

There remain several critical questions for something as broad as a global ethic. How can any global norm have moral suasion without a shared global religion? Or, put another way, how can human religious belief, with its great divisions and diversity, possibly be made a source for the common morality that is prerequisite for a common ethic? And finally, if the world's religions can indeed provide a framework for a global ethic, what, based on their own blatant shortcomings, provides the authority for its propagation in the global economy?

First, is it possible to have a global moral norm without a global religion? Yes. Humans have as many similarities as differences. Biologically, people everywhere share DNA that can be traced back thousands of generations to a single mother. Physiologically, people everywhere, of every culture and class, also share the same basic life needs: food, water, air, clothing, shelter. Psychologically, we are born into families and derive our identity and values from them and from our communities. Sociologically, we learn and mature, interacting with others in a social milieu, forming bonds, a sense of place and eventually our own families. Economically, we work to "earn" a living and for the right to consume. Religious symbols are used in all cultures to provide meaning, and rituals mark the major transitions of life, maturity and death. There are, in addition to these similarities, three fundamental aspects of human life that are especially conducive to a global ethic. As noted, people are all inextricably social. People also all experience emotions. And all people have the same rights. Since we are all social, we all need—and benefit from—a relational framework that protects our basic individuality while contributing to the cohesion, functioning and harmony of society. Since emotions are all and always a personal response to others, the capacity for both pain and empathy confirms that we also all have a basic capacity for empathy and responsibility. And since we all have equal rights, we all need a moral structure to ensure personal freedom, and at the same time fulfill the obligations to community that prevent one person's freedom from impinging on another.

Beyond our similarities in psyche and sociology, and beyond our common need, a global ethic reflects another shared reference point. Although still in its infancy, the study of comparative religion reveals that certain basic tenets are found in all cultures and spiritual traditions. The primary work of the Parliament of the World's Religions, as well as that of other similarly motivated organizations, has been to sift back through the dogma, ritual and moral teaching of various religions to expose these foundational ideas. To greatly simplify what is a difficult and nuanced analysis, human beings are divided, often irreconcilably, by the specifics of religious belief, but they are basically in unity on the motivations for religious seeking and moral conduct. This is the starting point for the global ethic.

But a shared foundation does not cancel out the exclusivity and even hostility that religions often manifest toward one another. This leads to the second large question: Why should religions, with their diversity and divisiveness, be accorded moral authority for a global ethic? This is dangerous territory for a business book to travel, but religion, as an institution, is very much like the world's economy. Both are works in progress, far from complete—if they ever can be—and are struggling to adapt. Like other political and social institutions that were primarily focused on local concerns, religions are confronting the now global reality of economic activity, ecological destruction and cultural homogenization. The concrete reality of intimate interdependence is causing many religions to respond like people—simultaneously retreating to the fundamental beliefs that confirm identity while going forward into deeper interfaith exchange. Swidler sees this as a progress from "monologue," when each religion, ideology and culture "tended to be very certain that it alone had the complete explanation of the ultimate meaning of life, and how to live accordingly," to "dialogue," an acknowledgment of the limitation of any single ideology or perspective, fostering a desire for "conversation with someone who differs from us primarily so that we can learn."[12] There is a growing, though tentative, recognition that the categorical beliefs that motivated conflict and sought conversion to a single universal faith are untenable in the new, global reality. The desire for religious hegemony is slowly giving way to the embrace of diversity.

This evolution is what Macmurray meant by "groping efforts" toward "maturity." Technology, commerce and cultural consciousness are enabling humans for the first time to see themselves in terms broader than local community and patriotic state. As the events that shape our lives and identity become increasingly global, the institutions of religion, again like those of the economy, will need to mature to provide relevant context and meaning. A global ethic, by acknowledging that we cannot live in adolescent isolation, also forces institutions to grow beyond their parochial territoriality. To paraphrase theologian William J. Bouwsma, since it is impossible to achieve perfect maturity in life, the duty of wisdom is simply to develop constantly toward it. This does not paper over differences. It simply means that the constitutive elements for the global community are at the same time diverse and interdependent.

This quest for maturity among religions has already begun. Sparked by different inspirations, scholars, theologians and teachers from the whole range of religious traditions have collaborated to define shared and compelling principles for a global ethic. For this analysis, I have examined the results of four initiatives. The first, mentioned earlier, is the Declaration Toward a Global Ethic that emerged from the Council for a Parliament of the World's Religions that met in Chicago in September 1993. The Declaration is so far the most broad-based expression, and has been theologically endorsed by Hans Küng, Karl-Josef Kuschel and Leonard Swidler, among many others. The second project was begun after a state visit by the British Royal Family to Jordan. Intending to break stereotyping and increase understanding, the Interfaith Declaration involved theologians and scriptural scholars, with bankers, businesspeople and politicians. This time the focus was "constructing a code of ethics for international business" based on the "shared moral, ethical and spiritual values inherent in the common Abrahamic tradition" embracing Judaism, Christianity and Islam.

The third effort had more modest roots and agenda. The Ad Hoc Interfaith Working Group brought together twenty-one teachers and leaders representing the aboriginals, Buddhists, Christians, Hindus, Jews, Muslims and Sikhs of Canada. The goal was to enshrine "six fundamental values" in the Canadian Constitution, and led to the submission *Mutual Responsibility: The Tie That Binds.* The fourth input derives its momentum more directly from the business community. The Caux Principles, organized by business leaders and politicians under the aegis of the INSEAD business school in France, sought to give dimension to the ethical values derived from the distinct European, American and Japanese business systems. The Caux Principles represent as well cross-learning, a sort of ethical "best practices" that each economic system can learn from the other.

Clearly, the call for a global ethic is coming from a host of voices, from a variety of places and from a rich diversity of professions and cultures. Reflecting exactly the dynamics of the global economy, some of these projects are global in scale with local implications; others start locally and project out to a global reality. As well, the spreading fervor for a global ethic is attributable to the growing recognition of the social discontinuity and damaging injustice resulting from the advances in technology, industrialization and the globalization of the economy. The global human community is awakening to its responsibilities and potential in managing its increasingly global institutions. All the voices, including those of business, religious and political leaders, do not seek to dismantle or undermine the economy, but they do condemn its abuses, growing corruption and criminality. The power accumulated and used by economic institutions is universally seen to be at the service of the human family, and not its master.

None of the principles, declarations and submissions assumes to be complete. The philosophy behind each initiative has been inclusion, and this ethos is projected forward to capture the commitment and creativity of all individuals striving to develop and deepen their ethical orientation. Hans Küng and Karl-Josef Kuschel explain in their introduction to *A Global Ethic* that "of course this Declaration Toward a Global Ethic—like the first Declaration on Human Rights in 1776 at the time of the American Revolution—is not an end but a beginning."[13] Maturity is a capacity that is not learned but experienced. Each of the groups was very clear and passionate about the disturbing problems requiring a global ethic, but the proclamations are all invitations for participation. An imposed global ethic is an automatic failure. Küng and Kuschel explain that the global ethic is "not directed against anyone, but invites all, believers and unbelievers, to make the ethic their own and act in accordance with it."[14]

The Declaration of the Parliament of the World's Religions

In its introduction, the Declaration expresses the concern found in all the other proposals, stating simply, "The world is in agony." Violence and warfare, the abuse of the natural environment, poverty, injustice and violence toward children are "condemned" as the source of the agony. The Parliament also condemns the "religious aggression" that has tolerated and so contributed to the world's pain. "The truth is already known," states the Declaration, "but yet to be lived in heart and action." Agony of this scale and damage demands a response from all human beings that reflects our inextricable "interdependence," as well as our "individual responsibility" for ethical behavior. The perspective of the Declaration is that we are all members of the human family, that we each have rights and dignity to be respected by others and for us to respect them. This reciprocity is fundamental. Hence, injustice is a concern for all, not just its victims. A critical aspect of the respect for individual life, dignity and justice is responsible management of our shared ecosystem.

The Parliament of the World's Religions bases its Declaration on four principles:

1. *Everyone is responsible for a global ethic.* The "fundamental consensus on binding values, irrevocable standards and personal attitudes" applies to protect each individual, so by necessity each individual is involved. This seems to contradict the notion of invitation, but in fact it does not. The global ethic works only as a personal commitment made out of personal choice, but that does not mean that its purpose is optional or its implementation anything but urgent.
2. *Every human must be treated humanely.* All persons have rights and "untouchable dignity" that create obligations for respect among both individuals and states. This principle includes two famous antecedents. From Kant, the principle states that people will be "ends, never mere means." And from the teaching of a variety of

religions, a version of the Golden Rule: "What you do not wish done to yourself, do not do to others. Or in positive terms, What you wish done to yourself, do to others."

3. *Four irrevocable directives emanate from these principles*: 1) A commitment to a culture of non-violence and respect for life, expressed in a commandment: "You shall not kill." 2) A commitment to a culture of solidarity and a just economic order, expressed as a commandment: "You shall not steal," or, in positive terms, "Deal honestly and fairly." 3) A commitment to a culture of tolerance and truthfulness, expressed as a commandment: "You shall not lie," or in positive terms, "Speak and act truthfully." 4) Finally, a commitment to a culture of equal rights and partnership between men and women. This includes respect for the elderly, children and families and is expressed in an attitude of "reconciliation and love."

4. *A transformation of consciousness acknowledges the difficult work ahead.* The world is too complex for any exhaustive, all-encompassing list of strictures and guidelines. The Parliament invites professional groups and associations from all walks of life to define norms that express the spirit of the global ethic in terms appropriate for them. The key though is a "conversion of heart."[15]

I have already noted that this declaration of a global ethic seems rather too simple. This, however, does not make its meaning any less profound, or its implementation anything but difficult. Even what seem like obvious principles like "You shall not kill" take on radical significance if applied to tobacco, CFC usage and black-marketeering, and other environmental waste, exploitation and destruction. In the next chapter we will begin to peel away these layers of implications for business. For now, we need only consider the latency of each principle, and recognize how this declaration represents a truly revolutionary consensus.

The Interfaith Declaration

The very starting premise of this interfaith initiative was clearly economic. Simon Webley, director of the British–North American

Research Association and one of the authors of the Declaration, explains that the intent of the group's work was to establish the still-vital common values of the three Abrahamic religions and "relate this relevance to contemporary business issues."[16] After referring to the Jewish and Christian Testaments and the Islamic Koran, the eclectic working group settled on four key concepts that recur in "respect to economic transactions." These values are:

- *Justice,* meaning "just conduct," "fairness" in dealings with all other people and using "authority in maintenance of what is right." In other words, those who have power, either political or economic, have a commensurate obligation to support and do what is right.
- *Mutual respect,* as primarily encoded in yet another version of the Golden Rule: "Love thy neighbor as thyself." In economic terms, this means accepting the commitment that "self-interest must take into account the interest of others."
- *Stewardship,* relating to the "care" and "proper use" of nature. The Declaration iterates that no one owns the natural environment. We are all its trustees.
- *Honesty,* extending to "thought, word and action." Referring to "dishonesty" as an "abomination," the group calls for an attitude of honesty that in its fullness is "integrity." The Declaration also confirms that "speaking the truth is a requirement for everyone."

Only four key values, in simple language, with common-sense requirements, yet once again, the simplicity masks a profound accountability. David Korten reports that there are now 25 percent more public relations agents in the United States than reporters. He explains that "these firms will organize citizen letter-writing campaigns, provide paid operatives posing as 'housewives' to present corporate views in public meetings, and place favorable news items and op-ed pieces in the press. A 1990 study found that almost 40 percent of the news in a typical newspaper originates from public-relations press releases, story memos, and suggestions. According to the *Columbia Journalism Review,* more than half the *Wall Street Journal's* new stories are based solely on press releases."[17] The point is that a commitment to "thinking, speaking and acting" the truth raises innumerable questions about spin doctoring and obligations for honesty in our highly wired and overcommunicated world.

The Interfaith Declaration went on to include some details of how to implement the values. It did not provide an answer about truth—nor could it—but offered some guidance for obligations to stakeholders, the community, the natural environment, business practices and employees. Perhaps the most important realization came from the process rather than the content. As business and political leaders in the forum struggled to define ethical values, they inevitably referred to scriptural sources and spiritual traditions, thereby confirming Daly and Cobb's observation that business is a consumer of moral capital and not a producer.

The Tie that Binds

As an exploration of mutual responsibility, this was an effort by a group in perhaps the world's most multicultural country to find a "common ground on principles." This document was prepared in 1991, not at the behest of world leaders but as an ad hoc submission to the Special Joint Committee investigating reforming Canada's Constitution and Charter of Rights. The group, comprising primarily religious leaders, wrote: "We believe there is a solid foundation for unity underneath the vast diversity of our beliefs and traditions. Pluralism, respecting differences, is not chaotic. This basis for unity must not, therefore, be made peripheral but rather foundational."[18]

The Tie that Binds put forth six "fundamental considerations" or principles that expressed the unity that can come from such immense diversity. These were:

- *Human Dignity,* the right of all people, both as individuals and within their communities, to be "treated with justice, love, compassion and respect." Integral to this principle is the "responsibility to treat others likewise."
- *Mutual Responsibility,* the "duty" of all persons to contribute to

the community "as they are able," and the reciprocal duty of the
community to look after all its members "regardless of ability."

- *Economic Equity,* the right of all persons and communities to the
  "resources necessary for a fully human life." Again, this right
  entails an obligation—in this case, using all resources with care.
- *Fiscal Fairness,* which means that everyone contributes "fairly
  for the well being of all."
- *Social Justice,* the right of all to "participate in life and decision-
  making," demanding that public institutions be accountable for
  their effects on individuals.
- *Environmental Integrity,* involving stewardship and the "duty of
  all persons, communities and institutions to live in harmony"
  with the natural environment.

A few terse "practical guidelines" were added to the principles,
condemning racism, sexism and practices that contribute to the fragmentation of families. Importantly, one guideline links "the true well-
being of a community" to the "well-being of its weakest members."
This articulates a concept only suggested in the other declarations. As
befits a multicultural group, there is also a call for nourishing the
distinctiveness of communities.

Finally, likely reflecting a cadence from its first peoples, the document states: "Before there is a people there is land, water, air, fire, trees
and animals—in a word, environment. Sustained care for this environment is a first principle for all economic and technological development." Most of the established, more traditional religions have only
lately come to understand that compassion and moral principle must
also embrace the human relationship with nature. Theologians like
Thomas Berry have borrowed from aboriginal religion to reenvision
nature not as a backdrop for human activity but as a sacred dynamic
adding immeasurably to human meaning and well-being. All the declarations for a global ethic include an explicit acknowledgment of our
responsibility to care for the environment. The environment (the
globe) is our host, the host on which all life lives. *The Tie That Binds*
reminds us that, as "a first principle," the environment is the "first-
bind"—the original basis of human unity and a world ethic.

The Caux Principles

Caux is a small town in Switzerland that hosts two philosophically related events. Since 1938, there has been an annual meeting of an organization founded by Dr. Frank Buchman. An American, Buchman founded a group that sought to counter the heavy arms build-up before the Second World War by emphasizing four values that are "common to every religion and ethnic group: absolute moral standards of honesty, purity, unselfishness and love." This group advocates conversation and one-to-one encounters so that people can experience the richness of our differences, as well as the unity of our essential humanity. Buchman's approach has been "that individuals must first undergo self-transformation in order to be able to change the world."[19]

The Caux Roundtable was founded in 1986 by Frederik Philips, former president of Philips Electronics, and Oliver Giscard d'Estaing, vice-chairman of the European graduate school of management, INSEAD. The work of this forum has been twofold: to develop understanding and constructive exchange between the quite different market systems of Europe, North America and Japan, and to "provide a forum for business to articulate its worldwide social obligations." Senior executives from around the world meet to discuss problems, and with a "common respect for the highest moral values" they seek to establish not "Who is right?" but, more essentially, "What is right?" The Caux Principles are but one product of that questioning and collaboration.

The language and concepts of the Caux Principles, developed in 1994, are similar to those of the other declarations yet with their own distinct perspective. There are seven principles:

1. *Extending the responsibility of business beyond "shareholders toward stakeholders."* The basic premise is that business has its priorities, "but survival is not a sufficient goal." There is an acknowledgment that "businesses share a part in shaping the future of communities." This brings obligations, particularly for honesty and fairness.
2. *Orienting the effects of business toward "innovation, justice and world community."* This is not a call for world government but a

recognition that multinational companies have an influence beyond any single state or community. This power carries responsibilities, for contributing to "human rights, education, welfare and vitalization" of the countries within which they operate, and for managing free and fair competition.

3. *Moving "beyond the letter of the law to a spirit of trust."* This is a commitment to operate with sincerity, to keep promises and to provide "transparency" to the communities and stakeholders that are engaged or affected by companies.

4. *Respecting "rules."* Some behavior may be legal but still be immoral. So in addition to conforming to regulations, companies must apply their own judgment for "fairness and equity."

5. *Supporting multilateral trade.* This is essentially a commitment to an even playing field in all markets and economies.

6. *Respecting the environment.* This suggests that various companies are at various stages of ecological management. A basic, universal responsibility is to "protect" the environment. But this is not enough. The commitment needs to develop and deepen—"where possible to improve the environment, promote sustainable development, and prevent waste."

7. *Avoiding illicit operations.* Corruption, bribery and money laundering are totally unacceptable. Companies are obliged to not only avoid but cooperate in eliminating these wasteful as well as immoral practices. The group also condemns trade in arms and other materials that may be used for terrorism, drug traffic or other organized crime.

Capitalism was until recently perceived as one economic system that functioned in opposition to communism. It turns out that capitalism is not singular but has as many flavors and variations as there are countries and cultures. The Caux Principles seek to do for the global economy what the Ad Hoc Interfaith Group sought to do in Canada—uncover the basic unity within this diversity. The goal for the Principles was a fusion of the values inherent in the three major types of capitalism: the "respect for human dignity" focus of the Europeans; the stakeholders' rights approach of North Americans;

and the *kyosei*—the concept of "living and working together for the common good" of the Japanese. Once again, although the make-up of this organization is more skewed to business, the final principles bear remarkable similarity to those of the other groups, including those mostly comprising religious leaders and theologians. This is probably not that surprising. Since we cannot even in business entirely escape our humanity, we cannot escape the responsibility for being human, for acting humanely. The great religious traditions have not so much set out an alternative path for humans as revealed something constitutive and defining about humanity. To be moral, then, is not a vocation or a chore. It is to be human.

The language of the Caux Principles also suggests some of the dynamics of "orientation" that I covered in Chapter One. The commitment to principle, as in the one for the environmental responsibilities of business, does not just set a minimum for compliance but projects a deepening development. The more companies practice ethical reflection and judgment, the more capable and perceptive they become at it. Ryuzaburo Kaku, the chairman of Canon, has taken this concept one step further and argues that companies, like human individuals, have degrees of social responsibility that vary by their "maturity." I will incorporate this thesis into a later section, but Kaku basically means that the societal obligations for an entrepreneur during start-up must be less developed and preoccupying than for a fully resourced multinational. Everyone and every company has a fundamental, inescapable responsibility, but obligations vary by development, resources and maturity. Orientation thus represents a progression of accountability as well as of commitment.

Committees may create camels, but what is remarkable is that such variously founded and constituted groups should repeatedly create the same camel. For purposes of analysis (although recognizing the danger of simplifying what are already summaries of complicated processes), I have created a grid to outline the key principles and values. Some of the values from the various declarations align almost perfectly, some suggest alignment and some overlap several categories and could comfortably sit in any of several boxes. My focus has been to show the flow, to demonstrate the continuity and commonality of highly different initiatives that attempted in their own sphere to do the same thing.

Two essential qualities pervade the language and principles of all four declarations. First is a recognition and acceptance of personal responsibility. All persons have rights, but these are inalienable, inherited by the nature of being human. Responsibility instead requires choice. Rights are realized only if responsibility is accorded from others. An inextricable dynamic of our own individual rights is our own individual responsibility for the rights of others. The message in all the declarations is that any action, for both persons and companies, starts with a clear recognition that "I am responsible." The second quality, implicit in the first, is that ethics are circular. Repeatedly, each of the proclamations used "reciprocity" and "mutuality" to express this give-and-take interdependence. Reflecting some laws of balance, the back-and-forth movement works on several levels: between individual and community; between rights and responsibility; between Bonhoeffer's "freedom and obedience"; between unity and diversity; between global and local; between rational and emotional; between material and spiritual; between reflection and action. This quality, which I call symmetry, is central to the model I will elaborate later that is designed to help companies develop a working ethical orientation.

The categories of values are declarative: Respect Life, Be Fair, Be Honest, Strive for Justice, Honor the Environment. Listing and enumeration suggest a priority, but none is intended. Indeed, the values are best seen as linked, a chain that works only if all the pieces are in place and accorded equal vigilance and rigor.

Table 6. Global Ethic Composite

	RESPECT LIFE	BE FAIR	BE HONEST	STRIVE FOR JUSTICE	HONOR THE ENVIRONMENT
Parliament of the World's Religions	• Treat all humanely • Do not kill	• Do not steal • Extend equality to all	• Do not lie • Speak and act with truth	• Moderation. • Partnership. • A *just* economy	• "Intertwined together in the cosmos" • Care for all life.
The Interfaith Declaration	• Extend mutual respect	• Mutuality: *Love thy neighbor as thyself*	• Honesty in thought, word and deed • Integrity	• "Exercise authority in maintenanc ofe what is right"	• Stewardship: charged with care and proper usage
Ad Hoc Inter-Faith Working Group	• Right of all to be accorded human dignity	• Promote equity in the economy	• Fiscal fairness • Mutual responsibility	• Diversity with equality • Fair to weakest	• Duty to live in harmony with nature as a "first principle"
The Caux Principles	• Obligations to all stakeholders	• Support fair trade • Avoid illicit activities	• Beyond the letter to the spirit of the law	• Justice within the world community	• Protect, improve and promote sustainable development
BASIC RIGHT:	• **Dignity**	• **Respect**	• **Integrity**	• **Justice**	• **Access**
BASIC DUTY:	• **Mutuality**	• **Reciprocity**	• **Truthfulness**	• **Care**	• **Sustainability**

Despite the remarkable synchronicity of these various efforts, many executives will still object that these tentative agreements about common ethical principles are insufficient for dealing with the complexity and diversity of the modern global economy. There are indeed profound differences between markets and cultures to be acknowledged and honored. But there is also a more developed basis of unity and cohesion for confronting the ethical dilemmas of multinational business than most cynics assume. Fons Trompenaars, the managing director of the Centre for International Business, in the Netherlands, has studied the difficulties of managing across cultures. "The implication of the research," Trompenaars writes, "is that universals exist at another level. While you cannot give *advice* that will work regardless of culture, and while the general axioms of business administration turn out to be largely American cultural axioms, there are *universal dilemmas* or *problems of human existence.* Every country and every organization in that country faces dilemmas *in relationships with people, in relationship to time and in relations between people and the natural environment.* While nations differ markedly in how they approach these dilemmas, they do not differ in needing to make some kind of response. People everywhere are as one in having to face up to the same challenges of existence."[20] Whether, like the Asians, we start from a universal perspective and work to the individual or whether, like North Americans, we start from the particular and extrapolate universals from there, both approaches increasingly acknowledge the validity of the other. With managers from Detroit learning to implement quality circles from Japan, and managers from state companies in Beijing learning accounting from Harvard business professors, the culture of the global economy is increasingly hybrid. Common ethical problems are creating the conditions for a common ethical response.

I believe that the global spiritual factory has begun to manufacture the moral principles for a global ethic. Now the work begins, for individuals and companies, of absorbing intent, imagining implications and creating the structures, attitudes and transformation necessary for an ethical orientation.

Table 7. A Universal Symmetry—The Golden Rule Across Cultures

Judaism and Christianity	You shall love your neighbor as yourself. Bible, Leviticus 19.18
Judaism	When he went to Hillel, he said to him, "What is hateful to you, do not do to your neighbor: that is the whole Torah; all the rest of it is commentary; go and learn." Talmud, Shabbat 31a
Christianity	Whatever you wish that men would do to you, do so to them. Bible, Matthew 7.12
Islam	Not one of you is a believer until he loves for his brother what he loves for himself. Forty Hadith of an-Nawawi 13
Jainism	A man should wander about treating all creatures as he himself would be treated. Sutrakritanga 1.11.33
Confucianism	Try your best to treat others as you would wish to be treated yourself and you will find that is the shortest way to benevolence. Mencius VII.A4 Tsetung asked, "Is there one word that can serve as a principle of conduct for life?" Confucius replied, "It is the word shu—reciprocity: Do not do to others what you do not want them to do to you." Analects 15.23

Hinduism	One should not behave towards others in a way which is disagreeable to oneself. This is the essence of morality. All other activities are due to selfish desire. Mahabharata, Anusasana Parva 113.8
Buddhism	Comparing oneself to others in such terms as "Just as I am so are they, just as they are so am I," he should neither kill nor cause others to kill. Sutta Nipata 705
African traditional religions	One going to take a pointed stick to pinch a baby bird should first try it on himself to feel how it hurts. Yoruba Proverb (Nigeria)

CHAPTER SIX

IMPERATIVE

The question of good is posed and is decided in the midst of each definite, yet unconcluded, unique and transient situation of our lives, in the midst of living with men, things, institutions and powers, in other words in the midst of our historical experience. The question of good cannot now be separated from the question of life, the question of history.

Dietrich Bonhoeffer, "History and Good," in Ethics

A global ethic will have global impact in the global economy only if it is practical enough to be of value. Most businesspeople already have drawers full of decision charts and mission statements as well as models for excellence, total quality, empowerment and customer service. The consulting industry (of which I am a small part) requires that new concepts be diagrammed, matrixed or modeled. Many people at most companies now know how to do the break-out sessions, creative ideation and action contracts that go with system, structure and attitude change. These good intentions, supported by smart seminars, have not often produced the expected results. Various studies have marked the failure rates of total quality, reengineering and the synergy goals behind many mergers to be as high as 70 to 80 percent. This terrible waste has in many ways polluted the atmosphere within companies for any new change. While managers and workers understand the need for continuous change, they are largely drained and frustrated by the general lack of constructive progress. They are concerned that new initiatives will, just like previous programs, not achieve the desired solution but only create more work. How do we translate the precepts of the global ethic into something functional but lasting, particularly given that its implementation is not always one of step-by-step simplicity? What structure can the global ethic take to provide workable complexity—something that is both practical and practicable, but also clearly beyond any "one-minute manager" reduction?

Some models already exist for ethical decision-making. Conceived for the most part by academics, these tend to operate like a series of sieves through which decisions are filtered. Using principles from ethical theories of duty, utility and rights and obligations, questions at each level sift out various aspects of ethical integrity and force managers to confront lapses, inconsistencies and problems.

Conventional Evaluation of Business Ethics

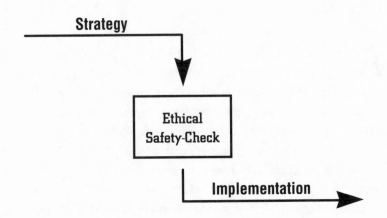

These approaches do raise awareness and develop the right questioning skills, and have been used by some companies as one part of their ethical practices. There are, however, some limitations to this approach, quite similar to those encountered during the initial efforts to raise quality in North America and Europe. This sieve process is akin to performing quality control after the manufacturing is complete. You catch mistakes, or at least some of them, but without changing the institutional and attitudinal dynamics that contribute to the poor standards of quality in the first place. Though such interventions catch some transgressions, they do not provide companies with the deeper intellectual and cultural learning upon which real, lasting change is built.

A second weakness of the sieve interception is that ethical considerations are rarely that linear or clear. It suggests that the strategic decision-making process and the ethical evaluation process are distinct and sequential, when they are actually highly integrated and simultaneous. And it creates the impression that there is a fixed set of rules or questions, or a set checklist, which validates or disqualifies decisions and actions on the basis of ethical merits. The real business world is more dynamic and complex than that. A final concern is that the people in the business trenches rarely have the time, understanding or inclination to distinguish between deontological (duty-driven) ethics and utilitarian (happiness-driven) ethics. Language, principles and structures must make sense and be accessible to win the attention and practice of harried workers. This is not to criticize the intent or input of other ethical models, but to help set the objectives for maximum engagement of a global ethic.

What, then, are the goals for a model for a global ethic? First, the model must integrate business and ethical considerations into a single decision stream. This is not automatic. It is hard to do, but the aim of an ethical orientation is a pervasive and consistent marriage of objective with obligation. Second, the model must provide a mechanism for substantive change to mission, structure and culture. We know from John Darley's lessons on corporate evildoing that information paths, group dynamics, fear of reprisal and compartmentalization of responsibility play a part in subverting morality and diligence to the law. An ethical orientation does not work as an ethical afterthought. Third, the model must create perspective on the complexity of ethical business management, as well as the depths of implication that result from individual decisions and actions. This is not to intimidate people, but to ingrain in their decision making and problem solving an automatic recognition of aftereffects and responsibility. Fourth, the model must incorporate the key principles of ethical behavior, allotting each equal weight, while also recognizing that they are interconnected.

The model is premised on a belief that managerial, group and individual shortcomings that scuttle other well-meaning initiatives like Total Quality are those that also resist ethical deliberation. Put another way, *the characteristics of bad management need to be addressed in order to reorient and recreate a good company.* From my experience and study, there are six variables that must be aligned: the Board of Directors must set the tone; the CEO must set the example; the strategy must be clear and compelling; the culture must be open and questioning; the group dynamics within the company must be based on trust; and individual managers and employees must make a personal commitment to the initiative. Companies are a system, not a structure, so the interaction and the cohesion of all these parts are critical for progress on any business issue or program of change. Misalignment creates failure, as when a CEO does not "walk the talk," or when a fear-of-failure culture strangles creative risk, or when strategy flip-flops from one great idea to another. This alignment of managerial factors will be studied in more detail as part of the implementation section that starts with Chapter Seven. The point to underscore at this time is that the first requirement for this ethical model is business competency.

The model is meant to be customized (specific examples will be discussed in Chapter Ten). Every company has unique issues and distinct pressures; it also varies in its development and maturity in both business competency and ethical sensibility. Uniformity within such variation is neither practical nor realistic. For purposes of initial exploration, I will demonstrate one iteration of the model as a cube. On the surface of each side of the cube are etched six boxes, which reflect the alignment of Board principles, CEO beliefs and behaviors, strategic direction, cultural reference points and reinforcements, group dynamics and personal understanding and commitment.

Ethical Orientation Model

Board Guidance	Cultural Supports
CEO Example	Group Dynamics
Strategic Commitment	Personal Commitment

Creating the awareness and acceptance for an ethical orientation requires, as it does for any smart business initiative, consistency in thought, word and deed within each sphere of a company's operation. Ethics are relational, so mutuality and common purpose are that much more important. Once the leadership, structure and people are united in the corporation's moral cause, specific ethical principles can be defined in three dimensions. Imagine the Alignment model in three dimensions, with its other sides in various colors—perhaps red for *Respect Life,* yellow for *Be Fair,* white for *Be Honest,* purple for *Strive for Justice,* and green for *Honor the Environment.* Finally, imagine that all these colors have the same demarcation as the blue business face so that six sections appear on each side. If you have in your mind's eye a customized version of a Rubik's Cube, you've got it.

Dynamic Model for an Ethical Orientation

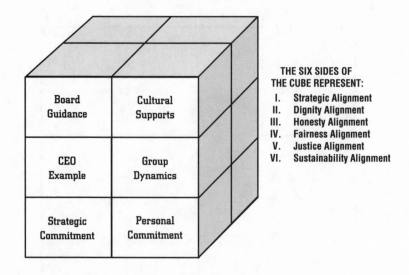

THE SIX SIDES OF
THE CUBE REPRESENT:

I.   Strategic Alignment
II.   Dignity Alignment
III. Honesty Alignment
IV.   Fairness Alignment
V.   Justice Alignment
VI.   Sustainability Alignment

The model I have developed for a global ethic is, appropriately enough, a puzzle, not a game. I know from having used this visual metaphor in groups that it immediately conjures up several associations that are important to ethical deliberation. The cube with moving parts is dynamic and three-dimensional, just like life and so unlike most straight-line graphical models. Immediately, there is recognition of the multifaceted nature of most business decision making. There is also an understanding of interdependence—the separate parts and colors ultimately all fit together as a single whole—and of the need for alignment—one single part out of sequence destroys the integrity of the whole. Finally, although the complexity is challenging, the puzzle is solvable. It takes time to think, to work out the implications of specific actions, but the coming together of separate parts into a comprehensive alignment is doable.

It is now important to break down those many interconnected parts of the EO Cube, but first, take this test. Can you imagine the puzzle cube? If you can conjure it up, then you know that it is easy to remember. Although it may take time to become familiar with all the sides and all the units within each side, most of us can readily imagine the puzzle and therefore visualize that every decision has a multitude of implications to be figured out and reconciled. This is workable complexity. It is not only easy to remember but, more importantly, once explained, it's hard to forget. Most people react to this iteration of the model by saying that every decision in business already involves a Rubik's cube of complexity. That is exactly the point: this model, rather than intruding on business reality, reflects and integrates with it. Strategy and ethics must be linked every step of the way. Over time, as the business and ethics process becomes seamless and spontaneous, the probing provided by ethical questions will also shed light on other managerial weaknesses. Every misalignment speaks to a problem, either in board direction, CEO leadership, strategy, culture, trust or individual commitment. Understanding and coming to terms with any breakdown prevents ethical or legal improprieties, but also highlights the thinking, structural or behavioral weaknesses that all organizations and individuals suffer. The EO Model is therefore an early warning system for managerial failure, as well as for ethical risk.

Recognizing the interplay between management and ethics, the *Economist* comments: "The rational pursuit of self-interest is the necessary basis of human activity but, if a country is to be worth living in, all those competing individual self-interests have to operate within an agreed set of rules. The rules may be derived from God, or they may be constructed by a consensus of non-believers; but in either case, they will draw upon the instinctive part of the mind—the tug of compassion, the intuitive sense of right and wrong—as well as the purely rational part."[1] By expecting business and ethical alignment in all dimensions, the EO Model engages both the analytical and the intuitive aspects of individuals and the organization. To extrapolate the *Economist*'s observation: If a *world* is to be worth living in, all those competing individual self-interests have to operate within an agreed set of rules. The rules of the model are based on the wide understanding and deep appreciation of the divine derived from genuine interfaith dialogue. As was shown by the Caux Principles and the Interfaith Principles for International Business, the model also represents an emerging secular consensus that includes government leaders, business teachers and practitioners, environmentalists, human rights advocates and persons from all walks of life.

The gulf between seeing and doing, recognizing and applying, is still vast. Several questions are critical to closing this gulf and moving into practice. The first is: How can a global ethic be both optional and imperative? As suggested earlier, the optionality is important because an ethic finally has value only if it is freely chosen and adopted. Companies learned from both Deming and Juran that their commitment to quality could not be achieved by corporate edict, but only through the dedication of single employees performing specific, individual tasks. To have tangible benefit and enduring impact, an ethical orientation also needs to be practiced with such incremental attention to detail, and personal understanding and involvement. The imperative is a result of both the consequences of operating without a binding ethic and the requirements of effective change. An unethical global economy affects every individual personally, in terms of livelihood (jobs and wages), natural basic resources (air and water), and opportunities (growth and creative development). The risk of leaving the global economy unattended, as well as the benefits of reforming it, belong to everyone.

This obligation to act reflects the symmetry that I noted earlier. Human law, design, art and relationships all involve symmetry. Physicist and professor at Cal Tech Richard P. Feynman wrote that "symmetry is fascinating to the human mind, and everyone likes objects or patterns that are in some way symmetrical." But although humans may appreciate and use symmetries, the concept itself is actually "proto-natural." Feynman explains: "It is interesting that nature often exhibits certain kinds of symmetry in the objects we find in the world" and symmetries "exist in the *basic laws themselves* which govern the operations of the physical world."[2] The symmetry of the Golden Rule is thus but a human expression of a much more cosmic process of relation.

Business is primarily defined by the relation of competition. However, "the survival of the fittest" is but one rule of nature. There are many other types, what John H. Holland of the University of Michigan calls "a wondrous panoply of interactions such as mutualism, parasitism, biological arms races and mimicry."[3] To focus only on one behavior—competitiveness—as natural law, is *unnatural*. To single out self-interest as the only natural motivation is *unnatural*. And to assume that there is only a linear natural path from self-interest to competitiveness to economic progress is *unnatural*. Symmetry, since it suggests multiplicity and reciprocity, is actually the more encompassing natural law. Philosopher John Rawls argues that a basic moral intuition of humans equates "fairness" to what is "right," so that the morality we intuit in "autonomy, agreement, human rights" all involve some dynamic of symmetry.[4] What's good for the goose is naturally what's good for the gander. Or, better still, what goes around comes around.

The EO Imperative uses symmetry, both as an overarching theme and as a specific expression of its individual elements. There are several reasons for this. First, symmetry emerged consistently and is implied in concepts like "reciprocity," "mutuality" and "justice." Second, symmetry links the individual to the outcome. Darley showed how the "diffusion of information and responsibility" undermined personal morality and allowed groups to commit conscious evildoing. Symmetry reminds us to always act as if our decision would directly affect ourselves—thereby helping making the abstract real, the impersonal personal and the distant immediate and near. Third, symmetry involves a tension toward balance. The ethical imperative for the global economy is to bring into equilibrium the self-interest that generates industriousness—but also abuses—with the legitimate social and environmental needs of the global community. Fourth, symmetry suggests a harmony rather than antipathy between business and ethics.

The objective is not to curtail strategic and management concerns, but to infuse these with an ethical consciousness. Professors James Collins and Jerry Porras have shown that enduring success involves a focus on ideology and values. Profitability for companies cited was not less important than for other companies, but the systems of meaning and belonging were much more important. The authors explain that "The corporate bonding glue will increasingly become *ideological*. People still have a fundamental human need to belong to something they can feel proud of. They have a fundamental need for guiding values and sense of purpose that gives their life and work meaning. They have a fundamental need for connection with other people, sharing with them the common bond of beliefs and aspirations. More that any time in the past, employees will demand operating autonomy while also demanding that the organizations they're connected to stand for something."[5]

A Practical Framework

Companies that manage by balance sheet are more successful, endure longer and master the tasks of continuous change much better than those that manage the bottom line alone. The lesson is that the workability of a model, no matter how valid its premise, rests first on the organization's ability to renew itself. Business disciplines are therefore integral to the Ethical Imperative, and have integral application in the decision making around each ethical principle. The model makes management competency an ethical goal, along with the five principles—dignity, fairness, honesty, justice and sustainability—described earlier. For each goal or dynamic, the model sets out three layers of engagement particular to it.

First, the *Principle* targets the ideal, setting the benchmark and focusing commitment. Second, the *Rule* expresses the ethical mandate for each principle as a specific command. This sounds authoritarian, but is intended to reflect the reality of ethical choice. In John Kekes's words: "The direction moral wisdom provides takes the form of us *not* doing what we are motivated to do and of making an effort *to* do what we are insufficiently motivated to do."[6] Third, the model defines a specific *Symmetry* for each principle. This is meant to provoke "transposition"—putting oneself personally into the shoes of another who may be affected by an action or decision. Not only does this help to engage the natural empathy of individuals, it also exercises the reflex of imagining and attending to implications. The practice of Symmetry over time encourages the growth of competence and eventually yields a spontaneous deepening of perspective. Finally, the model detailed on the following page includes some brief examples of *Application*—what the principles, rules and symmetries actually mean in practice.

Table 8. A Business Model for Ethical Orientation

	Strategic Clarity	Respect Dignity	Be Fair	Be Honest	Strive for Justice	Honor the Environment
Principle	• Manage assets *professionally*	• Conduct all interactions with *humanity*	• Practice business with *equanimity and care*	• Operate *truthfully*	• Balance business with *moral obligations*	• Manage nature *as an asset*
Rule	• Do not devaluate (build sustainable equity)	• Do not kill (enhance human life)	• Do not steal (give equitably)	• Do not lie (value integrity)	• Do not discriminate (honor intrinsic rights)	• Do not destroy (respect the ecosystem)
Symmetry	• "Offer value in the quality and with the qualities you seek in profit"	• "What you do not wish done to yourself, do not do to others"	• "Practice self-interest with equity for the needs and interests of others"	• "Be accountable for truth to earn the trust that you rely on, and expect in, others"	• Contribute to the formation of community that you would want to entrust yourself to	• "Use nature for only what you need, and in balance with what you put back"
Applications	• Innovations for future returns • Respect for all relationships • Long-term building of balance sheet	• Job safety • Stress relief • Job dignity • Compassion in balance with efficiency	• Fair wages for all • Equitable CEO pay • Fair value to customers and suppliers • Anti-corruption • Intellectual rights	• Transparency and access • Protection of privacy • Truth in ads, in PR, and internally • Listening with integrity • Provide genuine value	• Pay equity • Equal potential for all • Community priorities (education, human rights) advanced by business as member of that community	• Sustainability • Pricing to reflect cost of replacement and clean-up • Work toward "zero waste" • Fulfill Kyoto Commitments

Strategic Clarity

Some of the business examples we have already reviewed show that poorly managed companies are especially prone to moral and legal risk. The pressure to perform, either at unrealistic levels or in the absence of value-added innovations, encourages the cutting of corners and rationalization that leads to impropriety. This is precisely what happened to Sears before its more recent turn-around. In the late 1980s and early 1990s, the company responded to its loss of market share and profits to Wal-Mart by cutting wages and reconfiguring sales targets. Although strategy was in disarray, employees were forced to move more and more merchandise through the system. As Ronald Green reports in his 1995 analysis, workers in the Sears Automotive Center were "pressured to sell a specified number of shock absorbers or struts for every hour worked. If they failed to meet their goals, Sears employees told investigators, they often received a cutback in hours worked or were transferred to other Sears departments."[7] Bad decisions, compounded by bad policies, finally led to bad practices. In 1992, after numerous complaints and a probing investigation, California revoked operating licenses for seventy-two Sears Automotive Centers in that state. This unleashed a storm of negative publicity and raised the ire of several other monitoring agencies in other jurisdictions. After paying out fines and settlements to various states and offering a $50 coupon to all of the automotive customers who had purchased one of the products implicated in the "pressure-cooker" approach, Sears finally began to examine the fundamentals of its neglected business.

Many companies have been through a similar, widening spiral. First a strategic misstep or complacency on the part of the senior management team creates the conditions for the business to deteriorate. To recover lost sales, customers and profits, frazzled executives impose higher targets for managers, who in turn squeeze employees to cut costs and churn out extra volume. In the illogical vortex of trying to achieve more from less, judgment inevitably suffers. Norms and obligations are sacrificed to expediency, and long-term goals are mortgaged for the next immediate sale. As demonstrated by the Sears example, such a cascading of pressure screws not only customers. The average customer suffers from the deception of paying more for products, or being forced to buy something that they did not really need, or receiving less than their money's worth for service. As well, employees who by and large were not in a position to influence the company's most important business decisions are left paying the price for strategic mistakes. Some lose their jobs. Others face longer hours and more work at lower pay. Some are forced to suspend their better judgment and take their own workers and customers for a ride. Society takes on the costs of investigating, litigating and settling. And, finally, shareholders are cheated of value. In many companies that undergo this self-inflicted deconstruction—the situation for many years at Sears—the team at the top responsible for the slide in business and ethical standards remains unaffected. Like their car batteries, old managerial arrogance proved to DieHard.

Ethical codes are standard in other professions, such as law, medicine and engineering. These are in place because mediocrity or faulty judgment in any of those disciplines can lead to serious injury or death. There are no comparable codes for business practice, but the truth is that the potential for harm in economics is as great as or greater than for other professions. And that potential is growing. This means that managerial excellence is itself a legitimate norm, warranting conscious attention and measurement not only by shareholders, but also by peers and industry associations. Making managerial quality an ethical issue works to decrease the pressures to short-cut decency, while helping to intertwine the skills for success with those for moral responsibility.

Manage Professionally means managing short-term goals in ways that do not compromise long-term goals. This is one of those truisms noted by many analysts and conceded even by many managers, which nevertheless has been nearly impossible to apply consistently. One reason is that the short term can be relatively easily managed by pulling the levers of cost cutting or price increases. The longer term involves imagination, intelligent risk taking and the managerial capacity to lead people to do more. This requires a much higher degree of managerial quality than just squeezing more from less. It also involves exactly the interpersonal sensibilities that make up an ethical orientation.

Managerial excellence sets out a purpose as well as goal—to give meaning as well as scope to employees. Listening with respectful empathy to customers, shareholders and other strategic partners gives relevance and depth to management's vision. This openness also helps the envisioning of new opportunities, something too often neglected in too many companies. Respectful support is also essential for creating the environment of risk that is needed to fully engage people's creativity and get to breakthrough innovations.

The command *Do Not Devalue* attacks the tendency, so pronounced in this last decade, to generate profits by draining value from the organization. Devaluation may be strategic—such as when the North American car companies deliberately let quality slip throughout the profitable 1950s, '60s, and '70s, allowing Japanese and German manufacturers to zoom ahead. Or the devaluation can be ethical—such as when Dow Corning fought any liability for its faulty silicone breast implants. Although the scientific evidence about health risks is still being debated, the monolithic treatment of victims and the legal rigidity that sought to have key documents sealed by the court, devalued Dow Corning's credibility and reputation. Driscoll, Hoffman and Petry, in their study of this 15-year-long legal and ethical battle, write: "Dow Corning may be right in the end . . . But scientific proof may be beside the point. Because Dow Corning became embroiled in a national controversy with ethical implications involving one of its products, the impact has already been felt on its bottom line."[8] A multi-billion-dollar settlement has finally been structured, but the costs continue with more lawsuits and class actions entering the pipeline.

Devaluation affects shareholders, even though the impact may be obscured, such as when a chemical company is slowly creating the heavy liability of toxic waste at a dump site. Sometimes, the devaluation is cultural, for example, when change programs are implemented heavy-handedly, or when senior executives raise their compensation while rolling back jobs and wages for everyone else. The loss of commitment or trust among employees, customers or suppliers drains value and value-creating potential from an enterprise. This means that part of the managerial imperative is to create value for shareholders by building the long-term value of the company. Within this balance between immediate results and enduring capacities, managers are entrusted with attending to the motivations of employees, and the obligations to customers. *"Offer value in the quality and with the qualities you seek in profit"* expresses this mandate. "Quality-value" in products or services is genuine, innovative and continually replenished. "Profit qualities" are those that build the balance sheet and not just the bottom line. This means, in addition to revenue, sales and profits, attending to the relationships and commitments, both inside and outside the company, upon which future success depends.

Respect Dignity

One of the defining cultural shifts of our time, and one of the central pillars of postmodernism, is that diversity is legitimate. The rational-scientific construct had for several centuries assumed that a single, logically based and coherent universal would eventually melt away all differences between people. Rigid rationality imbued with transcendence led to the death chambers of Auschwitz, Buchenwald and the more than two hundred other concentration camps that for the Nazis comprised the "final solution." Perpetrated by thugs, the Holocaust represented to them an apex of scientific management. With the latest technology, employing the latest in logistics, that highly efficient and productive "machine" killed over six million people. Philosophers like Edith Wyschogrod point to this most dark experience as the birthplace of postmodernism. In this magnified capability to kill and destroy was dashed once and for all the modernist hope that science, rationality and technology would liberate and empower people to experience a richer life of opportunity and dignity. Genocide and ethnic cleansing did not end in 1945, but tragically continue to this day around the world. Human factual knowledge and scientific understanding have outstripped the growth of our collective wisdom. It is not that technology is the enemy of people, but that those with enmity have had their power for oppression and destruction magnified terrifically and terribly by technology.

The global economy is today's most potent power, and while not consciously cheapening human life, its rationality and technological orientation have in many cases brought about just such a depreciation. Human rights experts estimate that there are over 200 million children under fourteen years of age working full time. "Officials have documented the presence of children under fourteen in factories in Honduras who make garments for popular U.S. labels and retail chains. They are found as well in the orange groves of Brazil, where juice is turned into concentrate for American breakfast tables; in toy factories in China and Thailand; and on assembly lines in Indonesia, where $100 basketball sneakers are made."[9] What we buy, eat, wear and consume may be only a few degrees of separation from squalor, poverty and exploitation. Few consumers, and fewer companies, can escape that linkage.

Like many U.S. corporations, Alcoa developed plants in the Maquiladora corridor—that thin slice of Mexico across from the U.S. border that has become a prime location for multinationals like Toshiba, General Electric, Ford, Johnson & Johnson and Zenith. Companies invest there for the cheap labor and easy access to North America. As journalist David Schilling explains, "Alcoa and other U.S. companies rationalize paying poverty-level wages in two ways. They point out that wages paid to workers are competitive with what other companies are paying in a specific area, and that wages paid to workers are above the minimum wage set by governments."[10] Alcoa followed this pattern until religious and human rights groups pressured CEO Paul O'Neill to actually visit the area and meet with workers. What he found was that the minimum wage was in reality sub-minimum— below what made subsistence possible. A study in 1996 showed that "basic food items (not including meat, milk and vegetables) cost $26.87 a week while wages at Alcoa averaged between $21.44 and $24.60 a week."[11] Many rationalize that Alcoa is paying what the market will bear, but is this to take precedence over what a human being can bear? To his credit, O'Neill fired the human resources manager for not reporting the health and safety violations he encountered at the plants. He also put soap and toilet paper in plant bathrooms and raised wages. A small step on the long road to dignity, but a step nonetheless.

To *Treat All Humanely* is to acknowledge that all people deserve basic, minimum compensation for their work, as well as respect.

O'Neill encountered the human beings affected by his company's policies and observed their working conditions. This face-to-face experience gave specific dimension to the humiliation workers feel in relation to the company. It made cost-cutting measures like not supplying toilet paper seem ludicrous and petty. People had jobs, but for all their work they could not even make ends meet on basics. Providing amenities such as soap and increasing wages is not yet a policy of compassion, but it is an admission that the still prevalent rationalizations for many Third World labor practices are no longer tenable.

Working conditions, wages and firing practices are callous throughout the industrialized world. Indeed, statistics that show North American wages to be static for the last two decades actually conceal the fact that for many, wages are much lower and prospects much more constrained than ever before. Robert Reich, former U.S. Secretary of Labor, argues that the old divide between white collar and blue collar has been replaced by an even more pronounced gap between "groundworkers"—those doing the laborious, dirty and often hopeless jobs of hotel and food service, construction and delivery—and "skyworkers"—those managers and executives who work in towers, manipulating ideas and information, and thriving in the expanding possibilities of the knowledge economy.[12] Merit deserves to be rewarded, but only as an enhancement of a basic degree of dignity shared by all. Last year, more than 650,000 people were injured on the job in the U.S. alone. Basic safety, basic rights about dialogue with companies over issues affecting workers, and basic access to health care are some of the areas in which dignity has yet to be universally applied, even in the world's most successful economies.

Do not kill is the command that demands human life be respected. Compromised safety in work environments and faulty products are direct risks to life. As we saw with examples like the Dalkon Shield, these issues require constant vigilance. But in many ways, these are also easier to regulate or outlaw. Much more difficult are the indirect but still lethal and dehumanizing practices. Pollution is a killer. So are particulates released into the air. So is stress in the workplace. So are "sick" buildings. Many corporate practices take their toll very slowly, and only in combination with other factors do they produce serious risk to health and life. The point, though, is to stop the automatic and legalistic denial that most companies adopt in defense. In response to human dignity, companies must explore the issues openly, acknowledge those practices that may indeed contribute to the problems, and take responsibility for dealing with them in a proactive manner.

Most executives would say that *Do not kill* is so obvious and extreme that it does not apply to their organizations. In truth, it is not so clearly avoided. The statement of symmetry, borrowed directly from the Declarations reviewed in the previous chapter, sets the norm for human dignity as the Golden Rule: *What you do not wish done to yourself, do not do to others*. At the very least, the respect due each other means not violating the rights to which we are all entitled. This is a notion embedded in virtually every major religious tradition, but which as a norm transcends spiritual belief. In his study of the Golden Rule, Jeffrey Wattles explains that "Much of the meaning of the rule can be put into practice without any religious commitment, since it is a nontheologic principle that neither mentions God nor is necessarily identified with the scriptures or doctrines of any one religion. The rule is an expression of human kinship, the most fundamental truth underlying morality."[13]

An ethical orientation does not pose the unrealistic and therefore unpracticable burden of solving all injustices simultaneously. The key is to be oriented—to be open and responsive to the call of compassion. In Alcoa's case, this meant offering necessities like soap and increases in pay that at least take people up beyond subsistence and into the realm of hope. But Alcoa did not bring Mexican wages up to par with wages in North America. A few companies like W.R. Grace and Baxter International have already signed an agreement to participate with international human rights organizations to committing themselves and encouraging others to adopt a policy "to pay a sustainable wage whether workers are in Michigan or Mexico, Indiana or Indonesia."[14] The task now is not to simply acknowledge the universality of the Golden Rule, but to universally apply it.

Treat All Fairly

The commitment to dignity is to honor the inalienable rights of all persons. The commitment to fairness is to accord to each person the proportion of wealth they earn through their efforts and creative contributions. The widening wage gap between senior management and average workers is perhaps the most blatant unfairness. But it is only the tip of a slowly melting iceberg. William Wolman, an economist at *Business Week,* and Anne Colamosca characterize the current business environment as a "Judas economy." They write: "The effects of the betrayal of the worker reach beyond stagnant income to more subtle, and in some senses more disturbing ramifications. Many who have lived through the endless, grinding machinations of reengineering have noticed that despite the drama and trumpeted successes, companies following the new advice have been enormously successful at only one thing—increasing profits, at least temporarily, at the expense of workers. And many workers who had survived reengineering found that the purported flattening of management structures led to more, not fewer, procedures and control."[15] Unfairness, it turns out, is endemic to many business processes, and not just the outcomes. The brusque style in which many people have been let go in the name of restructuring, and the way in which people who retained jobs were assigned much more work with less support, are examples of the process of unfairness. That people are forced to compromise commitments to family is another. That workers paid the price with their jobs for management's strategic mistakes is an all-too-familiar unfairness that has been replayed at GM, IBM and many other companies.

Fairness is an issue that, as will be explored in the next chapter, has enormous implications for relationships with customers, suppliers and strategic partners. At a base level, fairness represents a commitment to provide genuine value for the price charged. Increasingly, however, customers, consumers, partners and even shareholders also expect the exercise of fairness to apply across the whole spectrum of business activities. Wages and employee policies in the Third World, including those of third-party subcontractors, are now under scrutiny. Some companies are making commitments to fairness. Levi Strauss and Gillette have both made investments to send child-laborers from the subcontractors factories to school.[16] These, however, are exceptions, and most companies come to accept the importance of equity only under pressure from the public, lawmakers or special-interest groups. The call of a global ethic is for a spontaneous commitment to fairness, working not out of resistance but with compassion toward processes and outcomes that are fairer for all.

Ironically, it is now business itself that is in many ways vulnerable to a reverse unfairness. As more and more value in the information economy is created through ideas and knowledge, the companies providing that value are often pirated. For software alone—not including entertainment videos and music CDs—the loss through illegal copying is estimated to be over $11 billion a year.[17] Hard-ball negotiations threatening trade sanctions have yielded little progress on this. Microsoft has recently decided to work with governments of the most offending countries in a new way; for instance, they are offering highly discounted software for education with the proviso that illegal software will be purged from the school system. "In the past, you'd have a bunch of cowboys going around the world threatening people," notes Orlando Ayala, Microsoft's vice-president of international operations. "That's not the way to do it."[18] Microsoft is probably being more realistic than magnanimous, but this only highlights how the reciprocity of fairness can benefit many companies.

The command for fairness is *Do not steal.* This means exactly that, as in, do not take part in insider trading; do not rip off customers; do not short-change employees; do not pilfer documents from other companies; do not undertake corporate espionage; do not plagiarize someone else's ideas; do not take wages disproportionate to contribution. Also straightforward are the implications for employees: do not download confidential files before changing employers; do not pad expense reports; do not take what is not yours. *Do not steal* has wider meanings as well. Environmental abuses steal from future generations the conditions for health, as well as potential economic well-being. Using the Third World simply as a low-cost supplier of natural resources and labor also robs populations of these developing countries of hope. Stealing operates on many planes, and part of orientation is a commitment to grow wiser in discerning such less obvious but potentially even more damaging misappropriations.

The symmetry for fairness expresses interdependence: *practice self-interest with equity for the interest of others.* This does not mean to stop competing. Rather, it means competing with the responsibility not to abuse the community or the natural environment, which make wealth creation for individuals and companies possible in the first place. Interdependence is not just a matter of interconnection, but of a much more intimate interreliance. To depend on one another compels us to take and enjoy what is earned, provided it corresponds to what is fair in relation to the effort of others. The key point is that none of us can thrive alone, so any imbalance is ultimately self-destructive. Again, fairness will always be an issue in human affairs, and no utopian solution will materialize to ensure equity. However, for an institution whose power is demanding an ever greater maturity, the fairness of business represents an acid test for its growth and future trustworthiness.

Be Honest

The truth may be incredibly hard to pin down, but honesty is not. To be honest is to be *intentionally* frank and open. So we know honesty not by its content but by our aim. The truth is also something in essence objective, a reality outside of our perspective that we try to fathom and understand. Honesty, by contrast, is primarily relational, an experience shared with, and expressed to, others. There is, of course, much self-deception in life—no less so, as we have seen from John Darley's studies of unethical corporate practice, in business. But, generally speaking, we are honest or dishonest *to* each other. Individuals often harm others by deceiving them, for example, by denying the faultiness of the Ford Pinto's gas tank design, or the risk of second-hand smoke from cigarettes. Such deceit to others usually involves an initial self-evasion or self-delusion, either to construct the rationalization for proceeding with clearly unethical action, or in the form of subscription to one of the lies diagnosed in Chapter Two. In this way, deception can be seen as the opposite of maturity, and dishonesty as the opposite of integrity and human wholeness.

I noted earlier that our wired economy is actually trip-wired. Databases, journalism and the Internet are among the media working in the information age that scour the validity and intent of messages. One thing we have seen repeatedly is a public reckoning of behavior. Decisions taken in the shadows eventually are flooded with light. This is a warning, another definition of what is ethical: that which you would not like to have reported in the next day's newspapers and broadcasts. But there is an even deeper urgency behind the command *Do not lie.* Not just the economy, but the very foundations of global society, are based on the information we share. Honesty has always been important to the integrity of any group, and it is therefore the very currency for forming and sustaining relationships on that much broader scale of global community. Lies, whether institutional or personal, contaminate the relations upon which community is based. Robert Wurman has explained that one consequence of the data overload of our times is "information pollution." Lies can thus be seen as the information economy's toxic waste.

Do not lie means more than do not deceive. In business terms, it means: do not promise what you can't deliver, do not misrepresent, do not hide behind spin-doctored evasions, do not suppress obligations, do not evade accountability, do not accept that the "survival of the fittest" pressures of business release any of us from the responsibility to respect another's dignity and humanity. Denials, cover-ups or the confrontational attitude of "prove me wrong"—seen so often in companies—are violations of the openness and self-reflection that characterize honesty. To be genuine involves providing substantive value to customers, open engagement with employees and forthcoming accountability to society. The symmetry inherent in *extend the integrity that you would want extended back to you* requires the vigilance to be attentive, to listen with empathy, as well as to express and explain in ways that do not deceive. In other words, honesty is an inward as well as outward process and requirement. An example I will explore at length in Chapter Ten involves the necessity for some companies to downsize. The points I make are that an ethical orientation does not diminish the validity of such a necessity, but it does provide guidance for how to implement difficult change in ways that honor the individuals affected. Honesty in this context means giving people as much advance warning as possible of the implications of strategy, and making financial, competitive and performance data about the company as transparent as possible to them. In some companies, workers are taken completely by surprise by downsizing or restructuring. In these cases, management has either been less than forthcoming, or was itself caught unawares, thereby suggesting a culpability in terms of strategic incompetence.

Another important dynamic of honesty is a company's response to exposure. Many organizations that have clearly established ethical codes still find it very difficult to deal with employees who uncover impropriety. The very term "whistle-blower" is pejorative, and very often the individuals who take moral stands and comply with the company's legal code have found themselves demoted, ostracized or fired for their intervention. Honesty may be more widely acknowledged as the best policy among businesspeople, but the policy for recognizing and rewarding honesty at work still has a long way to go. Such disclosures are threatening to companies in part because they represent a betrayal of the team. Often, unethical practices have had the implicit, if not explicit, approval or endorsement of many others within the company, including many layers of management. To call short a project or initiative on ethical grounds disrupts the cohesion of the team, but more fundamentally aims a criticism at all involved. Corrupt practices often also represent an even deeper institutional indifference to legal and ethical conformance. So an intervention, however honest, unleashes questions about the careers of those involved and the managerial intelligence of those supervising, as well as the integrity of the whole corporate culture.

An important aspect of an ethical orientation is to value honesty and reward it, to demonstrate it in small ways so that those examples can reinforce moral behavior on the bigger issues. A code is not enough; an orientation requires action as proof of commitment, and action as the experience from which more growth and confidence is realized. Hotlines do get used by employees who trust that their judgments will be respected and that the company will act. Any inconsistency between intent and action perverts that process and creates the cynicism which is to be expected in any encounter with hypocrisy.

Strive for Justice

The principles so far express obligations within the context of business management, performance and implications. The call for justice goes beyond that, and weaves all institutions and individuals into the larger fabric of community well-being. The community is best served by business if business is the best business it can be. In other words, ethical and efficient commerce and exchange are the best public service that the economy and its corporations and companies can provide. That said, it is also not enough. The economy consumes resources—natural, human and moral—so by its very activities it is engaged with the community on more levels than merely the creation of wealth. By removing these resources from the global community, companies are therefore inextricably bound to putting back contributions which further the social well-being of society as a whole.

In his book about responsibility, Professor Gabriel Moran of the department of culture and communication at New York University calls justice "the most important, most comprehensive, ethical term. Its roots go deep into both religious tradition and philosophical speculation."[19] Philosopher John Rawls defines justice within the context of a social contract in which people are "self-originating sources of valid claims." In other words, people share a moral equality. Will Kymlicka explains that "each person matters and matters equally, each person is entitled to equal consideration. This notion of equal consideration gives rise at the social level to a 'natural duty of justice.' We have a duty to promote just institutions, a duty not derived from consent or mutual advantage, but simply owed to persons as such."[20] Although an understandable symmetry, the problem with justice is that, unlike the previously discussed ethical principles, it requires not simply accountability for personal or individual behavior, but an advocacy to influence others to act justly. In their book *Applying Ethics,* Jeffrey Olin and Vincent Barry note that "people who are fair, loyal, honest, faithful and kind have great difficulty agreeing on principles for justice. That difficulty is largely due to the difficulty [of political action which] is coercive. All of us are in principle against coercion, but we also recognize the occasional need for it. Unfortunately, we don't always recognize it on the same occasions."[21]

A case in point is child labor. Companies defending, or at least deflecting, such practices cite differences in cultures and values as justification for not intervening. Many also note that the families involved would be even more impoverished if the children were not allowed to work. But to accept or profit from such exploitation is clearly unconscionable. Waiting for local laws or economic conditions to catch up to the just sensibility regarding child labor is an abrogation of Rawls's social contract that all of us—companies and individuals—participate in and benefit from. Such differences of opinion call for creativity and commitment. A few companies, like Levi Strauss, have found a way to influence justice in social environments that they cannot control by investing *of* themselves as well as *for* themselves. The company, as noted, pays children to go to school and commits to having a job waiting for them when studies, however rudimentary, are complete. An imperfect solution in an imperfect world, this nevertheless demonstrates exactly that commitment and incremental progress that is central to an ethical orientation.

GM, like so many other corporate giants, operates in Mexico. Although it has so far resisted raising wages following Alcoa's example, the company has made a commitment to invest in housing. Jack Smith, GM's CEO, and other executives from Detroit inspected the plant in Mexico. They also visited "workers at their homes in Reynosa, Mexico," most of which "are made from corrugated metal and have no running water or electricity."[22] In the face of such squalor, the company has launched a program to, in Smith's words, "make affordable housing a reality for thousands of its workers." Activists among its own shareholders have criticized the company for not raising wages, currently less than $26 per week. Barbara Glendon, of the Mercy Consolidated Asset Management Program explains that "The housing program is a generous and compassionate response to the deplorable living conditions of some of GM's Mexican workers. But compassion without justice is not enough to fulfill the obligations of our company to its employees. We are morally and ethically responsible to provide a sustainable wage to the people whose daily labor benefits us who are GM shareholders." Smith's example again reminds us that it is important to meet injustice face-to-face. It is important to be moved by compassion to make a difference. Glendon's point is that the steps must be progressive, that the orientation must continuously deepen in both commitment and practice.

The command of justice is *Do not discriminate*. As we have seen with Texaco and its black employees, and the attitude of business in general toward women, discrimination is not eliminated by laws or policies. Discrimination ends only when attitudes have been reformed and action taken. Many companies, indeed many individuals, have adopted equality out of the pressure for political correctness rather than genuine commitment to generosity and justice. This is notable because cosmetic niceness conceals an insidious resistance. The more prolonged such superficial conformance to an ethic, the more anger and bitterness entrench the original bias. Discrimination is not finally resolved by learning or training, although these are important. The only way to cease being discriminatory is to outgrow it, to achieve the personal or organizational maturity that recognizes and accepts the mutuality of interdependence.

The symmetry of justice from an ethical perspective is not that of blind equality from a legal perspective. Social justice requires that we care. If compassion is our natural ability to receive inside ourselves an empathy for another, care is how that empathy is expressed outward to others. The notion of care is one of the contributions to ethics made by feminist explorations of society and philosophy. An ethical action, in respect, honesty, fairness or justice, expresses both (masculine) duty and (feminine) care. This is many ways reflects the difference between men and women in their respective practice and framework for ethical conduct, but the insight for companies is that duty and care are intertwined in an ethical orientation. We are called upon to be just because we are called upon to care. *Contribute to the formation of a community that you would want to entrust yourself to* includes several dynamics. "Contribute" encourages participation. It is the action of giving, building and adding to. "Formation" means progress, the realization of an ideal or improved potential. "Community" is the shared forum from which no individual can justly extricate him- or herself. "Entrust" sets the norm as "cared for." To paraphrase, we must each work to create that society that we would entrust ourselves to if we needed to be cared for.

Honor the Environment

The economic battle lines in relation to the environment are well known. Some economists, like MIT's Lester Thurow, believe that environmental "institutions have to be linked with those promoting economic growth, since pollution and species preservation are inexorably linked with economic development."[23] Other economists, like MIT's Jerry Hausman, belittle any link, stating that "environmental economics is to economics what military music is to music."[24] Many companies have already adopted some degree of environmental management, if only to improve their image or keep up with the efficiency that such attention to waste reduction and conservation inevitably yields. But managers still tend to be on one side or the other of this ideological divide. Perhaps surprisingly, the view of the economy as being either *within* or *beyond* the environment has similarly affected the debate about ethical obligations to nature. Some environmentalists follow in the tradition of nineteenth-century thinkers like Ralph Waldo Emerson and John Muir, who saw nature as pure, industrialization as evil, and from that stark, black-and-white perspective, fought for the preservation of wilderness and the containment of economic activity. Others have followed the more utilitarian environmental conservation articulated by Gifford Pinchot early in the twentieth century. Pinchot did not condemn consumption and the attendant environmental degradation because he saw these as indispensable to human development and progress. He was appalled by injustice, by unfair exploitation of what are a "commons" and by the callous disregard for conservation, since profligacy not only destroyed nature but crippled progress. His view of conservation included "the greatest good, of the greatest number, for the longest time."[25]

J. Baird Callicott, a professor of philosophy at North Texas and Wisconsin universities, critiques both these perspectives. The first position of complete wilderness preservation splits human beings from nature, perpetuating the divide that contributed to people taking nature for granted in the first place. In Callicott's view, this split ignores the lessons of evolution that position humans within the continuum of nature. Since human beings are a natural part of the system, our activities may be destructive—even if they do not necessarily have to be—but they are still "only natural." What finally deflates absolute preservation is that it is natural for humans, as it is for other species, to use the abundance of nature for their ends. Conservation environmentalism, on the other hand, is premised on a utilitarian husbandry of resources. The flaw in this approach is that nature, as a complex system, is far beyond our ability to manage. Callicott explains that "the natural world is more than a collection of externally related useful, useless and noxious species furnishing an elemental landscape of soils and waters. It is rather a vast, intricately organized and tightly integrated system of complex processes. It is less like a vast mechanism and more like a vast organism."[26] More than ideological points are at stake, because the contrast in philosophical perspectives mirrors the ecological debate between the First and the Third World.

The developed world, having had its cake of industrial progress, now wants a clean and healthful environment, too. Leaving aside the irony of the most polluting and wasteful societies pressuring and lecturing Brazil and Indonesia to preserve wilderness areas, the preservationists are implicitly denying the right of people in developing regions to participate in the economic bounty to be drawn from nature. For developing countries, the utilitarian demand to use nature for jobs, raw materials and wealth creation represents an unwillingness to learn the lessons of exploitation. Drawing on the work of Aldo Leopold, Callicott suggests that only a synthesis is ultimately workable. In *A Sand County Almanac,* Leopold defines conservation as "a state of harmony between people and the land." The implications of this synthesis are not compromise. Although "harmony with nature" involves meshing the needs of utility with a commitment to preserve wild areas, it also represents a much more radical reenvisioning of possibilities. Callicott writes that the concept of harmony "endorses the human economic use and development of land as appropriate and natural, as they are necessary."[27] But to Pinchot's requirement that human exploitation of natural "resources" be fair and efficient, Leopold would add a third requirement: that human land use be compatible with the land's ecological health and integrity.

The principle of a global ethic to *Treat nature respectfully* and the command *Do not destroy* reflect a desire to reintegrate humans into their natural environment. That we are a part of nature suggests that the entire ecosystem is naturally deserving of the consideration and respect we afford to each other. That we are part of nature's continuum demands that we not destroy what cannot be separated from ourselves. We can, indeed must, use nature's riches for human development and well-being. The intimacy with which we are entwined in the natural world demands that this use be not only responsible but harmonious. Harmony in this instance means regenerative. As the symmetry expresses it, *use nature only for what you need and in balance with what can be put back.* Harmonious use is not a skill or competency currently evident or very well understood in our economy. Most environmental practices, however successful, are nowhere near regenerative.

Thurow provides an analogy for the degree of change required in our business and economic principles and priorities. He writes: "If the world's population had the productivity of the Swiss, the consumption habits of the Chinese, the egalitarian instincts of the Swedes, and the social discipline of the Japanese, then the planet could support many times its current population without excessive pollution or deprivation for anyone. On the other hand, if the world's population had the productivity of Chad, the consumption habits of the United States, the egalitarian instincts of India, and the social discipline of Yugoslavia, the planet could not support anywhere near its current numbers. Unfortunately, most humans seem to fall in the America-India-Chad-Yugoslavia category."[28] This suggests two important implications. First, the intelligence necessary for a smart and harmonious relationship with nature is within the skill-set of human beings; but right now there is only a scrambled, tentative and politically incoherent competence. Second, and the reason for including nature in the principles for a global ethic, is that what we do to the natural environment we do to ourselves. As the Canadian aboriginals reminded us in *The Tie That Binds,* the earth is inescapably "the first principle."

An Invitation to an Imperative

How General Electric Could Lead in Adopting a Global Ethic

General Electric is one of the world's most consistently successful companies. As such, it is also one of the most admired, studied and emulated business organizations in the world. Jack Welch, GE's CEO, has become probably the most influential business leader of our time, celebrated in numerous books, featured in countless articles and cited in almost every management seminar or speech since 1980. GE and Welch deserve their success. They have taken bold stands on strategy and structural renewal. And unlike IBM, Xerox, GM, Kodak and most other companies, GE, because of Welch, embraced change in advance of being forced to out of crisis.

Despite one of the most rigorous codes for ethical and legal compliance, GE has been stained by numerous and repeated offenses. In her 1995 article *The Smoke at General Electric,* Nanette Byrnes reports that "in addition to seventy-two Superfund environmental cleanup sites in which it is named a 'potentially responsible party' (total cost to GE to date: $500 million), GE has paid fines or settlement fees in sixteen cases of abuse, fraud and waste in government contracting since 1990 . . . According to the Project on Government Oversight, the Department of Defense and the U.S. General Accounting Office, GE paid $163 million in fines and settlements for fraud, waste and abuse in government contracting between 1990 and February 1994."[29] Visionary and determined in matters of business renewal, GE and Welch now have an opportunity to play the same leadership, paradigm-shifting role in relation to business performance and ethics by becoming one of the first major multinational to embrace the principles of a global ethic.

There are several reasons for undertaking such a bold step. First, the repeated and continuing nature of ethical scandals renders GE liable to the accusation that it is "not walking the talk." This is the most damaging of managerial indictments, undoing much of the renewal magic the company has achieved, and undermining its reputation for effectiveness. That the problems are so persistent suggests that they are also deeply embedded. A global ethic represents a total approach, macro in its coverage and micro in its relevance. As one of the great beneficiaries of the global economy, GE also has a parallel and equal responsibility to the global community that makes its commerce and profits possible. With its track record, GE would inspire many other companies to follow its lead. And with its authority, GE would force investors to debate and consider an appropriately patient approach to corporate social and environmental investments. Finally, with its training infrastructure and huge influence on what managers in other companies learn and do, GE has that rare chance to influence the meaning of work as well as its processes and outcomes.

Adopting a global ethic involves several steps:

- Welch and the management team must first proclaim their adoption of its principles. Having formulated some of the most visionary strategies of our time ("Be Number One or Number Two. Or Get Out" and "Workouts"), Welch and his planning team will need to create that pithy synthesis of ethical intent that galvanizes staff and forces an ongoing reassessment.
- As with any other capital expense or major decision of strategy, the board of directors must be involved in setting GE's ethical standards. Through its own committees and governance, the board must then set compliance norms and structure for rewarding or penalizing executive ethical performance.
- The training and learning machinery within GE—one of its greatest assets—must be deployed to create the models and message most appropriate for GE's practice of a global ethic. The task is integrative, requiring the inclusion of ethical considerations in planning, performance, measurement and compensation systems.
- GE's culture has so far been immune to ethical measures. A critical aspect of GE's ethical renewal will be to define the

variables of culture that have proven so resistant. Perhaps the first priority is to apply the principles of a global ethic internally, to identify the obstacles and vent any of the employee cynicism that may sit beneath GE's managerial success.

- GE is a pioneer of participatory management, so it is but an extension of current practices to form groups from various parts (and levels) of the company to take on the implementation of specific principles. One group may deal with *Dignity,* another with *Justice* and so on. Just as Welch has led renewal by his own example, his voice and actions in support of a global ethic are essential to its success.

- Welch has admitted that he has been frustrated in the past by how long it takes for large organizations like GE to change. Central to his success has been his willingness to stick to it, to attend to the details of excellence and to repeatedly communicate his vision and personal commitment to the plan. Ethical reorientation involves an even deeper reversal of values and thus requires the patience, consistency and perseverance that have been devoted to previous efforts of strategic change.

- The cost for GE's ethical transgressions has been in the hundreds of millions of dollars. This sets the benchmark for the investment GE should be willing to make to reform its culture and practices. To advance ethical ideals without investing money in the practical implementation of these ideas would be a hypocritical waste.

- An ethically reformed GE will have a profound influence in the world, simply because of its size. But even more important, because of its stature, GE will also pull thousands of other executives and companies into ethical renewal. A company and manager of impressive achievements may thus create a legacy that is meaningful for human history as well as economics.

CHAPTER SEVEN

BENEFITS

The right of the individual is the power that upholds the right of the community, just as, conversely, it is the community that upholds and defends the rights of the individual.

Dietrich Bonhoeffer, *"Suum Cuique" in* Ethics

Businesspeople for the most part will accept the argument about the need for an ethical orientation, but only if they are convinced it is a sure thing. They want categorical proof that ethics will not impede short-term results, or compromise competitiveness, or limit aggressive pursuit of opportunity. In short, most want ethics to achieve a return on investment (ROI). This, however, is a faulty expectation. Managers want of ethics what they know and accept that they cannot get from any other dynamic or decision in business—risk-free results. Hundreds of billions of dollars have been squandered in strategic misadventures like IBM's take-over and sell-off of Rolm in the 1980s, Matsushita's marriage and divorce of MCA in the early 1990s and, more recently, Wells Fargo's debacle-plagued assimilation of First Interstate. For the market economy, these are costly risks that did not pan out, strategies that had an initial compelling logic but failed because of unexpected competitive conditions or managerial inadequacies. I am not arguing about the intelligence or stupidity of management's decisions in these particular cases, but merely pointing out that risk, and the costs of failure, are accepted as intrinsic to business. Hypocritically, the only risk that many in business will not take is the one to be ethical.

Since at least the 1970s, those arguing for ethical practice have provided reams of substantiation, case examples and rationale. Yet, "despite a variety of contentions of the 'ethics pays' sort," writes Robert Cialdini, "a look at the misdeeds, fines, criminal prosecutions, and scandals regularly reported in the business press suggests that much of the business world has not been persuaded. Indeed, there remains a persistent belief that ethics don't pay, even in the long run."[1] A small movement in genuine ethical orientation at some companies is overshadowed by the ever more commonplace misdeeds at so many others. During a three-week period in the summer of 1997, the CEO of Columbia, the U.S.'s largest health maintenance organization (HMO), was indicted for allegedly overbilling Medicare; Honda executives and one of its major dealers were convicted of bribery over preferential car allocations of hard-to-get models; tobacco executives admitted to the Florida attorney general that cigarette smoking may indeed cause health problems; a cargo jet that crashed in Miami seems, by the Federal Aviation Administration's initial assessment, to have been grossly overloaded; Canadian banks aroused the anger of civil libertarians because cross-marketing programs between financial institutions eroded yet another layer of customer privacy; Mitsubishi settled one of two sexual harassment suits with twenty-nine of its female employees; journalists James O'Shea and Charles Madigan released a book about management consulting that exposed a contract between Andersen Consulting and O'Neal Steel of Alabama that included a bonus for every hundred jobs cut; major drug companies, including DuPont Merck, were reported contributing to a fund that spent $500,000 monthly to fight state attorneys general on any legislation that would advance the introduction of lower-cost and lower-margin generics; and it was revealed that for the past twenty years Ontario Hydro, North America's third-largest utility, had knowingly and consistently discharged radioactive waste into the water system in violation of the country's laws and the company's own policies. Without trying to simplify the complexity of each situation, the pattern that emerges is of large companies using their considerable power not simply for leverage against competitors but for every possible advantage—including illegal and immoral ones—against society, its laws, norms and individuals.

By no means complete, this litany of brazen or borderline behavior suggests that if anything the center of unethical gravity is shifting from the shadowy margins into the very mainstream of the economy. These infractions or ethical fudges touch millions of lives, embroiling some of the most important sectors of the economy in crimes that affect some of the most valued aspects of modern life. Laws, penalties and logic about values-based performance enhancement have done little to curb impropriety or the impulse to maximize selfish advantage. What this means is that a deeper listing of ethical benefits—and more anecdotes about successful ethical companies—will not be enough to reform the rigid institutionalized bias against ethics. *The task is not just to change minds but to change values.* Fundamental to any shift in business values must be a shift in the very concept of value. In other words, corporate equity must be reconstituted to appreciate the importance of social and ethical equities. This sounds difficult, and it is, but for a host of reasons a momentum is already building to value companies for more than their financial results. Publicly held corporations, writes Edward J. Waitzer, a lawyer and former chair of the Ontario Securities Commission, "are a work in progress—they always have been. The only constant has been their fundamental purpose: the development of wealth for shareholders. Today, that narrowly defined purpose is being challenged as employees and other 'stakeholder' rights are weighed against the traditional rights of shareholders."[2]

Slowly but inevitably the bottom line is becoming plural. Now, as in the past, company worth is primarily based on revenue-producing assets. The modern economy, however, is widely understood to operate differently. Human capital and intellectual assets are the reason that Microsoft's capitalization is greater than IBM's, although the software company has only a fraction of the latter's employees, machines and manufacturing plants. We have heard this comparison repeatedly in the 1990s, but few companies behave as if they understand what it means.

When worth is derived more from human creativity and intellectual capacities than from traditional bricks and mortar, then the market is itself valuing a very different managerial and productivity capacity. I call this new valuing relational equity.

Where conventional equity is based on return on investment, relational equity recognizes that value increasingly involves a return on relationship. Management of customers, employees, suppliers, strategic partners and global brand reputation are but some of the relations that are now of critical strategic importance to managers. These relationships are growing in complexity and now involve satisfactions that are not just functional but also emotional and moral. Since the worth of companies depends more and more on its varied relationships, the point is no longer that ethics must provide an ROI, but that ROI without ethics is much riskier and often unachievable. This is an opportunity that the process-and-results focus of most businesspeople prevents them from realizing. Waitzer concludes: "Companies generally are better equipped than government to respond sensibly to many of today's pressures on behalf of all stakeholders. Indeed, if employers, more than ever, will be defining society's well-being, then with it comes added responsibility. In the end, embracing voluntary changes in corporate governance is nothing more than enlightened self-interest."[3]

Relational equity involves two planes: the first represents a graduation of loyalty; the second defines the progressive interactions that contribute to the growth or strengthening of that loyalty.

Relational Equity Model

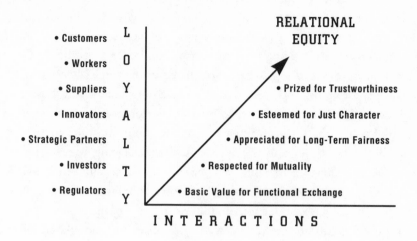

RELATIONAL
EQUITY

- Customers   **L**
- Workers   **O**
- Suppliers   **Y**
- Innovators   **A**
- Strategic Partners   **L**
- Investors   **T**
- Regulators   **Y**

- Prized for Trustworthiness
- Esteemed for Just Character
- Appreciated for Long-Term Fairness
- Respected for Mutuality
- Basic Value for Functional Exchange

I N T E R A C T I O N S

Customers Count

One of the most surprising developments of the 1990s has been the dramatic evaporation of customer loyalty. IBM, Sears, American Express, Bell Canada, GM, Apple and AT&T are among the corporations that have had long-entrenched customers uproot with shocking frequency. Even packaged-goods companies like Coke and Procter & Gamble have found that up to half of their customers are shopper/swappers who readily follow the lowest price or settle for any readily available alternative. Some organizations, among them IBM, Sears and Bell, have bounced back, but returning customers are not any more secure. Indeed, the ease with which customers switch between companies indicates a much greater comfort in venturing to a new supplier or vendor for a product or service. Companies often assume that this represents a growing fickleness, but it is actually a pragmatic response by customers to the push and pull of the global economy. Drawing on data from the Economic Policy Institute, Wolman and Colamosca conclude that since 1989 "there has been a sharp increase in the return to capital compared to the earnings on work." The same study also shows that "for those who earn their living from work, real wages (money wages corrected for inflation) have been stagnant since 1973."[4] With more than two decades of this diminishment, is it really surprising that the average customer is conditioned to seek the best deal or lowest price? Kellogg's, for one, ignored this reality, and after a century of brand building it raised prices greedily for a decade. In the midst of a prolonged jobless recovery, the company carelessly opened a price gap of up to 30 percent between some of its brands and those of generics. The company has yet to recover after dropping from ownership of half of the U.S. cereal market to only about one-third in 1997.

The lesson, though, is not just about price. Having been reengineered and downsized, customers have in turn reengineered their expectations of the companies they buy from. Numerous surveys point to the growing dissatisfaction in the workplace. Many people have responded in kind to the treatment they experienced at work, curtailing personal loyalty toward their own employers and regarding business in general with more cynicism. Unmitigated self-interest on the part of companies has only intensified the self-interest among customers. As a result, insouciance has replaced preference, even in markets with high switching costs, proprietary technology or highly developed rewards systems like frequent flier programs. Harvard Business School Professors Thomas O. Jones and W. Earl Sasser made "a startling discovery about customers in such markets. Whenever these customers have choices and feel free to make a choice, they act like customers in markets with intense competition: They will only remain rock-solid loyal if they are completely satisfied."[5] The authors stress that a satisfied, or even highly satisfied, customer is vulnerable. Xerox, for example, found that "totally satisfied customers were six times more likely to repurchase Xerox products over the next eighteen months than its satisfied customers."[6] Any relationship that is less than outstanding for customers is therefore disposable for them. No CEO would deny that their company derives a large part—if not all—of its worth from customers. With four out of five quintiles of customers up for grabs, corporate equity must be acknowledged as much more fragile and slippery than any revenue pattern might suggest.

If it takes total satisfaction to earn customer loyalty, then the real question is, What constitutes total satisfaction? Obviously, the product or service must fulfill the quality, value and performance criteria set out by the customer, matching or exceeding that delivered by the competition. Excellence in these variables is critical, but also only the start. More and more, full satisfaction involves dynamics of a relationship. This includes the reputation of the company, the experience that the customer encounters in interactions with the organization and the service, access and dependability after the sale. In *Working Wisdom*, I called this a progression from value-added to service-added. Nordstrom, British Airways and L.L. Bean are among the masters of service-added. Customers who encounter great respect and fulfilling service in one exchange transfer their expectations to virtually all other companies they encounter. If Disney can make me feel special, why can't my local gas station? In this way, the excellence of a few also works to exacerbate the disappointment most customers encounter in most purchases and corporate exchanges.

The market never stands still, so the pressures of competitiveness work to keep advancing service levels and to progressively deepen relationships with customers. Companies have no alternative but to build this relational equity with customers, if only to survive. Surrounded by choice, and courted on the full spectrum of human need and relationship, customers are increasingly using the power of their discretion to express their values and beliefs. In a 1993 survey by the Chartered Institute of Marketing, 64 percent of respondents indicated that "a company's record in environmental matters and social behavior influenced their purchase decision."[7] Another study, by MarketVision in 1994, found a similar trend of social concern, this time with new evidence that up to a quarter of all consumers and customers had boycotted a product, service or company in the previous year because of dissatisfaction with values or practices or reputation.

In this context of less loyal but more demanding customers, competitiveness involves improving the inherent value of the offering while simultaneously, and with equal fervor, improving the dynamics of interaction, experience and relating. Since 1985 British Airways has set the standards for service innovation and profitability within its industry. Sir Colin Marshall, the now retired CEO who revitalized the company, explains that as a price of entry, all companies must meet a basic set of expectations. Quality, value, timeliness and responsiveness are fundamentals for being in business, but these are not in themselves the resource for competitive differentiation and customer loyalty. In Sir Colin's case, "Our research shows that customers now take the basics for granted and increasingly want a company to desire to help them, to treat them in a personal, caring way. Fulfilling those desires is the centerpiece of how we wish to orchestrate our service."[8] Note that the concept of value is expressed almost completely in relational terms: desire—help—personal—caring. Features such as showers in airport lounges motivate customers to choose British Airways and to pay a premium for its service. But even the improvements are an expression of the company's caring and desire to help. When the product is an experience, the value is relational.

An ethical orientation contributes to and enhances relational equity in many ways. First, the inherent reciprocity of an ethical bias helps companies to put themselves into the shoes and situations of their customers. Since ethics involve considering the effects on others, the empathy and openness that are critical to listening, learning and more insightful research are already at work. Second, the principles of a global ethic all work to build a more dynamic intimacy between the company and its individual customers. The commitment to dignity demands respect for the health, well-being and values of the individual. Honesty imposes a scrupulous attention to real value and the avoidance of any deception. Fairness contributes to mutuality, and the possibility of an expanded sharing beyond a simple commercial transaction. Justice creates a bridge to the issues of pressing concern to customers and society. And sustainability acknowledges our larger interdependence. Not every principle has the same weight for every company, but the overall ethical orientation helps create the dynamic responsiveness that is indispensable for delivering total customer satisfaction.

Table 9. Relational Equity with Customers

Ethical Orientation Principle	Examples	Relational Equity
Dignity	BA's "Well-Being in the Air" stretch and health program for fliers.	Highest transatlantic service satisfaction scores. Premium pricing of only 5 percent generates $400 million incremental profit per year.
Honesty	First denying culpability, then suggesting they had no control, Nike finally, in 1997, issued a code to cover all its employees, which includes guarantees of freedom from workplace harassment and abuse.	Although suggesting important progress, the code seems to have been introduced in response to the complaints of customers. Nike is learning that marketing is indeed about image, but that image increasingly includes dimensions of responsibility.
Fairness	Motorola executives and engineers donate time to schools in three states, offering training in team building and problem solving.	"In the workplace of the future, kids will need problem-solving skills more than specific bits of information [William Myers, District 21 Assistant Superintendent]. "Many companies give money. But Motorola gives time, and that puts them in the forefront."[9]

Justice	After much analysis and delay, Levi Strauss withdrew from China because of human rights violations.	Although awkwardly handled, this showed how a company can respond to issues and expresses Levi's aspirational values.
Sustainability	Office paper consumption has doubled in the last two decades and is expected to double again by 2010. Xerox has achieved a recycling rate of almost 80 percent and reduced overall waste by 50 percent.	"Waste reduction improves the bottom line, both in reduced disposal costs and in revenues from sales of recyclables. In some instances, proceeds are funneled back into the community. For example, Xerox of Brazil's recycling proceeds help maintain a day nursery for disadvantaged children in Rio de Janeiro" (Paul Allaire, chairman and CEO).[10]

Relational equity is not a replacement for shareholder equity, but rather works as its constructive complement. It should be obvious that companies need customers. Now, it is also clear that companies can rely on the loyalty only of their most highly satisfied and committed customers. Improving relational equity is therefore an imperative of competitiveness. Relationships grow more trusting only with reciprocity, which is a key attitude derived from an ethical orientation. Ethics therefore contribute value to the company by deepening the values connections with customers. Put another way, to be distrusted, to be regarded as dishonest or to have a reputation for disrespect only imperils and diminishes shareholder equity. This is because, with so many options and so much information at their disposal, customers will go with their hearts as well as their wallets. "In such markets," explain Jones and Sasser, "it is the companies, rather than customers, who ultimately have no choice."[11]

Workers Win

A decade of downsizing has dramatically shifted the relations between a company and its individual managers and employees. In their study "Loyalty in the Age of Downsizing," Linda Stroh and Anne Reilly of Loyola University of Chicago confirm that the way in which laid-off employees are treated profoundly affects the pride and commitment of those workers who survived the cuts.[12] In many cases, the draconian style in which cuts were made left both those forced to depart and those still holding jobs alienated and dispirited. More recently, as the successive and substantial profit growth of companies failed to cascade down to workers, people have begun to resent being cheated of any reward for their longer work, growing productivity and personal sacrifices. The difficult 1997 strike at UPS—a company with a tradition of cooperation between management and labor—signals the deep anger of workers. Now that costs have been largely wrung out of operations, executives are slowly coming to recognize that growth—through innovation, and by adding value—depends on the very people whom they have by their behavior made angry and distrustful. Productivity has been achieved by pounding more value out of human assets. But competitiveness requires more than just productivity, and can be achieved only by developing more confidence, trust and accountability.

Relational equity is important for three reasons. As Stroh and Reilly point out, the pride and sense of identification employees feel for their company correlates to their commitment. High performance is based on high passion, and it is counter to every human intuition and experience to expect bullied and bloodied employees to be caring and proactive. Stroh and Reilly explain that "there are systemic links between employee loyalty and organizational performance, manifested in employees' willingness to assume responsibility for their work and to perform their tasks in a highly reliable way."[13] Employees who are accorded respect and dignity learn better, do better at problem solving, and are better able to provide highly satisfying service to customers. Indeed, it is just short of impossible to establish and deepen trusting relationships with customers without fostering with equal passion trust among workers. "Managers who want to build an organization that can survive many generations," writes Arie de Geus, "pay attention to the development of employees above all other considerations. They give a high priority to questions such as, How can we organize for continuity from one generation to the next?"[14]

One of the reasons it is so hard to manage in the 1990s is that the relentless intensity of the global economy keeps ratcheting up the definition of "competitiveness." Only a few North American companies, such as Ford, mastered Total Quality, only to be challenged by new standards for speed in global product development. Many others have streamlined systems with reengineering, only to have the competitive benchmark on innovation raised significantly higher. In such volatility and unpredictability, the majority of companies seem to be forever deconstructing themselves without ever completing any new reconstruction. This flux may be the defining management reality for the foreseeable future, but what it again emphasizes is the critical role of relational equity. Structures will change continuously as new technology, products and competitors come onstream. Such destabilizing variability is best managed by companies and workers bound together and supported by relational equity.

Take speed as an example. Ford's global car project, the Mondeo-Contour, took more than four years and $6 billion to develop. Honda by contrast took under two years and spent less than $700 million to develop its 1998 Accord. Part of Ford's cost and time involved creating the systems and global cohesiveness for future global products. Already having mastered intercompany teamwork, Honda achieved with the new Accord what many in the auto business thought impossible, a flexible, expandable and contractible platform and wheelbase on which to build Accords, mini-vans and sport utility vehicles. Perhaps more incredibly, Honda turned over its Marysville, Ohio, plant to produce the new Accord in only one day. One day it was making 1997 models; the next day its workers were assembling totally new 1998 cars. Such seamlessness in model changeover has never been seen before. *Business Week* reports that, by contrast, GM lost production of 152,000 vehicles in one particularly difficult plant changeover, and another company's downtime to reconfigure the plant cost $900 million in lost sales—a figure that exceeds the Accord's entire new model development.[15]

Honda is not reaping the benefits of some magic bullet or miracle technology. Just the opposite: its advantage comes from the creative and unconventional management of its employees and their knowledge. To begin with, Honda is only the sixth-largest of the world's car companies. It has therefore always had to make the most of fewer resources. Duplication and territoriality are wasteful practices that Honda cannot afford; it has stressed concepts like "oneness of body and mind" and "self-organizing teams."[16] In their exhaustive study of organizational knowledge creation, Professors Ikujiro Nonaka and Hirotaka Takeuchi provide three concrete examples of Honda's "oneness" in action. Many companies have begun to employ cross-functional teams. Honda went a step further and brought American and European engineers to Tokyo to help with the early-stage planning of the new model. Everyone had experience and ideas relating to the design, manufacture and customer acceptance of the older model. This created the opportunity to share ideas, so that the tacit knowledge of individuals could be formalized as explicit knowledge to be used for the new car. The key concept here is that ideas, creativity and solutions come to life not just in information exchange but in socialization. Memos and e-mail are no substitute for face-to-face engagement.

Honda took this socialization another step by having sixty American production engineers and their families move to work in Japan for three-year assignments. Nonaka and Takeuchi explain that "one of their key roles was to make sure that each part could be easily and cheaply manufactured at Honda's plants in Marysville." For teams to be self-organizing requires familiarity, camaraderie and trust. This happens only when people work together and, in Honda's case, play together on company retreats. Honda's third step involved "a contest among Honda's design studios in Japan, the United States, and Europe" to choose the new design. In the interchange of proposals, Honda determined that its one car for the world would need very different dimensions for each market: more interior space to accommodate the expanding girth of North American baby-boomers; narrower wheelbase and tighter handling to suit Europe's smaller streets; and a sportier and high-tech-laden version for the more youthful customer expected in Japan. The cross-continental and cross-cultural collaboration persisted until the very end of the design phase, when CEO Nobuhiko Kawamoto challenged his team to jazz up what he perceived to be a boring back end. The American designers leaped that hurdle.

To get the car from finished design to dealers without interrupting manufacturing, Honda had its assembly-line workers start studying the new model one year in advance of the turnover. It also teamed engineers with plant people to study problems and solve glitches in a way that maintained the product's design integrity while meeting the assembly line's needs for efficiency. And in the course of the year, Honda built four hundred prototypes so that the whole team could have practical experience with the assembly issues peculiar to each model. Honda's remarkable and standard-setting achievement was not the result of random cultural differences. Nor did it rely on any new technology or management theorem. Honda nurtured and used its employees' knowledge. But more than that, the company exploited its rich reservoir of relational equity. According to Nonaka and Takeuchi, "The two major traditions of the oneness of humanity and nature and the oneness of mind and body have led the Japanese to value the interaction between self and other. While most Western views of human relationships are atomistic and mechanistic, the Japanese view is collective and organic."[17] Knowledge and learning and creativity are assets for companies only if they are shared. The skills of interaction are therefore the base upon which intelligence can be leveraged into value. In other words, the critical competency of self-organizing teams is not organization but trust.

This must not be dismissed as yet another Japanese management idea that does not apply outside Asia. An important lesson from the work on a global ethic is that this orientation for belonging and group partic-ipation is not culturally based. No doubt, North Americans are more self-oriented, while Asians are more devoted to group. But in the global economy, cultures are drawing ever closer, with some Asians demanding more of the individual rights that we associate with West-ern values, while people in the West, by force of our environmental problems and economic challenges, appreciate more and more the values of interdependence and collective responsibility. Under this melting pot of ideas and cultures lie the shared moral principles expressed by a global ethic. All the major religious traditions define morality in relational terms, seeking the harmonious integration of the individual within the constructive and creative interactions of society. This is Bonhoeffer's point in explaining that the community draws its "power" from the "right of the individual" and that it is the commu-nity that "upholds and defends the rights of the individual." Compa-nies that operate in accordance with such principled reciprocity are creating a relational equity that not only fulfills obligations to individ-uals and society but also provides an enduring competitiveness.

Nonaka and Takeuchi's lessons about trust building apply to human nature, not to a specific country or culture. They write that "the indi-viduals' emotions, feelings and mental models have to be shared to build trust . . . At Honda, team members shared their mental models and technical skills in discussing what an ideal car should evolve into, often over *sake* and away from the office. These examples show that the first phase of the organizational knowledge creation process corre-sponds to socialization."[18] Companies in which workers are trusted— and trust each other—collaborate more readily, solve problems faster and take more creative risks in innovation. By contrast, de Geus notes that "in organizations in which benefits accrue to only a few people, all others are outsiders, not members."[19] Not attending to relational equity not only squanders the opportunity for greater speed, smarts and innovation. Such neglect contaminates the corporate environment and wastes productivity on things like the protection of territory. I noted earlier Peter Drucker's observation that many workers not only distrust management but regard senior executives with "hatred, contempt and fury." The point is that like capital, relational equity is either an asset or a liability. The companies that do not manage to have a surplus of relational trust will therefore have to deal with its deficit.

Table 10. Relational Equity with Workers

Ethical Orientation Principle	Examples	Relational Equity
Dignity	Southwest Airlines has built its low-cost but high-value-added business and profits by extending to employees the respect and "fun" that the company expects employees to extend to customers.	"CEO Herb Kelleher makes fun a priority at innovative and wildly successful SWA. But he has also persuaded his team that the airline has an exalted mission. Southwest doesn't simply provide customers with cheap flights from Dallas to Tucson. It offers passengers something far more precious—the 'freedom of travel'" (Warren Bennis).[20] Purpose, then, is not simply an objective for people but something in which they participate.
Honesty	Hewlett-Packard has made *integrity* a competitive factor, as well as internal competence.	"Bill Hewlett and David Packard constantly emphasized the importance of never compromising quick profits . . . David Packard pointed out in 1976 that any time he discovered an employee had violated HP's ethical principles in order to increase short-term divisional profits, the individual was fired—no exceptions no matter what the circumstance, no matter what the impact on the immediate bottom line. HP's long-term reputation, in Packard's view, had to be protected under all *(cont.)*

		circumstances."[21] As a result of this commitment to principle, the culture and company at H-P are not only self-organizing but largely self-regulating so that people who cannot be trusted simply do not fit in.
Fairness	3M is a paragon of innovation, deriving 25 percent of sales from products introduced within the previous five years.	"3M's minimization of corporate rules leaves plenty of room for experimentation. It consciously tolerates—even approves of and rewards—the innovative failures essential to ultimate success." "Researchers, marketers and managers visit with customers and routinely invite them to help brainstorm product ideas." "If an idea can't find a home in one of 3M's divisions, a staffer can devote 15 percent of his or her time to prove it is workable. For those who need seed money, as many as ninety in-house grants of $50,000 are awarded each year."[22] Rewarding risk rather than success requires two-way trust and accountability. Mature management begets mature workers.

Justice	Konosuke Matsushita built a business that by his death generated more revenue than "the combined sales of Bethlehem Steel, Colgate, Palmolive, Gillette, Goodrich, Kellogg, Olivetti, Scott Paper and Whirlpool."[23]	"His incredible success generated billions of dollars in wealth which were not used for villas in France but for the creation of a Nobel Prize–like organization, the founding of a school of government to reform Japan's political system, and a number of other civic projects." Matsushita told his early employees in 1932 that "the mission of a manufacturer is to overcome poverty, to relieve society as a whole from the misery of poverty and bring it wealth." Matsushita believed that "big idealistic/humanistic goals and beliefs are not incompatible with success in business. They may even foster achievements, at least in a rapidly changing context, by supporting those habits which encourage growth."[24]
Sustainability	In March 1996, 3M received the President's Award for Sustainable Development.	Since 1975, 3M employees have developed and implemented more than 4,400 projects, which prevented 1.4 billion pounds of pollutants and saved 3M more than $750 million. L.D. DeSimone, chair and CEO, states that "3M is moving beyond

		an era of compliance with environmental regulations toward one focused on sustainable development. We are convinced that, in the future, the most environmentally responsible companies also will be the most competitive companies."[25]

Relational equity works just like money. It does have a cost, requiring conscious and consistent investment to build and maintain it. But like money, relational equity can be drawn upon to support new ventures, structures and strategies. Collins and Porras's formula for enduring success—"preserve the core and stimulate progress"[26] —is possible only if sufficient relational equity is in place to provide individuals with the confidence and trust to leave behind the old and familiar for the unproven and the new. Relational equity can be borrowed against, as, for instance, when Louis Gerstner shut down the traditions and cultural attitudes of IBM as part of reinventing its business practices and customer relationships. Crisis sharpened the mind, but IBM succeeded in changing cultures so effectively because its commitment to culture never wavered. In other words, old equities made it possible to create radically new ones. Like money, relational equity also collects interest. Both Bill Hewlett and David Packard are long gone from their company, but to this day, employees ask themselves what Bill or David would do or say in a particularly difficult situation. With experience and consistency, principles take on a life of their own, refreshing and renewing the stock of relational equity for the company to use in the future.

This is basic managerial wisdom for an economy of global ideas, information and intelligence. Yet most senior managers and their companies have done more to deplete or destroy the critical relational equity with their employees than to nourish and harness it. A poll released on Labor Day in 1997 indicated that, while most workers are happy with their jobs and colleagues, less than half would recommend their company to a friend as a good place to work. More damaging, two-thirds of respondents did not trust their management, believing that senior executives had made decisions that not only dampened job prospects but also compromised value to customers. Workers feel distanced from the very companies that they are hired and paid to help grow. This can only depress commitment and curtail innovation. It is up to managers to reactivate this most essential asset. And it is the company that must initiate the process of restoring dignity, respect, honesty and justice to the workplace.

Producing Partnerships

Mercedes-Benz has arguably the world's best engineering resources, yet in 1997 it announced an alliance with tiny Ballard Energy Systems of Vancouver, B.C. The two companies will invest $300 million to develop vehicles powered by Ballard's zero-exhaust-emission, hydrogen-based fuel cell technology. Buses using this technology are already in trials in Chicago and Vancouver, and the alliance plans to start marketing fuel cell cars by 2005. Mercedes has already produced a totally new car from another unlikely partnering. With the design and engineering help of Swatch, the plastic watchmaker, Mercedes developed a super-subcompact, smaller than the Honda Civic, in Europe. Luxury cars are still the staple of its automotive business, but by these moves Mercedes acknowledges two strategic imperatives.

First, energy consumption and environmental impacts will become much more important dimensions of competitiveness in the immediate future. Smog kills hundreds of thousands of people each year. Gridlocked highways and crowded city streets suggest that any marginal gain in environmental efficiency of combustion engines is more than offset by the sheer growth in the number of cars on the road in the developing world, and in North America and Japan by the increasing popularity of sport utility vehicles and trucks. New research in the U.S. and Canada shows that particulate pollution is especially harmful and dangerous to humans. North American car companies have gone on record denying the validity of this research, and have played the all-too-usual delaying game of calling for more studies. Mercedes, meanwhile, has placed its bets on technology that reduces emissions.

Second, through its affiliation with Swatch and investment in Ballard, Mercedes is again demonstrating the extension of reach and capability afforded by alliances and partnerships. Success in the global economy requires imaginative stretches for both the largest and the smallest companies. Strategic alliances began coming into vogue in the aftermath of conglomeration, but their real importance has become clear only as technology and deregulation have come together to create a truly global marketplace. An analysis by consulting company Booz–Allen & Hamilton shows that there were at least 5,539 strategic alliances in the U.S. during the year ending September 1995. Virtually every industry sector—software, communications, medical, retailing, industrial and financial—has seen the formation of hundreds of new partnerships and multicompany webs. Booz–Allen vice-president David G. Knott explains that "alliances, often more so than contractual relationships or outright purchase, can help companies achieve competitive advantage by complementing their own core competencies with the different capabilities of extended enterprises."[27] Industries are overlapping and choices for customers proliferating. No company, not even powerhouses like Microsoft or Citibank, can singularly control the evolution of its own business. Proof of this is that the average return on investment for alliance-involved companies is six to eight points higher than for the average stand-alone.

Both the ecological and the alliance imperatives are advanced by a more defined ethical sensibility. Beyond the damage to air, land and water, automotive pollution can also cause serious injury, discomfort and death. This violates the basic dignity of all persons, and their right to life, health and a renewing natural environment. That some companies deny the scientific evidence or want more study can be seen as dishonest. Certainly companies have the right to ensure the data are accurate, but the tactics of refutation are hardly constructive. Car companies have in the past had to be regulated into making cars safer and less toxic. Now they risk repeating the damaging pattern of tobacco companies: fighting the social good for self-interest, using obfuscation to undermine damaging evidence and pretending that there is nothing to be done about the status quo, only to finally capitulate to public or governmental pressure. Pollution from cars also involves considerations of fairness and justice because, just like secondhand smoke, many of those affected are not necessarily the ones doing the driving. To be fair, Chrysler, Ford and GM have for several years been in their own strategic partnership with government to develop the battery and drivetrain technologies for an electric car. Chrysler is also involved in an initiative to transform abandoned rail lines into a nature trail that will straddle the entire breadth of Canada. And automotive managers and employees are working as hard as anybody to reduce waste and toxic pollution to meet government standards, adopting, for instance, water-based paints and non-CFC-based coolants for car air-conditioners. Nevertheless, attitudes toward the ethics of pollution from the industry as a whole seem to be the outdated ones of confrontation and denial.

If the problem of pollution represents a defensive application of an ethical orientation, then strategic alliances and partnerships represent a more positive and opportunistic one. In explaining their concept of "co-opetition," Professors Brandenburger and Nalebuff see "two fundamental symmetries" at play in the creation of a "value-net." First, "on the vertical dimension, customers and suppliers play symmetrical roles. They are equal partners in creating value." What this means is that the creation of value is advanced in proportionately equal terms by listening and responding to suppliers and partners, as it is in listening to customers. Sometimes, as with Federal Express, the link between customer need and supplier competency is direct. Often, suppliers and partners have expertise or learning that affords new leverage in serving customers, provided that the company with the relationship with the customer has the skills for tapping in to it. Those skills are primarily the relational ones of attentiveness, empathy, open-mindedness and a willingness to share knowledge as well as rewards. The second symmetry in Brandenburger and Nalebuff's model is that between "complementors"—the universities, research labs and social infrastructure that any company can draw from—and competitors.[28] An example of this symmetry is the test-launch of the Mondex electronic cash card in Canada. The global network of ATMs makes possible the underlying infrastructure for supporting such a card. But the encryption and track-ing difficulties are major, so rivals CIBC and Royal Bank formed a partnership to manage this radically new product.

David Knott stresses in his analysis that among the challenges for such alliances is "to build the competitively advantaged capabilities to execute chosen strategies effectively."[29] The inverse at work here is that the capabilities of cooperation are actually the capabilities of competition. Companies do not need to put aside their competitiveness, but rather need to mature that self-interest sufficiently to handle the obligations and reciprocity that are essential for enduring and constructive cooper-ation. Recognizing this need for radical sharing, consultant James Moore has developed the metaphor of business as ecosystem. He writes: "Companies and their executives are reconceptualizing the business world as a place bristling with coalitions, camps and communities— allied interests working together on shared visions with powerful poten-tial for innovation."[30] Many groupings have been attempted for strategic reasons like synergy, and have failed. The reason is that "community" requires more than strategy. In Moore's terms, there must also be an "alignment of the community around a shared vision of the desired future" in order to produce a "co-evolving, symbiotic, self-reinforcing system of strategic contributions."[31] Capital is still important to the building of strategic competitive advantage. But it is relational equity that is critical for building strategic *cooperative* advantage.

An ethical orientation alerts companies to the particular needs of cooperation, community building and partnership. Dignity, honesty and fairness are commitments to mutuality that help make organiza-tions and their people more open to others. These provide a basis for listening, and for resolving the inevitable conflicts and disagreements that occur in any relationship. Perhaps most important, the genuine and consistent manifestation of these virtues earns the trust and respect of partners. Charles Handy notes that "unlimited trust is, in practice, unrealistic. By trust, organizations really mean confidence, a confi-dence in someone's competence and in his or her commitment to a goal."[32] Such confidence is developed by the actual behavior and prac-tices of companies and individuals. It is an outcome of character, of principle in action. Justice and sustainability are commitments that go

even beyond mutuality and recognize that the common good sometimes requires sacrifice. As Moore and de Geus have shown, the lessons
from nature, particularly in the diversity of relationships, provide a
more lasting and successful paradigm for corporate success than the
simplistic, self-centered concepts of competition as the survival of the
fittest. The rich lessons provided externally by a commitment to
sustainability are mirrored internally by developing a deepening sensitivity to issues of social justice. Strategic alliances are webs that reflect
the much wider and more intimate interconnection between the global
economy and the world community. The obligations for just action
within this wider interdependence reinforces the obligations of the
narrower strategic interdependence.

Is this overstating the importance of relational equity? No. Arie de
Geus's data show that corporations in North America, Europe and
Japan have a life expectancy of well under twenty years. He answers the
question "Why do so many companies die young?" by explaining that
"mounting evidence suggests that corporations fail because their policies and practices are based too heavily on the thinking and language
of economics. Put another way, companies die because their managers
focus exclusively on producing goods and services, and forget that the
organization is a community of human beings that is in business—in
any business—to stay alive. Managers concern themselves with land,
labor and capital, and overlook the fact that *labor* means real people."[33]

Table 11. Relational Equity with Partners and Suppliers

Ethical Orientation Principle	Examples	Relational Equity
Dignity	Hewlett-Packard has developed a series of strategic alliances, including a far-reaching joint program with Microsoft on networks, and another with Siemens to develop a platform for telecommunications management networks and market them worldwide.	H-P's reputation for respecting its employees and encouraging their innovation has made it a much sought after partner for strategic alliances. The ethical style that has been embedded by the founders also provides partners with the assurance that H-P's commitments can be trusted. Partnerships based on respect are more productive than those of competitive convenience like the on-again/off-again cooperation between IBM and Apple.
Honesty	Intel underestimated its obligations to customers when it delayed owning up to flaws in its Pentium chip, and then delayed taking corrective steps. It took action by IBM to move Intel into a recall.	CEO Andy Grove has admitted learning that "Intel Inside" is not just a promise about technical capability, but ultimately a promise of relationship. It is "Intel Values Inside"— the capability to manage innovation and consistently improve its products —that contribute to the company's alliances with Compaq, Microsoft and others.

Fairness	Foiled in its attempt to take over London Life Insurance for $2.4 billion, the Royal Bank instead opted to buy $10 million worth of technology, software and training from phone sales pioneer Co-operators Group.	With a brand among the most trusted in the financial services sector, Royal's venture with the Co-operators allows it to trade on its reputation, sidestep traditional sales agents and use technology to reach and serve customers. As technology distances customers from companies, the reputation for fairness and trustworthiness becomes the essential relational assurance and differentiator.
Justice	Toyota has launched a venture with the Doe Fund, a nonprofit organization serving the homeless, to set up a computer training and direct mail center in Harlem. The program is providing a business and much needed training opportunity, and has already resulted in career placement for some of the participants.	This is only one of a group of community-oriented programs launched by Toyota to advance education and training opportunities in its "adopted" North American market. It is working with Maryland's Chesapeake Bay Foundation, using a $2-million grant to involve 946 schools, 3,225 teachers and 96,000 students in activities and learning geared to cleaning American watersheds. This and other programs recognize that the learning skills derived from total quality manufacturing can be an asset for dealing with intractable social problems.

Sustainability	Shell's recent announcement to involve environmental and other special interest groups in strategic decision making brings together experience from diametrically opposed points of view to solve common problems.	The partnership of adversaries provides both with new learning as well as with credentials for effectively engaging other audiences. "Among the values I would rank most important within any organization is tolerance, which allows us to learn from others and improve. Similarly, taking responsibility for our own actions (rather than blaming others or being victims) is vital to organizational transformation. Learning begins with the recognition that none of us has all the answers. Thus, I would rank humility as another core value."[34] (Edward Waitzer)

Like money, relational equity can be misspent and wasted on a nonstrategic issue (like the UPS strike that seemed to be played out against an agenda no party sought or controlled). Even if a company does nothing with its relational worth, this asset can still be devalued by competitors that learn to give more, by customers who demand more or by the natural inflation in virtually every sector of ever higher performance and service expectations. British Airways' success must be refreshed (hence some of management and labor's recent run-ins) if the company is to continue to earn high marks from customers and employees. Microsoft similarly must remake its relations, shifting from sheer quantity—having relations with everyone—to more quality—meaning deepening interactions with individual customers to make their products easier and more ennobling of the individual. Nike's relational growth, in the words of social marketing consultant Eric Young, will come from evolving the company's positioning and sensibilities from "Just Do It" to include "Do It Just."[35] (Or now that it is "I can",

"They Should".) An ethical orientation provides the commitment for at least consciously managing this asset, and often for adding to it. Ethical questioning is fundamentally relational. When business logic asks, Where is the advantage? ethical logic asks, How does this decision affect the dignity of others? Over time, this question evolves into a combined and interactive one: What business advantage serves dignity? And how can the advancing of human dignity toward customers, employees, partners, suppliers and the community add to competitive advantage?

Table 12. Business Benefits from an Ethical Orientation

An ethical corporate character wins trust.	In a world of globalization and market convergence, reputation is a critical and ever more important differentiator.
A trusted company earns greater loyalty from customers.	Saturn and Xerox have achieved outstanding retention and satisfaction rates from customers by focusing on issues of integrity.
A trusted company attracts and holds on to trusting people.	The people with the skills that companies most covet are in short supply and will gravitate to, and perform for, those companies like Hewlett-Packard that provide a sense of purpose.
A trusted company attracts responsible strategic partners.	Companies, like people, want to link up with organizations that are not only successful but responsible enough to manage a fruitful relationship.
A trusting work environment creates the support that fuels creativity.	People will innovate if they trust that they will not be arbitrarily punished for failure. All the scientific research into innovation, including Professor Warren Bennis's work in *Organizing Genius*, confirms the importance of group support and mutuality.
A trusting work environment is faster and more responsive.	When people do not have to look over their shoulders, they can focus all their energy on looking ahead. Trust minimizes "cover your ass" tactics that only slow down work.
A trusting work environment is more open to change.	Trust begets trust. Trust is also the only antidote to fear.
A trusting company is motivated to produce excellence in both revenues and social results.	Enduring companies are defined by their beliefs and traditions, never just by their products.
A trusting company creates personal growth opportunities for its people.	Particularly in the knowledge economy, companies that neglect the intellectual and wisdom growth of their people are risking joining Arie de Geus's list of prematurely expired organizations. Ironically, in business it is *not* the good who die young.

CHAPTER EIGHT

ALIGNMENT

Development of the vital force and self-denial, growing and dying,
health and suffering, happiness and renunciation, achievement and
humility, honour and self-abasement, all these belong together in
irreconcilable contradiction and yet in living unity. The unity of life
is irreparably destroyed if any attempt is made to render the one
independent of the other, to play off the one against the other, or to
appeal to the authority of the one against the other.

Dietrich Bonhoeffer, "Good and Life" in Ethics

As a consultant, I have spent the last seven years working with senior executives to improve results. My expertise involves combining the strategic with the human, and I originally saw this groundwork in ethics as the next phase in promoting organizational effectiveness. The performance benefits of an ethical orientation have turned out to be more tangible and dramatic than I had thought, and these are part of the support for ethics as an imperative that will be detailed below. What was more surprising was the realization that among the victims of unethical business behavior are the unethical. I had set out in my own small way to save society and the environment from predatory companies and ended up trying to save these companies from themselves.

Some of the lessons and contradictions I encountered provide a warning about this topic. With ethics, we never know it all and never really know it enough. Long-held assumptions are often reversed. Even judgments, which would seem to be the currency of ethics, are never absolute. This is not because what is right is relative, but because determining what is right is an ever deepening process. We live in a complex world, with interconnected causes creating intertwining effects. There are no easy answers and very few instant determinations of right or wrong. The issue is propensity, the desire for and consistency toward right effort over time. Ethics, it turns out, are doubly important, first for helping organizations discern the most proper or right outcome in real-life situations of great ambiguity, and second, for exercising the very analytical skills and weighting of implications that improve overall decision making. Rather than function as abstract ideals, ethics derive their value in concrete action, "in the midst," as Bonhoeffer notes, "of our historical experience." Rather than provide fixed norms, ethics contribute what law and sociology professor Philip Selznick calls "moral knowledge in the problem-solving experience of human communities."[1]

It may seem that the momentum toward a global ethic is beyond any of us as individuals to affect. Yet it is exactly because this is an exercise in community reimagining that we have no choice but to start at such a specific, personal level. Peter Senge explains: "You cannot command people to change how they think. Instead, small pockets of people or organizations will start operating differently. They will develop new skills in understanding complexity, in building shared aspirations, in learning how to reflect on their own assumptions, and in challenging assumptions without invoking defensiveness. Some of these 'small pockets' may be at the top of organizations, but even that will not alter the basic organic nature of the change process. Changes in mindset don't start on a large scale."[2] We may be living on a quiet street in the far corner of a small town, but we remain the only agents for forming, practicing and benefiting from a global ethic.

There are no ethics without community. Whether their ethics derive from deep spiritual conviction or an ingrained sense of duty, individuals are ethical only in relation to each other and only because the community, through persuasion, pressure and enforcement, is able to elicit compliance. Right and wrong are therefore not a perspective, but outcomes. They live not in ideology, which is abstract, but in action between people, which is real. The task we face from a business perspective is twofold: first, contributing our personal action to the creation of a global community within which to share a global economy; and second, creating the community within our companies that will support the organizational growth toward an ever more responsible ethical orientation. The key for creating this internal community involves a commitment to principle and an equally important dedication to consistency. This requires an alignment of intention and action, stretching from the most exalted board member to the lowest-paid employee. Goals, messages and measures must also be harmonized to activate and reinforce the expected or desired result. As noted in an earlier chapter, this alignment includes six variables: the board, the CEO, the strategy, a company's culture, the dynamics affecting group behavior, and commitment from individuals throughout the enterprise.

The Board of Directors

As the representatives of the shareholders, a board is charged with overseeing direction, management and results of the organization. It has duties to the owners, including the astute allocation of capital and resources and the earning of a fair and sustainable return. Boards vary in their activism and influence on management, but generally the role of custodian is expanding to include that of conscience. There is now great legal pressure for companies to comply with regulations, and there is great fiscal risk for not doing so. To fulfill their fiduciary responsibilities, the boards have no choice but to exert diligence on and guide behavior other than financial. Although building slowly, the recognition of ethical obligations is gaining momentum for other reasons as well. As Lynn Sharp Paine points out, "to be agents of shareholders with a fiduciary obligation to them" does not mean that the company and its directors "have no obligation to other parties or that ordinary principles of morality cease to apply."[3] Any company operates within a web of interdependencies. Neglecting the obligations that go with such links can as easily diminish revenues and competitiveness as make a bad product.

Board accountability for ethics is also expanding with the recognition that values affect value. This equation has both internal and external validity. From within, companies that build trust and treat employees with respect are more successful. Robert Waterman, co-author with Tom Peters of a landmark study of corporate excellence, concludes: "Companies that set profits as their No. 1 goal are actually less profitable in the long run than people-centered companies."[4] Further proof of this proposition was shown again and again in the study by Collins and Porras. Profit is important, but profit is most readily achieved when it shares priority with values of relationship building and trust. There is a strong reason for, and tangible benefit to, values. Amitai Etzioni explains: "Moral commitments reduce what economists call 'moral hazards.' Specifically, the stronger the moral underwriting of implicit contracts, the lower the transaction costs, resulting in less of a need to buy hedge protection."[5] Efficiency, therefore, is a result not just of streamlined processes and cost control but of smooth and reciprocal interaction between people. As noted, one consequence of reengineering has been to create fear among employees. While steps in processes have been reduced, the excessive stress has only caused many people to retreat to their specialization, thereby only compounding the compartmentalization of silo-thinking.

The external manifestation of values is no less important to corporate value. Boards are beginning to realize that equity exists not only in the revenue that accrues to the bottom line but also in the beliefs, perceptions and confidence of customers and the public. As Nike, Levi's and others have discovered, brand equity is a critical variable in the global marketplace that can be diminished as much by perceived ethical improprieties as by performance failure or disappointment with product quality. Customers have become as activist as shareholders, and the board, to do its job, must manage obligations to those who buy a company's products and services as well as to those who own its shares. Shell's move to bring nongovernmental groups into its policy and decision making exemplifies this understanding. The chairman of Shell Transport and Trading, John Jennings, admitted: "We should use the increased scrutiny of nongovernmental organizations as a tool to strengthen performance."[6] Response to customer issues and concerns, instead of a being seen as a public relations issue, is finally understood to be strategic, affecting satisfaction, sales and profits.

Boards are in many ways suspect of being disconnected from the business reality affecting the company, or of being immune to any of its improprieties and failures. ADM responded with aggressive denials to authorities and threats to its own people in response to allegations of price fixing. It was finally proven culpable by the companies it had conspired with. As already noted, the senior management on whose watch the crime and cover-up were perpetrated did not suffer any career dislocation. Nor did the board, which includes a former prime minister of Canada and several other former senior government officials. Obviously, these board members did not in any way participate in or sanction the price fixing, but the company's prolonged resistance to enforcement officials, the cover-up and the closing of ranks around the besmirched management team suggest a moral laxity that can only undermine any ethical directives from the top. *Business Week* has expressed the judgment of peers, naming ADM's as one of the ten worst boards for both 1996 and 1997.[7] Ethical priorities cannot be achieved part-time, nor in one pocket of the company in isolation from the others. "An integrity strategy," explains Paine, "is characterized by a conception of ethics as the driving force of an enterprise. Ethical values shape the search for opportunities, the design of organizational systems, and the decision-making process used by individuals and groups."[8] Only the board can be the motor behind this driving force. And thus the board itself is as accountable for right and wrong as it is for success and failure.

Some of the directors at Barings Bank were worried before the crash of the company, with one complaining: "The fact is that 90 percent of us don't know what is going on 90 percent of the time." Other boards are no doubt better informed, but few understand the complex problems or products or complicated selling conditions that introduce moral challenges in day-to-day operations. Boards cannot envision every exigency, or control every choice or act, but they do set the moral tone of the company. James Gillies, professor of policy at York

University, writes: "By defining the ethical stance of the organization, fulfilling its social responsibilities and representing the views of all stakeholders, the board can do a great deal to determine the 'culture' of the corporation. Indeed, it is from the board that the 'culture' must come—it cannot be created anywhere else. The board cannot meet this obligation if it is not significantly involved in governing the enterprise."[9] Any alignment of executives, strategy, culture and employees can be seen only as a response to the board's direction and a reflection of its moral priorities.

Boards seeking to infuse or strengthen an ethical orientation can start by reading minutes of past meetings to establish which issues led to moral deliberation. This is not just to identify possible types of problems but to benchmark how much of the board's attention and time have been devoted to ethics. The board is responsible for supervising the mission of the company and for ensuring that obligations—moral, social and environmental—are expressed, understood and consistently delivered. In practical terms, this means calibrating senior managers' rewards to reflect the board's ethical priorities, and expecting specific and regular updates on ethical issues, including conformance, training and slip-ups. It also involves raising the ethical implications and probing the company's moral preparedness on virtually all business and strategic presentations. And it means measuring and reviewing ethical performance in parallel with, and to the same degree as, financial results. The trick is to set the moral tone, expect problems and issues and use the wisdom and perspective of the board to help people in the thick of operations to understand and stay on course. An ethical orientation is a long-term commitment, one of ever deepening appreciation for obligations. In time, managers will change, strategy will be reworked and culture will evolve, so it is up to the board to encode and preserve the company's ethical stance.

Leadership

Perhaps the most critical element affecting the ethical constitution of companies is their CEO. Leadership is acknowledged as vital for any organizational success or renewal effort. It is axiomatic that performance starts at the top. But leadership is even more vital for realizing an ethical orientation within a business enterprise. Leaders must set the context in which the business operates, and provide the rules for achieving its results. This, though, is only the beginning. To be effective in the sphere of ethics the CEO needs that inner discipline and vision to balance the self-interest and competitive instincts demanded by the market with the legal and moral responsibilities expected by the community. In a *Harvard Business Review* article Edmund Learned, Arch R. Dooley and Robert Katz appropriately call this "the terrible task of leadership," which means "to live with conflicts and tensions, to make discriminating judgments where necessary, and to find mutual relationships where possible."[10] Terrible for having to make tough choices. Terrible for sometimes having to check the very impulses associated with success to achieve moral balance. Terrible for having to weigh and choose between the sometimes contradictory demands of stakeholders.

The terribleness, though, is far more sinister and threatening than the choices. It is not just the ambiguity of the demands that makes leadership terrible, it is that leaders are mostly terribly prepared to deal with moral discernment. This ineptitude is apparent in the growing number of legal and moral infractions committed by companies, but Bausch & Lomb, Olivetti, Elf Aquitaine, Barings, Sumitomo and Nomura are emblematic of a far wider ethical laxity at the top. In several studies, including one of more than five hundred managers, the vast majority of executives emerged as stunted in their personal ethical development. These findings are hardly surprising. Corporate leaders have spent their career fulfilling their quest for power and self-advancement by advancing the interests and power of the company they serve. What would be uncharacteristic would be to find corporate chieftains reformed of their own competitive and aggressive instincts to the point of being able to engage the cooperation and expansiveness of their own organization. As Bonhoeffer noted, success becomes its own right, and the people who sacrificed so much to succeed are not necessarily going to have the wider perspective and self-knowledge to stand up to success when it is morally wrong.

This terrible truth of moral immaturity at the top is substantiated by

Benyamin Lichtenstein, Beverly Smith and William Torbert in a 1995 article that appeared in *Business Ethics Quarterly*. They looked at four studies that similarly established seven or eight categories of ethical sensibility in the course of personal growth and development. Seven such developmental positions or stages of personal ethical growth became the focal point of the authors' analysis. These are described as:

- "Impulsive," representing the least maturity and reflective development.
- "Opportunist," seeking "symbols of power" and resorting to manipulation to win them.
- "Diplomat," working toward group acceptance and striving to avoid an alienating conflict.
- "Technician," treating people as "technical systems" that are activated by a hot-button.
- "Achiever," striving for excellence and seeing the wider inter-connections behind results.
- "Strategist," developing the "multiple perspectives" and open-ness for making change.
- "Magician," interacting with a situation, transforming self and others toward a potential

Again, these are development steps that emerged as consistent phases (with slightly different names) across all four studies. The authors concluded that most managers operate at the Technician stage or below. Only 10 percent of all managers measured operate at the Strate-gist stage where one realizes "that entirely different world views and ethical perspectives are among the issues that require mediation in ethi-cal action, and that timing is of the essence in determining the mean-ing and the effects of an action."[11] Rewind to Sharon Daloz Parks's study of Harvard MBA students. Intellectually strong, confident and curious about business, this group largely failed to appreciate that corporate decisions and actions—of which they would soon be a part—had implications that warranted ethical consideration. Fast-forward to Benyamin, Smith and Torbert's findings. Senior executives, despite their experience and managerial proficiency, are basically as morally developed as an MBA student. The abuses of business—the environmental degradation, worker displacement and even criminal activities—are more understandable in light of such ethical under-development among corporate leadership.

In the previous section I noted the dearth of effective strategies. This research shows why. Remember that Strategist is the first of the stages beyond Achiever. This means that, for the most part, corporate leaders do not have the emotional and mental dexterity to entertain the validity of conflicting options, or the conceptual ability to envision alternative courses of action. The authors explain that Technicians "treat people and events as technical systems that can be influenced by finding the 'key' to their inner workings. Their attention is on analytical coherence."[12] This explains the popularity of reengineering, which was never a strategy but only a tactic. Offering a truly technical system and analytical coherence, reengineering provided managers with the perfect substitute for the much harder, more mature task of forging a new direction and creating oppor-tunities. Ethical wisdom partakes of the same breadth of vision, and the same creative ability to construct new interconnections, as the ability to be strategic. Moral adolescence is thus a symptom of a similar strategic immaturity. The authors note that "the research results . . . exemplify the fact that extremely few managers are found in these three post-formal stages of development."[13] There may be institutional reasons for this widespread stunting, but that does not mitigate the terrible consequences for company performance as well as for company morality.

In light of these findings, resistance by senior managers to including the ethical in decision making signals a managerial as well as a moral gap. Put in positive terms, an ethical orientation provides not only safe-guards against legal and moral impropriety but also the major opera-tional and performance benefits that go with confidence in the face of unpredictability. Quoting a 1983 study by Bartunek, Gordon and Weathersby, Lichtenstein and team write: "As one matures develop-mentally, one becomes increasingly able to (a) accept responsibility for the consequences of one's actions, (b) empathize with others who hold conflicting or dissimilar world views, and (c) tolerate higher levels of stress and ambiguity."[14] The messier business gets, the more important is moral leadership.

Leadership has never been solely about intelligence or strategic smarts. A leader must not only choose the optimum direction but also inspire people to do their best, individually and within teams, to realize the organization's goals. This requires moral authority—the regard and trust earned by example that the leader understands not only the difficulties of the situation but also the difficulties of the people being led. Many companies have strong financial, marketing or strategic leadership, but do not have leadership that would qualify as moral authority. The proof of this is the fear present in so many companies, used to motivate and intimidate people into conforming to company direction.

To have moral authority requires of leaders that they be moral and that they be developing morally. Boards, then, have the first responsibility, to choose CEOs not only for business performance but also for their character and moral maturity. Most boards already value integrity, but for most, this means only that basic honesty of "keeping their word" and therefore delivering the results as promised. Integrity is a far more involved concept. It literally means wholeness—the full development and flourishing of all aspects of the human person. Integrity for business leaders involves, using Goodpaster's terms, growing toward "moral excellence" as well as "business excellence." The CEO, by assuming responsibility for the results of the enterprise, also assumes responsibility for the means in which those results were achieved. The two are so intimately intertwined that an ethical failing or criminal activity besmirches the reputation of the leader as well as that of the company. Thus, a major priority for CEOs is to develop character in parallel to results, both in a deepening moral maturity for themselves and in a more far-reaching ethical orientation for the enterprise. Since CEOs are responsible for succession, the development of moral character in subordinates throughout the company is one mark of leadership success. Since CEOs are responsible for strategy, the appreciation of and responsiveness to ethical implications is another indispensable acumen. And since CEOs are the ones who imbue values with authority and relevance, the example of their actions and choices is central to the company's own ethical maturing.

Warren Bennis and Burt Nanus have written extensively about business leadership. They have developed a four-step "vision retreat" to help CEOs express and focus the values critical to success and sustainability. The first step involves a "Vision Audit, which examines the character of the organization, including its current mission and values." The second step is the "Vision Scope, in which decisions are made regarding the desired characteristics of the new vision."[15] Setting the cross-hairs for "vision" on "character" suggests that leadership is not just a matter of direction and guidance but inevitably also of virtue. The quality of character nurtured by the leadership is even more important than the quality of the results because it is the character of the company that is ultimately the source for endurance and resilience. CEOs must initiate the development of corporate character by being the example of those characteristics that are seen as strategically and ethically essential. Those that practice ethics by "do as I say, not as I do" undermine the corporate character in the same way that inconsistent parents produce inconsistent children.

Strategic Sensibility

Strategy is management's highest art, but, unfortunately, the 80/20 rule applies here as well. All companies have strategies, but only a small minority of those are truly strategic. The difference is the difference between a plan and an insight upon which to do business. A plan sets an objective—usually a financial share or sales target. An insight perceives an opportunity—usually an intersection of unique relationships involving company skill and customer need. Against plans, all activities throughout the company are focused on realizing results. Against strategies, activities are instead geared to developing the relationships that maximize opportunity to achieve results. In most companies, the drive for results in the 1990s has meant more and more operational pressure to hit more and more elevated profit targets. The relationships and competencies of strategy have therefore been consistently compromised for the expediency of higher profit.

More aggressive results with looser strategic guidance have created the now ripe environment for ethical short-cuts and outright criminality. If the numbers are all that matter to management, then how I deliver those numbers is just a lower priority than getting them. This seems to be the poisonous logic that led to widespread impropriety at Bausch & Lomb. If numbers are all that matter, and the strategy is unclear or ineffectual, then the temptation to cheat and deceive is that much greater. Senior Barings executives admitted that they did not really understand the alchemical business of derivatives, so their guidance for Nick Leeson was not strategic but quantitative. Rather than set long-term vision, with controls and attention to relationships, they simply asked Leeson to deliver more of the profits to which they had become accustomed. Was Leeson wrong? Yes. But so was the strategy, or the lack of it.

Henry Mintzberg of the Business School at McGill University has studied both the basic need for strategy and the often abysmal failure of corporate strategic process. Mintzberg notes, "Planning is fundamentally a conservative process: it acts to conserve the basic orientation of the organization, specifically its existing categories. Thus, planning may promote change in the organization, but of a particular kind: change within the context of the organization's overall orientation, change at best in strategic positions within the overall strategic perspective."[16] He distinguishes between strategies that are fixed, formal positions, and those that reflect a flexible attitude to shifting circumstances. The first is intellectual, while the latter is relational. Others see strategy as a script that everyone adheres to. Mintzberg instead regards strategy as more of a performance, in which the words of the actor take on their meaning and power from interaction with the audience. By recognizing strategy as a dynamic involving the managers who conceive it, the employees who deliver it and the customers who buy it, Mintzberg also links obligations to strategies much more intimately. Most businesspeople would separate the two, regarding strategy as a process to do only what is best for the business, and ethics as only the consideration of the aftereffects of strategy. Yet if strategies are about relationships, then obligations are intrinsic to strategy.

This is especially important in the highly competitive pressure of the global economy. Senior managers have become in many ways dismissive of strategy because it seems impotent to deal with the uncertainty of this new, fiercer business reality. As a result, there is even greater priority on financial targets, and even less strategic context to guide managers and employees. Any ethical initiatives in this situation are usually cosmetic and unconvincing. One investment house, in the aftershock of Procter & Gamble's lawsuit against Banker's Trust for less than full disclosure regarding risks in P&G's derivatives portfolio, sent all the marketers in its trading pit a written Code of Ethics. People were told to read it and sign it. Everyone followed the instructions, or at least the second one. But the code became an instant joke. There was no training. No programs were launched to deal with gray areas. And there were no signals from management except those reinforcing business as usual. The employees saw the code for what it was—some legal ass–covering at a time of greater client scrutiny. Whatever the intent, reactions suggest that individuals, rather than being more ethical in their practices, were just that much more cynical that the ethical commitment of the company was for real.

An ethical orientation deserves to be woven into strategy precisely because of the unpredictability of the business world. Since strategy cannot adequately prepare people for all eventualities, ethics can at least provide a belief structure to guide the creation of solutions and the realization of new opportunities. Gael M. McDonald, an associate professor of management at the Asia International Open University in Hong Kong, provides a different angle on the often used Tylenol recall to make this point. Johnson & Johnson is justly celebrated for pulling Tylenol off store shelves after several people in Chicago died when pills were tampered with. Students of the crisis point to J&J's fifty-year-old Credo as the moral inspiration for the decision. But, as McDonald writes, the reality was both more subtle and more powerful than that. "James Burke, chairman and CEO of Tylenol (J&J) at the time, has an interesting view of what happened. Burke is on record as saying that the $100-million recall decision never happened, because in reality there was never just one decision. According to Burke, dozens of people had to make literally hundreds of decisions, and then had to make them work. But by making the hundreds of decisions that led to the recall, Johnson and Johnson regained their market."[17] Strategy could not have foreseen such a tragic eventuality, but the moral sense pervading the company allowed people to participate by their decisions in creating ad hoc the most compelling strategy of all.

Many companies have sought to imitate J&J's crisis management strategy, but this has proven to be very hard. First, the strategy turns out to have been not a strategy at all, but an ethic. Second, that ethic was not thrown together in some three-day off-site session with crisis management consultants. J&J's ethos was set by senior management in the 1930s and has been inculcated year after year in plans, employee training and rewards. In fact, strategies have changed often and plans have been redone at least yearly, but the commitment to what is right based on the company's principles has been constant. Third, not only are these long-term values but they are also questioned and tested by successive management teams. This helps the words and concepts take on relevance and meaning in whatever the contemporary context. Corporate mission statements were originally meant to imbue company practices with values, but most of these statements have been made anachronistic by the speed with which senior executives reverted to a profit-at-any-cost mentality. More than most, J&J practiced what they preached so that at that moment of crisis, hundreds of employees could practice doing the right thing without being told from above.

One critically important dynamic of strategy is the use of power. Corporations have enormous clout, not only in their operations but in the global and local communities. The attention to corporate charac-ter and virtue is so important precisely because this power has been growing, and because it is never neutral. There are two concepts, already briefly discussed, that in combination provide an ethical refer-ence point for the exercise of corporate power. The first is the British trade association RSA's concept of inclusion; the second is the idea of *kyosei* promoted by Canon and its former chairman, Ryuzaburo Kaku.

Inclusion involves many dynamics, which RSA defines in part as follows. "TOMORROW'S COMPANY is managed by people who can hold collaboration and competition in their heads at the same time, and see the company's identity as including all stakeholders. YESTERDAY'S COMPANIES are managed by people who see only themselves and their immediate colleagues as *us,* and everyone else as them."[18] Successful corporate governance and management hinges on strategies that share power and fulfill its obligations. Contrast the old IBM, which used its power to push customers into products and pricing that did not serve their best corporate interests, versus the reinvented IBM, which in 1995 included competitive machines and software in one-third of its customer sales because that combination best solved the client's problems. The first tangent of this more responsible use of power is deepening collaboration.

The second tangent involves a corresponding deepening of obligation. *Kyosei*, as explained by Kaku, is the "*spirit of cooperation* in which individuals and organizations live and work together for the common good."[19] In Kaku's view, the common global good is imperilled in at least three ways by three imbalances: that of trade deficits and surpluses; that between "wealthy and poor"; and that between the current generation and future ones in terms of access to and consumption of the earth's natural resources. The model Kaku has worked out for practicing *kyosei*, which has been used at Canon since the late 1980s, acknowledges that companies, like people, develop through different stages. Each level of maturity brings both more power to correct the imbalances, and more obligations for doing so. Kaku defines five stages: *Economic Survival*, in which the priority is building the financial base for viability; *Cooperating with Labor*, in which the internal partnership and "sharing" for realizing future growth is shaped and institutionalized; *Cooperating Outside the Company*, in which relations with the local community are formalized and made reciprocal; *Global Activism*, in which multinational companies use their investments and resources to address imbalances on a global basis; and *The Government as a Kyosei Partner*, in which *kyosei* companies and their *kyosei* partners work directly with national governments to address justice and social issues.

The progression of a company from entrepreneurial start-up, to local firm, to national competitor, to multinational corporation involves a parallel progression in size, resources consumed and power. It is only natural that this progression also involves maturing and a corresponding deepening of moral commitment. By implication, the strategies of fourth- and fifth-stage companies that are fixed on profit to the exclusion of all other responsibilities represent that danger of an underdeveloped character managing adult power. Kaku notes: "There is nothing wrong with the profit motive per se—even companies in the later stages of *kyosei* must increase profits. But making profit is only the beginning of a company's obligations. As they mature, businesses need to understand that they play a role in a larger, global context."[20]

Strategy must reflect and respect three basic inputs. First, the analysis of problems and opportunities that brings competitive advantage. Second, the critical variables that strengthen internal and external collaboration. And third, the growing obligations that justify any growth in power. Kaku notes: "Because multi-billion-dollar corporations control vast resources around the globe, employ millions of people, and create their own incredible wealth, they hold the future of the planet in their hands. Although governments and individuals need to do their part, they do not possess the same degree of wealth and power."[21] The exercise of power is automatically moral, whether we choose to see it or not. In strategies, companies can begin to condition their power to achieve results of justice as well as profits. This full use of strategy must be clear, to directors, CEO and staff. It must also be measured in results.

Open Culture

The concept of corporate culture is now very familiar, but what exactly is it? Some call it style. Others see it as attitude. Most definitions split culture from function, and even though the link between the two is underscored, the dichotomy between the concrete role of performance and the intangible role of culture is retained. This is a false division. Companies do not have cultures. They *are* cultures. Operations and competencies cannot be separated from the emotional and relational conditions prevalent within the organization. Car companies have learned this in relation to improving quality and deploying cross-functional teams. And IBM learned this in remaking itself from a hardware provider into a solutions specialist. The reason brands are so important is that customers no longer just buy what companies make but now relate to who companies are. The first major lesson, then, is that culture is strategic because without a culture there is no strategy.

Cultures change very slowly. Made up of history and experience, memory and expectation, cultures have the resiliency, even rigidity, of personality. Attempts to change corporate behaviors to master programs of quality, or high-value-added renewal, are often frustrated by culture. It is not that the logic of such change is unclear. It is that the receptivity is clouded by the biases and entrenchments of the organization. Culture is what happens in between the boxes of an organization chart. It is the white space on a process flow chart that ultimately determines whether the flow happens at all. Consultants may have cures for culture, but culture itself is latent with ethical possibilities by virtue of its nature as a context for interaction. Reduced to its essence, corporate culture equates to the quality and qualities of relationship. How people interact with each other within a company, and how they engage those outside the company, is culture in action. Any interaction between executive and employee, between workers and peers, between company and customer manifests cultural beliefs about the importance of relationships. The second lesson, then, is that, whether acknowledged or not, ethical orientation is already ingrained in every corporate culture because all cultures are merely the terms of relationship.

All companies have cultures, and all cultures involve an ethical orientation, but it does not follow that all companies are ethical. In some cultures, the ethical is denied, ignored or suppressed. Companies always on the edge of moral propriety, or those intentionally breaking social norms and laws, are not without ethics, but are more accurately cultures in which ethical obligations have intentionally been disconnected from business practice. This is an important distinction. The absence of an ethical code is not the natural condition for human relationships, so companies without them are consciously choosing to operate without their guidance. This heightens their culpability, and may indeed be why federal sentencing guidelines in the U.S. are so much more severe for companies without formal ethical norms than for those that have made the effort to encode them. The third important lesson about culture is that it is nonethical behavior that is unnatural and discretionary, involves conscious corporate choice and therefore holds the greater accountability (or culpability).

After differentiating between companies that do and those that do not have formal ethical codes, it is important to recognize that not all those that do have equally developed ethical cultures. Paine distinguishes between ethics strategies of compliance—those geared to not breaking any law or norm—and those of integrity—those geared to a deeper moral realization, fulfilling the spirit as well as the letter of the law. She explains: "An integrity-based approach to ethics management combines a concern for the law with an emphasis on managerial responsibility for ethical behavior." Strategies and cultures may vary, but "when integrated into the day-to-day operations of an organization, such strategies can help prevent damaging ethical lapses while tapping into powerful human impulses for moral thought and action. Then an ethical framework no longer becomes a burdensome constraint within which companies must operate, but the governing ethos of an organization."[22] The same lesson drawn earlier in relation to CEOs applies to companies as a whole. Ethical maturity for organizations provides the same benefits beyond morality that are available to ethically mature individuals. While not breaking the law or an ethical norm is a start, practicing ethical behavior in a more substantive and integral way builds exactly the competencies—like trust, conflict resolution and action within ambiguity—that are essential for business success in the global economy.

Orientation, as discussed earlier, represents a movement to growth. Not all individuals or companies are at the same stage of ethical maturity, but orientation is a commitment to keep developing toward wisdom. To more accurately reflect the gradations in that progression, I have modeled three stages or phases of ethical development: "Compliance," like Paine's definition, is ethics by reason of not getting caught; "Compromise" is ethics with a recognition that self-interest can also be advanced by adherence to a moral norm; and "Commitment" is ethics based on a wiser sense of beliefs and purpose. Below are some of the attributes for each stage in this model for organizational maturity:

Table 13. The Three Stages of Ethical Development

	Compliance	Compromise	Commitment
Motive	Avoid punishment	Advance self-interest	Express moral beliefs
Terms	Contract	Compact	Covenant
Impact	Minimum	Median	Maximum
Authority	The law	Marketing	The individual
Mechanism	Rules	Optics and rules	Responsibilities
Emotion	Fear	Confidence	Trust
Measurement	Statistics	Benefits	Innovations
Source	Top-down	Outside-in	Within
Maturity	Knowledge	Understanding	Wisdom

The recognition that cultures vary in ethical maturity is important, just like self-awareness and self-knowledge are critical for personal growth. As well, the understanding of progression dissuades companies from adopting, as many did for total quality or reengineering, some cookie-cutting mechanism for implanting an ethical consciousness. To have cogency and validity for a company, ethical values must be home-grown, developed from within its unique culture and not grafted on as some "best-practices" appendage.

Group Dynamics

Why would tobacco CEOs stand before the U.S. Congress and risk perjury, the ignominy of jail and the opprobrium of history to lie about the addictiveness and health dangers of smoking? The answer is that the code of the group is stronger than the code of law or code of morality. Groups invest their members with power, and that power is protected by the loyalty individuals give back to the group. The spell of this power and its web of relations makes the group the dynamic most inimical to a global ethic. Groups have many roles and vary greatly in their make-up, but all groups confer on their members some special-ness, some exclusivity for belonging. The global ethic challenges the specialness inherent in any group with an unexclusive expectation of equality for all. Groups thrive by being apart, whereas the global ethic recognizes any group, regardless of its power and status, as merely part of a larger interdependence.

The power of the group is not only formidable but enduring. Operating by their own code has given tobacco companies the forti-tude to fight long battles with governments, special interest groups and world public opinion. Groups construct their own principles, and sometimes those principles are lies: in the case of the tobacco companies it is the crusade to protect free speech and sell their legal product. Amazingly, such principles have cogency and are compelling to members of the group, even when the group's norms are by historical, social and religious norms heinous and indefensi-ble. So strong is this hold on the moral imagination of the group that defectors are made pariahs, even if defectors are right by society's moral standard. This was the group dynamic at play both when tobacco companies turned against Liggett & Brown after its agree-ment to cooperate with federal authorities investigating nicotine addiction and when Morton Thiokol fired the one engineer who objected to the group's decision to proceed with the ill-fated launch of the *Challenger* space shuttle. To the group, being loyal is more important than being right.

Companies tend to underestimate groups, which is why so many change initiatives and new strategies come to such inglorious ends. Executives also tend to underestimate the moral construct of such groups. In the corporate world, the prevailing assumption is that ethi-cal development is a personal capacity, best learned from family, school, religion and society. Companies recognize an obligation to follow the law, but consider ethical orientation more the domain of personal choice and responsibility. This means that for most managers, corpo-rate groups function as a composite of individuals, each guided and held in check by their own personal code, and in total, guiding and holding in check the group as a whole. When something goes wrong, someone like Nick Leeson is sought out for blame. The group usually remains intact and largely unrepentant because, in being regarded as a morally neutral entity, any immorality is just an aberration—an abuse or manipulation or deception by an errant individual. As we have seen with ADM, and even GE with its repeated ethical offenses, corporate moral mistakes are judged to be mostly a case of individual bad apples rather than a spoilt basket.

Individuals do indeed commit the crimes, but the group dynamic is more than just a backdrop, and often facilitates, reinforces or even encourages people to step over the moral and legal line. Groups are organized for functionality, as what Selznick calls "a special-purpose tool, a rational instrument engineered to do a job, a lean, no-nonsense system of consciously coordinated activities."[23] But groups involve human interactions as well as functional tasks, so values, issues of identity and belonging, and symbols of power are all rolled into their make-up. Groups have a life of their own that sometimes expresses itself beyond the beliefs and general orientation of its members, and even beyond the expectations and rules of the larger community that instituted it. The FBI under J. Edgar Hoover became a law unto itself, beyond the laws of the government institutions that had created it in the first place to safeguard the rule of law. Unruliness is commonplace in business as well, with groups within companies often sabotaging the strategic goals of their own management and shareholders. Change consultants call this a resistance to change, but it goes deeper. One of my clients explained that employees regarded a new management team as short-term turn-around artists. Some workers were intentionally thwarting new programs in the belief that the measures were wrong for the company and that "loyal, long-term" employees would have to pick up the pieces after the leadership moved on to the next turn-around target.

Groups create and operate to their own standard. History has shown that groups magnify exponentially the human capacity for both good and evil. There is indeed a fearsome power in numbers, but more than sheer quantity is at play. The group provides an identity, an anchor, that takes on more and more importance in times of great difficulty and transition. The more threatening the external reality, the more assuring and comforting is membership in the group. Much of the reaction to the uncertainty and change of the global economy has been the retreat noted by Huntington and others to a tribal, religious or nationalist group and subgroup. Identity with group provides a barrier against the foreign or unknown. It also provides a barrier as a mask for its members. Behind this mask of groupthink and groupface, individuals have the assurance of belonging but with a degree of anonymity and invisibility. By belonging, persons are emboldened, but by their lack of visibility, they are also freer from direct personal liability for their actions. It is this mix of group-inspired boldness without personal consequence that makes teams dangerously irresponsible.

The exclusivity and self-perpetuation of group decision making is one reason the world and its economy now need a global ethic. How can groups be engaged to include a commitment to global values that are embracive, thus depreciating the very privilege of belonging to a group? How can an institution structured for amassing power be reformed to appreciate the obligations and discretion that go with that power? There are two pre-change (pre-ethic) prerequisites. Emile Durkheim noted: "A society is not simply the mass of individuals that incorporate it, nor the territory it occupies, nor the things it uses, nor the movements it carries out, but above all it is the idea that it has of itself."[24] Groups tend to define themselves by function and to follow norms that set high professional standards. The idea of the group must be challenged to understand its purpose and power beyond its function.

A second precondition for changing meaningful values is to recast the group's fundamental motivation. This is the real job of management, to influence constructive change without the alienation and discouragement of having imposed it. Most companies and managers use what social scientists call extrinsic motivation to promote legal and ethical behaviors. These tend to be the rational and physical rewards of corporate performance. Rosabeth Moss Kanter notes that such "extrinsic motivation often produces compliance with the rules, followed by attempts to get around them and a shift of behavior if the rules change." Extrinsic changes the externals, but not the internal idea the group has of itself, so old beliefs eventually undermine the new goals. Kanter argues for "intrinsic motivation," which asks employees to do what is right because, in addition to producing higher performance, it also "creates goodwill in the marketplace and community, or is the right thing to do based on societal or individual values."[25] The way to transform a group is to engage and connect to the larger reality around it. In other words, companies and groups become good when the opportunity to do good is made available to them. Instead of deflating the idea of the group, a global ethic may well provide the purpose and values for revitalizing and preserving their diversity. Groups operate on the premise that there is power in numbers, and that may well confirm the inevitability of a global ethic, since there is no bigger number, and therefore no bigger power, than everyone.

After fifteen years of repeated programs of change, most managers understand that renewing organizations without attending to corporate culture is impossible. Strategy provides the rationale, but culture fuels the motivation. Lewis Platt, CEO of Hewlett-Packard, is famous for repeating in every possible employee forum that the key to H-P's success is its flexibility to change business and its commitment to *not* change values. That said, most companies suffer an enormous gap in their cultures that has attracted little commentary and less attention. Culture, fostered by senior management, and inherited from history, is an almost exclusively masculine construct. Even in its most expansive expressions of "teamwork," and even in the newly learned egalitarianism of "win/win," corporate cultures remain primarily male cultures. Many companies have adopted hiring practices and family policies that are more respectful of women, but these companies are a minority. A few companies have senior female executives, but these too are far from the norm. Indeed, it is the conspicuous absence of women CEOs that confirms business to be a cosmetically neutral but essentially masculine institution.

There has been some progress in addressing the gender imbalance. And women are recasting the tone of business, albeit slowly. One big change is that many women, frustrated by the inflexibility of most corporate environments, have chosen to go into business for themselves. This means that much of the feminization of business—the incorporation of feminine values within practices and cultures—is happening primarily at the periphery of the economy. Another change relates to the widening appreciation within the business community of "emotional intelligence," or "emotional IQ." Prodded by companies like British Airways, managers in most industries now consider relationships with customers as part of their business planning and performance measures. One study of eight thousand workers showed that both employers and employees acknowledged this priority and were adapting training and skills to this new reality. In that study, men emerged as more confident in problem solving, and women more confident in "relating."[26] Men and women obviously share these attributes, but the differences in development are also clear. Companies that want to improve relationship skills need to develop the listening, empathy and openness that tend to be feminine characteristics, or at least characteristics of the feminine side of human nature that psychology pioneer Carl Jung referred to as the "anima."

The feminization of business has only begun to feminize business ethics. Academics Gerald Cavanagh, Dennis Moberg and Manuel Velasquez have been studying business ethics for almost twenty years. In 1981, they introduced a model for business ethics based on bringing scrutiny to a decision or action's "Utility," implications for "Rights and duties" and on its impact on "Justice." In 1995, the "URJ Model" was updated to include the rich lessons drawn from feminist moral theory and discourse. They note: "Although there are significant dangers in generalizing about feminist ethics, one important claim underlying much of this sub-field is the view that traditional moral theory has been dominated by a male perspective that has given women's moral concerns no voice. In particular, while traditional ethics has centered on impartial moral principles, feminist ethicists have emphasized the importance of partiality based on caring."[27] While the male moral model focuses on rules, rational analysis and independent accountability, the female moral model emphasizes relationships, emotional attachment and interdependence. Ethicist Nel Noddings describes this as the difference between talking ethics in the language of the father or in the language of the mother.[28] Both are valid, but the two integrated into a more comprehensive scheme for life are better and personally more fulfilling than any one approach alone.

Caring is not one "virtue" but is itself a more fundamental "orientation." In fact, caring works both ways—as an impulse driving us to be ethical as well as an expression of our commitment to be moral. Caring thus precedes ethics but also is its outcome. We encountered in an earlier chapter Bonhoeffer's warning that duty alone limits the involvement and responsibility of the individual practicing it. With caring, principle can never be abstracted or left to a rigid implementation that overrides the emotional participation and moral commitment of the person involved. In the case of business, traditional ethics represent a benchmark, the standard for performance, while caring represents the personal excellence—the actual participation in relationships—for realizing that performance. In the case of this example, caring is the ingredient to foster within corporate cultures to place a positive emphasis on building relationships while building resistance to treating any individual person as only a means to an end. "Caring behavior," note Cavanagh, Moberg and Velasquez, "is often at the core of solutions to contemporary business issues. Good personal relationships, better communications, teamwork and trust are commonly viewed as essential for a business firm to be competitive. These elements can be better evaluated through an ethical norm of caring."[29]

One of the reasons a Global Ethic is so timely is that business structures are evolving from functional to relational. *What* is done, produced or sold is no longer the only or most important source of value. Increasingly, the value to customers and to companies is achieved in the *how*. The tone of service, the attitude toward learning and the cooperation between people in problem solving are more and more the true sources of competitiveness. This seems like an enlightened realization of the information age, but, as Arie de Geus showed in his study of long-enduring companies, it is actually the most basic of management principles. Now retired, de Geus spent his career at Royal/Dutch Shell and as a teacher at the London Business School. After studying the records and characteristics of twenty-seven companies, among them DuPont, Mitsui, the Hudson's Bay Company and Kodak—organizations that had survived and evolved for over a century, and in some cases seven centuries—de Geus concluded that these organizations "have a personality that allows them to evolve harmoniously."[30] Having survived several generations of technological revolution and management theory, these highly successful companies are proof that it is the human and relational variables that provide both longevity and results.

Calling these adaptive survivors "living companies," de Geus provides some of the lessons they hold for managers. The key is to recognize stewardship, the responsibility to pass along the company or function with the same opportunities and potential that had been inherited. "To do that," writes de Geus, "a manager must let people grow within a community that is held together by clearly shared values. The manager, therefore, must place commitment to people before assets, respect for innovation before devotion to policy, the messiness of learning before orderly procedures, and the perpetuation of the community before all other concerns."[31] The average corporation operates with reverse priorities, especially in usually putting the needs of assets before those of people. The penalty for this short-sighted reversal is dramatically shortened survival. De Geus's study shows that the average company has a lifespan of less than twenty years. Between 1970 and 1983, fully one-third of the Fortune 500 companies ceased to exist, most subsumed by merger, or reconfigured by acquisition, or dismembered in liquidation. Profits are a lot like ice cream. Rich, tasty and particularly satisfying as a treat or reward. But without moderation, a diet of mostly ice cream clogs the instincts of responsiveness and is even potentially lethal.

A global ethic starts with principle but comes to life with the practice of its key symmetry. Putting people ahead of assets initiates the reciprocity that supports a larger trust building between employees and the company, among employees themselves, and between the company and its customers, suppliers and communities. Trustworthiness deepens in parallel with a deepening ethical orientation. Like a virtue that is practiced and delivered by an individual and becomes a feature of that person's character, trust once earned and reinforced becomes a dynamic of reputation, quality, pricing, new products and overall corporate performance. "Trust is the heart of the matter," writes Charles Handy. "That seems obvious and trite, yet most organizations tend to be arranged on the assumption that people cannot be trusted or relied on, even in tiny matters."[32] So, when Canadians complain about high bank profits, or Americans decry CEO salaries, implicit in these criticisms are a mistrust about intention, about the proportion between reward and risk. People are not saying, "We don't like the numbers"; they are saying, "We don't trust you."

Handy explores the issue of trust from the perspective of the virtual organization. With outsourcing and intranets, this mode of collaborative working to solve problems, engineer products and deliver services is now standard. However, the advantages of this approach are not just systematic but, most importantly, relational. "If we are to enjoy the efficiencies and benefits of the virtual organization," Handy writes, "we will have to rediscover how to run organizations based more on trust than control."[33] Trust works the same way in business that it does in our personal lives. Trust grows only in human interaction, so the people involved must be experienced and known, never abstracted. Trust also works within boundaries, defined and contained by rules and expectations. Open-ended trust is the foolhardy opposite of zero trust. Trust is not really needed in stability, but it is incredibly valuable in situations of uncertainty or change. People then must be focused on learning, having the intelligence, skills and confidence to address constant change. This is very difficult, and not everyone can rise to the demands of trust. In this way, in not tolerating the untrustworthy, trust must be acknowledged as "tough" and managed with "toughness." Trust comes to life when people bond, when they share an experience, crisis or success that strengthens links and confirms expectations of each other. Trust also requires what Handy calls touch—human interaction around human issues. Those of us that have run companies or consulted to companies in times of change know that the real commitment to new strategies or programs is forged in the hallways and around water coolers. Finally, trust grows from trusting and trust-inspiring leaders.

An ethical orientation feeds the growth of trust, and is itself further developed by trust. Dignity extended to employees and customers by the company creates the foundation for trust to be exchanged. Honesty, fairness and justice set the terms of interaction, and provide the integrity that earns trust in even unpredictable and ambiguous situations. And sustainability demonstrates the commitment to our shared natural environments that warrants trust for the long term. Conversely, unethical or amoral behavior completely undermines trust. Self-interest invites self-protection. Dishonesty erodes credibility. Unfairness invites a reciprocal exploitation. Injustice displaces trust with cynicism. And environmental profligacy suggests a wider irresponsibility. A commitment to trust, essential in this economy of intellectual exchange, is therefore inextricably a commitment to ethics. And an ethical orientation, by practice, builds trust.

The Individual

All ethical discourse is premised on choice, between good and bad, right and wrong, constructive and destructive, moral and immoral, holy and evil. But life is rarely so categorical. Most decisions and actions involve more complex discerning, trading off and compromising to arrive at the better of two imperfect goods, or the lesser of two bedevilling evils. It seems as though, in another time, ethics were a much easier concept to deal with because they represented the absolute guidance from a universal source. But in fact, just as today, ethics have always been about two steps behind reality.

The tension between ethics and reality is not new but a fundamental part of the ethical process. As an answer, ethical theory is always just behind new questions, and subsequent questions and new issues often surpass the assuring guidance of current ethical norms. As Joseph Des Jardins notes in his essay "Virtues and Corporate Responsibility," "No ethical principle has been shown to be categorically binding on all rational agents; that despite the ideal of unambiguous practical advice, principles seldom offer any determinate and clear prescriptions; and that principles often leave an unbridgeable motivational gap between judgment and action."[34] This though is not a defeat of the ethical. Ethics are in flux because life and human society are in continuous change. This churning affects personal human dignity and community well-being, so although ethics may not provide all the instant answers, the ethical process itself is necessary if we are to rediscover the workable equilibrium within the uncertainty. Once regarded as a compass pointing out true good with the inexorable pull of magnetic north, ethics actually work much harder but less precisely—more like a gyroscope that keeps rebalancing and centering individuals in situations of confusion, conflict and morality. Not a fixed and final point, ethics are instead a journey. Not an edict, ethics are instead a dynamic orientation.

While the principles may be given expression by the community, ethics remain inescapably personal. Classic philosophers such as Plato, Aquinas and Kant, as well as such contemporary philosophers as Alasdair MacIntyre, who has sought to renew the relevance of virtue, stress that the ethical is historical, that it works not as a theory but as a practice, and that it involves personal choices by individual persons in the real, concrete demands of life. More than just a norm, the ethical represents a process of growth through the intellectual, emotional and spiritual struggle to make personal life and community history the best that it can be. "Responsibility," Selznick reminds us, "is something more than accountability." It involves integrity, living with the "wholeness and soundness" that "respects the autonomy and plurality of persons and institutions."[35] The ethical is therefore necessary for society to harmonize the unpredictable demands of unexpected conflicts and for the individual's personal maturity with which that complicated life with its irregular relationships can be fully engaged.

What does all this have to do with business? First, directors on the board, CEOs and members of various corporate groups and subgroups are human beings before, during and after their career, professional standing and roles. To belong to one stratum or special group does not abnegate membership in the broader human community, nor does it dissolve for individuals the rights and obligations that go with being human. Unless we practice ethics personally, as conscious discerning individuals, there are no ethics. John Macmurray distinguished between individual life and social life, and what he called personal life. This "is the life which we live as persons, and we can only live it by entering into relationships with other people on a fully personal basis, in which we give ourselves to one another; or, to put the same thing the other way round, in which we accept one another freely for what we are, and in which therefore there is and can be no purpose other than the sharing of our lives in fellowship. The impulse to do this is simply the

impulse to be ourselves fully."[36] Humans are constituted to be in relation, and the natural progress to personal maturity inevitably involves
deeper engagement, realization and mutuality in relation. An ethical
orientation is therefore not a discretionary capacity but a fundamental
and defining part of being human.

Integrity Through Integration

Lessons in Ethical Alignment from Hewlett-Packard

Do the small things well. Hewlett-Packard's ethics start with how
it perceives its people and how it hires, trains and treats them in the
day-to-day tumble of business. Small acts of decency that prove the
company's principles of fairness build an environment of respect that
eventually sets its own ethical expectations and monitors its own
ethical compliance. H-P legal counsel Hal Michaelson believes that
founders David Hewlett and Bill Packard would be upset if the
company needed to formalize a function like a chief ethics officer.
"We don't have an ethics guru," explains Michaelson, "because our
CEO is responsible for ethics overall, and all of us who work here
are expected to solve problems responsibly ourselves."[37]

**Act with the understanding that culture is more important
than systems**. H-P has a formal ethics policy in use around the
world, plus the usual training and video supports to communicate
expectations and develop competency among its employees. More
important than this formal program is the culture that values new
ideas, does not try to impose one solution on everyone and operates
first and foremost with respect for people. Recognizing the importance of senior input on culture, H-P not only has a board committee auditing ethical compliance but "trains" the board to scrutinize
decisions from the perspective of H-P's ethical tradition.

Respect history but make history. The spirit and sense of social responsibility of H-P's founders lives on well beyond their managerial tenure. Words spoken years ago by Hewlett or Packard, or examples from their own actions, are used as reference points for modern-day decisions. But the process is not merely that of preserving tradition. New managers create H-P's ethical tradition every day. This is critically important because ethics are relevant if they are dynamic, formulated and expressed not out of some traditional respect for principle but from an active belief that the principle makes a difference today and in the future.

Do not pretend to have all the answers. An ethics code cannot anticipate every exigency. And rules too rigidly applied only thwart the human development of a more creative understanding of ethics. At H-P, rules are made, but they are also open to adjustment and flexible reconstitution. For example, Michaelson notes that H-P instituted a "no gifts" policy for H-P employees. In Asia, such intractability proved offensive to some customers and suppliers. This policy was then revised to "No gifts over $100." This too proved unworkable, as employees embarrassingly tried to assess the worth of a proffered gift before deciding whether to accept it. Finally, H-P created a norm that allowed managers discretion about which gifts were appropriate. All such gifts are now received by the company and once a year auctioned off for charities.

The judgment of the company is only as good as the judgment of the individual. People matter more than policies. The best way to get people to respect the law and respect the ethical code of the company is first to be respectful to them. Working in different cultures requires vigilance to make everyone aware of the H-P way. But the company sees diversity not only as an accommodation of differences but as the opportunity to learn and benefit from those differences. H-P invested in special training for its employees in Eastern Europe to untangle some of the historic and behavioral patterns that were rooted in the corruption of the communist system and introduce Western management practices and norms. But H-P also imports new ideas, as when it adopted the flexible-hour work style of its German plants to the whole international company.

Mistakes are inevitable. Ethics are not about perfection, but about commitment and learning. An ethical company, like an ethical person, will make some mistakes. The key is the totality of conduct, the intention and the overall orientation displayed over time by words and actions.

Profitability is imperative, but equally so is character. For Hewlett-Packard, profit is not any less important than it is for other companies. It is critically so. The difference is that the importance accorded profitability is equally applied to its moral responsibilities. The impact of holding both priorities in equal importance is that they ultimately support one another. "All these ethical considerations," says Michaelson, "make us money. Our principles are important to our customers and partners. Any impropriety risks that long-term loyalty. We all try to make sure that short-term maximization [of returns] does not interfere with the cooperation we need for ventures in the future."

CHAPTER NINE

PRAXIS

*The attempt to define that which is good once and for all has, in the
nature of the case, always ended in failure. Either the proposition
was asserted in such general and formal terms that it retained no
significance as regards its contents, or else one tried to include in it
and elaborate the whole immense range of conceivable contents, and
thus to say in advance what would be good in every single conceivable case; this led to a casuistic system, so unimaginable that it could
satisfy the demands neither of general validity nor of concreteness.*

Dietrich Bonhoeffer, "The Concrete Place," *in* Ethics

Just like wisdom, an ethical orientation is not a theory, not simply a
formulation of ideals, but a practice undertaken with understanding.
Management, especially under pressure, seeks understanding in short-
hand. For any problem or system issue, businesspeople are hungry for
models that explain the dynamics and offer a simple, standardized,
repeatable and consistent solution. Thus, there are fourteen steps for
quality, seven principles for leadership, squares modeling strategic
development and circles demonstrating business ecosystems. Impatient
for results, executives want workable models that have worked in other

places to apply to what are assumed to be similar situations in their own companies. There is of course much to learn by exploring the experiences of others, and there is a rich validity to many of these grids, schemas and checklists. Nevertheless, most companies have found that the solution that worked brilliantly for GE or Xerox or Wal-Mart usually works only partially, or only for a short time, or not at all when applied to their own company, culture and circumstances. To borrow a solution from another company simply does not provide the depth of learning that comes from originating a solution from within. And to buy in to a model constructed elsewhere fails to exercise the native problem-solving creativity that is ultimately needed to derive the full benefit from any solution. "Paint by numbers" management is increasingly understood to be not management at all.

A global ethic for the global economy provides a framework for morally responsible business habits, but the day-to-day practice requires customization and nurturing highly specific, highly personal competencies. Although all companies may subscribe to a global ethic, the terms of participation will vary according to the conditions confronting that particular organization and its own maturity, confidence and culture. Consider the United Nations Charter of Rights. Written in 1948, this document encoded the principles of human dignity that were largely derived from the institutions, constitutions and charters of the democracies that had defeated fascism in the Second World War. The majority of the world's nations, involving countless other social and political traditions, did not necessarily have the same mores regarding the value and potential of an individual person. At various speeds and to varying degrees of commitment, the appreciation of, and aspiration to, these human rights has grown around the world. Most countries now include the principles of human rights in their own charters and constitutions. These are highly varied in their structure, expression and practice, but the point is that there is an orientation, an inexorable progress, toward fulfilling the intent of the UN Charter. That it is an irregular progress, that some of it is more cosmetic than substantial, and that it is not a universal, does not diminish the truth or benefits of that continuous achievement since 1948.

Similarly, companies that adopt a global ethic are subscribing to an aspiration that will tolerate and require endless variety in practice. Küng makes two critical points in this regard. First, he reminds us of the reality that "as in the question of human rights or ecology, or peace and disarmament, and the partnership of men and women, this [global ethic] will happen in a very complex and long-drawn-out process of change in consciousness."[1] There is an urgency to assume responsibility, an urgency that grows with environmental degradation and social displacement, but it is a responsibility that each individual, group and company must fashion, define and assume for itself. If this seems unreasonable, we need only review the spread of environmental consciousness, which within a generation has gone from the radical fringe to the global mainstream. This evolution is neither easy nor automatic, but it represents a new, learned habituation that is still growing in momentum and influence. Küng's second point is that "a global ethic does not mean a new global ideology, or even an attempt to arrive at one uniform religion. The call for a global ethic does not aim to replace the supreme ethical demands of each individual religion with an ethical minimalism; it is not meant to take the place of the Torah, the Sermon on the Mount, the Qur'an, the Bhagavadgita, the Discourses of the Buddha or the Sayings of Confucius." In corporate terms, this means that a global ethic is not a replacement for strategy or culture but a consciousness that is integrated into the company to affect both. The goal is not a single, standardized conformity, but a deepening of the awareness, and a widening of the corporate habit, for ethical consideration and accountability.

Although infinitely variable in its expression, a global ethic is neither random nor ad hoc. Yet, like strategic planning, there are also some common steps or stages. While the final expression of a global ethic will necessarily be unique, relevant to the specific reality of a specific company, the common steps arise as responses to some basic, inescapable questions.

Table 14. Ethical Orientation Process

Process Step	Central Question
Ethical Assessment	What "ethical temptations" challenge an ethical orientation?
Critical Ethical Factors	What are the "critical ethical factors" for successfully maintaining an ethical orientation?
Corporate Ethical Virtues	What skills, procedures and competencies are necessary for resisting temptations and deepening an ethical orientation?
Ethically Oriented Strategy	What is the ethical expression of the business strategy that integrates an ethical orientation?
Ethically Oriented Plan	What are the concrete steps for implementing and measuring an ethical orientation?

An Ethical Assessment: Resisting Temptations

As noted earlier by Gary Edwards, president of the Ethics Resource Center, two-thirds of companies seeking ethical programs "came off the front page as a result of serious wrong-doing."[2] This suggests that ethics are largely a tactical response to a problem, rather than a strategic commitment to a more enduring opportunity and obligation. From this perspective, most ethical initiatives aim to avoid repeating the mistakes that caused that particular crisis. Texaco blundered on race, and structured programs for racial equality. Nike stumbled on sweatshop management, and hired a former U.S. ambassador to the UN to audit its operations. But this ethical renewal is one situation where the rifle-shot approach is clearly not enough. Codes and procedures targeted to an impropriety may highlight the specifics of one problem, and usually assign blame to one individual, but without addressing the wider cultural, competitive and personal factors that contributed to it. At

Texaco, race is but one expression of a more problematic managerial arrogance. At Nike, sweatshops are but one issue of its maturing from rebel upstart to a more responsible multibillion-dollar multinational. The point is that ethics as a reflex are never as comprehensive or as motivating as the thinking and commitment applied to ethics as a pre-emption. That so many companies are repeat offenders is directly due to the narrowness of seeing ethics in relation to a one-time problem rather than in the context of the whole operation.

Companies hire smart people but do not leave them only to their wits to manage. Organizations expect strategies to be planned, analyses to precede decisions, and measures to be put in place to monitor progress and results. Smart companies, as learning organizations, also invest consistently in training and skills development. An ethical orientation involves the same disciplines. In addition to understanding the dynamics that contributed to an error of ethical judgment, organizations need to explore the deeper tensions and contradictions that may put ethics at risk in the future. Just as strategy requires a situation analysis, ethics requires a temptation analysis. What moral and legal issues have raised ethical concern in the past? How are these changing and testing the behavior of the company and its individual employees? What are new pressure points, created by changes in technology or competition or globalization? How do corporate behaviors and policies influence the perception of those ethical conundrums? The process here is one of scanning the horizon with an ethical perspective, of expecting new confusions and temptations and of anticipating risk.

Central to this exercise is understanding not only the scope and scale of temptation but also the moral strengths and weaknesses of the company for withstanding and overcoming them. This may involve an audit of past ethical performance, an analysis of transgressions or near-misses or an evaluation of the ethical concerns of employees. Bell Atlantic reports having had more than nine thousand calls a year on its ethics hot-line. An assessment asks: What are the nature of those calls? What are the common concerns or pressure points behind them? What are the key lessons behind the intervention of an ethics officer or ombudsman? What do customer and employee surveys reveal to be priorities or problems that affect ethics? How well developed are the company's awareness, sensibility and confidence for dealing with new ethical issues and challenges? New strategies, competitive innovations or technologies may change either the ethical problem or the ethical competency for dealing with it. The Internet, as an example, provides much more intimate access to customers, but it also raises new issues of privacy and respect. So, in using this new medium, are the company's ethical skills maturing in concert with its technical competencies? What customer "ethical hot-buttons" are emerging from this more personal involvement? And how well equipped is the company for dealing constructively with the new temptations afforded by the new technology?

As with strategy, the objective is not to compile a laundry list but to explore new possibilities, problems and opportunities in order to discern patterns and establish priorities. What ethical issue is central to the strategy? What ethical principle is put at risk by the strategy? What ethical competency is to be tested or developed to best fulfill the strategy? The key is to see the ethical and the strategic as connected, simultaneous and mutually indispensable, as opposed to separate, sequential and discretionary. Bonhoeffer wrote that ethics must strike a balance between general validity and concreteness. This means approaching them not as fixed and irrevocable principles, nor as a definitive checklist for every eventuality, but as living ethics that are given expression by questioning, and that are worked to completion through personal involvement and creativity. A strategic assessment sets the course for *what* must be done. An ethical assessment investigates the *how*. As we have learned from total quality and other programs of corporate renewal, the *what* and *how* can no longer be separated.

Critical Ethical Factors

Rather than being premised on practicing what is preached, business ethics are mostly a function of practicing what is presumed. Various studies, including that of the Ethical Resource Center, show that even among companies with established codes of conduct, employees often break rules, laws or ethical norms without much remorse simply because they believe in their heart that their illicit behavior is sanctioned by the company or the group they operate within. Saul W. Gellerman studied three famous ethics cases from the 1980s, the decades-long silence of Manville executives about the health and death threat posed by asbestos, the clearly ruinous loan practices at Continental Illinois Bank and the fraudulent billing practices at E.F. Hutton that "bilked" millions from more than four hundred banks. In each case, there emerged to varying degrees four presumptions, or what Gellerman calls rationalizations:

1. "A belief that the activity is within reasonable ethical and legal limits—that is, that it is not 'really' illegal or immoral."
2. "A belief that the activity is in the individuals' or corporation's best interests—that the individual would somehow be expected to undertake the activity."
3. "A belief that the activity is 'safe' because it will never be found out or publicized: the classic crime-punishment issue of discovery."
4. "A belief that because the activity helps the company the company will condone it and even protect the person who engages in it."[3]

All of these rationalizations involve presumptions: "It's not really a crime anyway"; "It may be technically wrong but everyone else does it"; "It may be wrong but if I don't do it someone else will"; "No one will ever know, so it doesn't make any difference;" "In these circumstances it may be wrong but the company expects me to do it"; and "In these circumstances it may be wrong but the company will back me up anyway." On one level there is a recognition of rules, norms and laws. On another level are the perceptions and reinforcement for breaking those rules. Most ethical programs address recognition without delving into the perceptions. Policies and structures are put in place to make awareness of rules, norms and laws more direct, but without necessarily piercing the presumptions that supported the deviant behavior in the first place.

The process of defining a company or group's critical ethical factors operates at this level of presumption. By asking analytical questions (What are the real drivers for this business? What are the expectations directed toward employees? Which are the behaviors that are rewarded and reinforced? What historical biases in attitude or countenance are in place? How deep and how wide is the understanding of the organizational ethical orientation?) people can begin to discern the most essential ethical attribute or dimension for a given company at a specific time. This analytical process for ethics again mirrors that for strategy. It requires going beyond the basic, most obvious definitions and seeking the deeper motivations and interactions upon which success and ethical integrity are based. Peter Drucker is famous for asking managers to think beyond the functional and see the relationships that are essential for business. "In 1989 C. William Pollard, chairman of ServiceMaster Co., took his board of directors from Chicago to meet Drucker. In a back room of Drucker's utterly unpretentious home, the sage of Claremont opened the meeting by asking the group, 'Can you tell me what your business is?' Each director gave a different answer. Housecleaning, said one. Insect extermination, said another. Lawn care, said a third. 'You're all wrong,' Drucker said. 'Gentlemen, you do not understand your business. Your business is to train the least skilled people and make them functional.' "[4]

Drucker's point is that in this instance it is not the task or the system that creates value and provides a point of difference but rather the skill, confidence and ability to learn of employees. Hence, the business of management is not just functional expertise around manufacturing or distribution, but in recruiting, training and motivating personnel. The revolution in information technology and "intellectual capital" are adding important dynamics to this redefinition of basic business. When senior executives move from one company to another, they carry in their expertise and experience a huge chunk of the knowledge and skills developed at the company they are leaving. In some cases, people on the move take documents, strategic models, new manufacturing plans and even working prototypes of new products with them. This is what happened when hard-nosed purchasing chief Ignazio Lopez left General Motors for Volkswagen. Pilfering confidential documents is clearly an ethical violation. Less obvious in the prolonged fight between GM and Volkswagen is the recognition that the value engineered into products is not simply in the physical manufacturing and performance characteristics of products but in the knowledge, intelligence and creativity of employees. Since individuals are the primary source of value, the critical managerial competence in this knowledge economy is relational. And since success is determined by the interactions of people, competitiveness is thus dependent on the ethical.

In cars, the business is manufacturing transportation, the core competency is quality, and the critical factors for success are the internal teamwork, training and supplier coordination that contribute to that quality. The same deepening, the same recognition of more subtle influences and implicit motivations, applies to ethics. For media and news information companies, the ethical imperative is to create trustworthiness. The core competency is thus honesty, and the critical ethical factors, or CEFs, are the unique combination of skills and attitudes essential for a specific company in particular circumstances to fulfill that honesty. For CNN, with its propensity for instant news, the CEFs may be "substantiation" and "reflection." For the *Wall Street Journal,* the CEF necessary to counterweight its widespread use of corporate press releases may be "transparency" of attribution. And for ideologically oriented papers like those of Rupert Murdoch and Conrad Black, the CEF may be "fair accessibility" and "inclusion."

A global ethic asks that all its principles be attended to without exception, but the CEF acknowledges that life is never so regular or predictable. As a result of circumstance, situation or need, one or two ethical attributes may assume greater relevance and importance for an organization or individual. Determining the critical ethical factors requires burrowing beneath the obvious to get at the pressures, presumptions and inconsistencies that plague ethical performance. What, then, are the organizational biases toward ethical conduct? What are the gaps between statement and action? What are the insights and lessons that must be absorbed for individuals to assume full responsibility for ethical integrity? What are the corporate attributes and characteristics that are needed, or missing, or in place and in need of amplification, for realizing a growing ethical understanding and compliance? And finally, what are the preconditions or prerequisites for corporate ethical development? As Gellerman notes, "The point is to prevent misconduct, not just to catch it."[5] Critical ethical factors provide one tool for working back from effect to cause to achieve just such prevention.

Corporate Ethical Virtues

Historically, ethics have been preoccupied both with outcome (Is a decision or action good or bad?) *and* with character (Is the individual or organization responsible for that decision or action good or bad?). The study of outcome tends to focus on ethical norms. The study of character instead tends to define the virtues—the habits of behavior—that are necessary for satisfying that norm. Aristotle provided the classical definition of virtue as acting "appropriately, or well, or successfully in any given circumstance" in reference to "the *teleos* or goal of action," which for him meant "human flourishing." But, as Cambridge management professor Jane Collier explains, since the eighteenth century "ethics has concentrated exclusively on deriving criteria of right action."[6] Bolstered by belief in the rational, ethics have focused on the universal norms for what is "right" through the discernment of logic and the conclusions of observation. In another presumption of rationality, other motivations, characteristics and emotions of the individuals and organizations that exercise choice were assumed to be secondary and ultimately malleable to rational argument.

As discussed, the Holocaust interrupted the veneration of the rational and all too tragically showed the limitations of focusing only on a logically deduced "right." Two Oxford philosophers, Elizabeth Anscombe and Alasdair MacIntyre, have since the mid-twentieth century shifted the study of ethics, in Anscombe's case from a focus on what is "right" to what is "good," and in MacIntyre's case from an exclusive preoccupation on "norms" to a more balanced interaction between norm and personal character or "virtue." It is the balance and interaction between norm and virtue that is key. Too strict adherence to norm alone produces an unthinking, impersonal and potentially immoral conformance to duty. This is what Bonhoeffer noted in the

Germany of the 1930s: "In this confinement within the limits of duty there can never come the bold stroke of the deed which is done on one's own free responsibility, the only kind of deed which can strike at the heart of evil and overcome it." Bonhoeffer added the warning that "the man of duty will end by having to fulfill his obligation even to the devil."[7] To be ethical involves an orientation to what is "good," both in recognizing and respecting its norms, and in development of the virtues or characteristics that advance that good.

The modern concept of virtues has largely been reduced to cartoon-character qualities like courage and crime fighting. Virtues, though, are both simpler and subtler, what Collier calls "dispositions or tendencies to act in a certain way in certain circumstances."[8] Decisions and actions come and go, so the relevance of ethical norms is in a sense transitory or situational. Character, though, is a constant—who we are is fundamentally the same regardless of the situations we confront. Virtues are those habits of character that precondition our response toward what is right, good and ethical. As Collier explains, virtues represent a latent power. Virtues are not inherited or automatically downloaded as some cultural DNA. People become virtuous only through the practice of virtue. Charles Hampden Turner calls this a cybernetic loop, in which "virtues are acquired by practice and strengthened by habit, so that the contribution of virtue to action becomes continually more powerful."[9] Companies that slip into unethical behavior are violating a norm, and most of the remedial actions that organizations take are to advertise those norms, entrench their importance and clarify the penalties of nonconformance. This, though, addresses only half of the equation laid out by MacIntyre. Unethical decisions and actions not only are a violation of norm but tangibly represent the neglect, or suppression, or underdevelopment of a virtue or virtues. So the "disposition" of the corporation—involving both its culture and character—must be attended to as rigorously as the norm set for it.

Virtue is also important because its opposite is vice. Companies have habits—predilections and biases of attitude and action that are derived from history, competitive situation, corporate culture and leadership example. If those habits are not attuned to what is right and good, chances are that they will not remain neutral but regress to that impulse for advantage at all costs that may include deliberate exploitation and evildoing. The price fixing at ADM, the inflation of military billing at GE and the payoffs to criminal extortionists at Nomura were not one-time aberrations but longtime habits. These negative practices, not necessarily sanctioned by senior management, nevertheless represent consistent tendencies to abuse the rules, and are examples of corporate vices. To ignore corporate virtue is therefore to invite its antithesis.

This raises several questions. First, is it even possible for organizations to have "virtue"? Companies are composed of people, but they also have purpose, methods and style that stand apart and operate independently of the aggregate. Companies make plans and take decisions, and they continue to act toward those plans even when personnel and management changes. As Collier notes, company "identity is not exhausted by the identity of persons." Purpose and goals reflect choices that have weighted pros and cons, optimization and minimization, success and failure. All these weightings involve a sensibility of value and implication, of choice and consequence. Indeed, there can be no planning, no expectation of results, without such evaluation. This intentionality and independence of thought and action are exactly what warrants ethical scrutiny and legitimizes the expectation of corporate virtue. J.E. Garrett explains: "Corporations are moral agents because the reciprocal adjustment of individual intentions and plans that takes place in such organizations yields a corporate intentionality that is more like human intentionality than it is like the efficient causality that might be attributed to blindly operating social wholes such as markets."[10]

Companies have indeed always had both virtues and vices, but these have largely been subsumed in the category of corporate culture. So the second question is, What indeed are those virtues? As the capacity to do good, or not, virtue basically involves moral discernment. Richard T. De George, director of the International Center for Ethics in Business, suggests two variables in this discernment: "moral imagination" and "moral courage." The first includes the skills and processes for evaluating moral implications of decisions and actions. The second involves the fortitude and discipline for consistently choosing and acting in moral ways. These are both habits—tendencies or orientations that are made stronger through practice. And although the initial motivation is ethical, both these habits also tend to strengthen overall management.

By its layers of questions and preoccupations, the exercise of moral imagination encourages managers to confront the full implications of an action. In a business environment of great uncertainty and ambiguity, this skill of "seeing beyond" the obvious helps develop managerial anticipation, responsiveness and confidence for dealing with slippery and interconnected variables. Moral courage involves having to act with responsibility for consequences. The numerous failures at empowerment show how difficult it is for people to take on any but the most prescribed and specific accountability. Courage in moral terms is premised on a trust and confidence that enhance the individual ownership of implications, the collaboration of teams, and the authority of group and corporate leaders. Lynn Sharp Paine points out that this also speeds up managerial analysis: "In a fast-paced business environment characterized by rapid technological change, managers often face conflicts between competing responsibilities or novel moral claims which cannot be resolved by appeal to familiar general level-one principles. Such problems are often complicated by factual ambiguities. Hence, the need for moral thinking at the critical level."[11]

That moral virtue raises general managerial competencies is only natural for Ian Maitland, since in his view it is the market itself that demands and hones those habits of character. Maitland argues that business success is predicated on four such market-motivated virtues. First is *trustworthiness,* the "conventional, mutual standards of honesty and trust" that are "necessary inputs for much economic input." Customer satisfaction and loyalty, supplier commitment and the generosity of strategic partners all hinge on trust. Economic decisions, whether for derivatives trading involving hundreds of millions of dollars or for the purchase of a single box of Tide detergent, require some expectation and fulfillment of trust. The second virtue is what Maitland calls *self-control,* the discipline for keeping promises, trading off benefits, compromising and collaborating. These, like trust, are essential to any commercial negotiation, as well as to the corporate processes for creating products and services that the market values. Third is *sympathy,* that ability to recognize and value the perspective and biases of others.

Creating and selling something means satisfying someone else's needs and wants. This evaluation requires at least a modicum of empathy, of transposing interest from self to others. Maitland explains that "participation in the market develops and reinforces the capacity to share the feelings or emotions of others" if only because "commercial success depends on the courteous treatment of people who have the option of taking their business elsewhere." Fourth is *fairness,* the mutuality that fosters ongoing exchange. Unfair or one-sided business practices are obviously self-defeating because, in a market of choice, and in the awareness of reputation, customers and other stakeholders will eventually seek out and engage more respectful, reciprocal partners.[12]

Far from burdening business and taxing its managers, virtues are, in Maitland's analysis, "a source of private advantage in the marketplace."[13] Since we tend to associate virtue with self-sacrifice and self-restraint, this language is slightly jarring. But there is an important lesson in this. Virtues are not abstract feats of heroism but living and practicable traits. Bill Shaw defines virtues as "habits of character that advance excellence in all one endeavors [to do]."[14] In Shaw's view, that excellence is prescribed not only by the market but by the sense of "good" that operates in society and the noneconomic community. This wider notion of accountability is central to the direction of "Tomorrow's Company," as formulated by the Royal Society for the Encouragement of Arts, Manufactures and Commerce (RSA) in the U.K. Launched in the early 1990s, the RSA's inquiry sought to establish the corporate characteristics and competencies necessary for success in the global marketplace. Involving interviews and consultations with more than eight thousand business leaders and opinion formers, including the chairpersons and chief executives of forty-eight of the U.K.'s largest companies, the five-year inquiry has resulted in the most exhaustive survey of its kind.

The final report, published in 1995, set out both the impediments and the requirements for effective global competitiveness. Among the obstacles the RSA noted are a "complacency and ignorance of world standards" and an "over-reliance on financial measures of performance." Companies are essential monodimensional entities in a multidimensional world. In their mono focus, companies have for the most part overlooked interdependencies, to the point where "public confidence in the legitimacy of their operations and business conduct" are in jeopardy. The RSA concludes that companies must learn to manage and behave in ways that "maintain their *licence to operate*." As explained in the RSA vision, "The companies which will sustain competitive success in the future are those which focus less exclusively on shareholders and on financial measures of success—and instead include all their stakeholder relationships, and a broader range of measurements, in the way they think and talk about their purpose and performance." In essence, this comes down to what the RSA terms an "inclusive" approach to management.[15] (This approach was explored in the previous chapter.)

The RSA identifies these virtues of inclusion as clarity of purpose, performance beyond financial, reciprocity in relationships, learning, and earning through responsible behavior the "licence to operate." As with moral courage and moral imagination, the virtues of inclusion are geared to a larger social good, but are also good business and good management. In the global economy, natural and intellectual resources are proving scarce. To warrant access to those resources, companies need to prove that the benefits will be optimized and larger than just corporate profitability. Another way of looking at this is to realize that Maitland's virtues are in fact bare minimums. For example, trustworthiness represents a basic condition for engagement. Overlaying the RSA's concept of purpose on trustworthiness provides a much greater motivation for employees, and an opportunity for an involvement with customers and other stakeholders that goes beyond functionality to include shared beliefs, passions and values. Similarly, self-control is a precondition for relationship. Adding the notion of reciprocity to the passive latency of self-control provides a much more active, tangible and compelling reason for relationship.

There are three lessons in this. First, virtue is necessary in business. Second, the dynamics and definition of virtue are changing. Third, in the global information economy, the trend of change is for virtue to be more and more focused on mutuality.

How, though, are corporate virtues developed? Aristotle argued that virtue is learned by the regular repetition of right actions. Here again is the interplay between norm and character. People are virtuous, not just because they are cognizant of the "good" but because they have developed the habits for thinking, deciding and acting toward that good. What, then, are the habits needed to avoid temptations and deepen the company's reorientation to the good? What are these habits in an individual? And how can they be transplanted and developed within the company? Which are also the behaviors that counter those habits or contribute to vices? How are policies, actions and examples of senior management inconsistent with those desired habits?

Again, most company ethical programs focus more on communicating the norm of "good" than on fostering the repetition and inculcating the habits of ethical orientation. Shaw argues that "character habits (vices as well as virtues) are shaped early in life by training and conditioning." In organizational terms, this means for most companies setting forth and developing new habits as well as identifying and breaking the old, entrenched ones. It is in underestimating the power of these old habits that even well-intentioned corporate efforts to change business practices, or reform morality, finally come undone. What are these old habits? How do they contribute to or impede ethical practices? What are the functional steps for unlearning them? How are these old habits being tracked and transformed? Ethics are personal, but they are also a corporate responsibility in that organizational policies and practices profoundly affect the habits of individuals and groups. What, then, is the corporate character? Which have been its greatest or most frequent ethical lapses? How will this character be prompted to grow and mature? Which strengths of character are underdeveloped or underacknowledged? How is the company now known? What is its reputation? What should be its reputation? And finally, How will the company get there and manifest its desired reputation?

Strategic Ethical Plan

"I deeply apologize for having caused this trouble. I am overwhelmed with shame." These are the words with which Tomichi Akiyama, president of Sumitomo Corporation, addressed stockholders and stakeholders just after the revelation in 1996 that trader Yasuo Hamanaka had been caught cooking the books in copper futures, resulting in losses (so far) of $3.6 billion. Numerous investigations, by the company and by various trading commissions and authorities, have been launched into Hamanaka's illegal practices. The company, though, has also chosen to follow the lead of so many others and blame a single individual. "Hamanaka abused the name of Sumitomo Corp.," noted Akiyama. "He carried through the trades entirely on his own initiative."[16] Having managed two sets of books for more than a decade, Hamanaka clearly knew he was doing wrong. But for Sumitomo management to have enjoyed the profits of this duplicity for ten years without ever questioning, monitoring or exercising any controls suggests very shoddy business practice. Reducing this staggering loss to an isolated aberration also suggests that the company is not dealing with the internal conditions and systems that allowed and perhaps encouraged such flagrant abuse of laws and morals. One transgressor had been caught—by accident—with disastrous consequences, but the company did not own up to the issues and policies that caused them. The message seemed to be, our strategy is sound and our problem is that of a single immoral individual.

Strategy, as noted earlier, is primarily focused on commercial and business issues. Professors James Collins and Jerry Porras have proven the inadequacy of this approach, showing that exceptional and enduring companies operate more from a "core ideology" than from a pursuit of profit. Organizations, like persons, need purpose, which Collins and Porras define as "the organization's fundamental reasons for existence beyond just making money—a perpetual guiding star on the horizon; not to be confused with specific goals or business strategies."[17] Advocating "co-opetition," business professors Adam Brandenburger of Harvard and Barry Nalebuff of Yale argue that success depends on a "virtuous circle" involving the company with its customers, "complementers," suppliers and competitors. Essential to the constructive interchange of value in this virtuous circle are various symmetries. Again the story is clear that success depends on values as well as value, on obligations as well as objective.

Yet, although a mountain of evidence shows that strategies directed only to fiscal results are less effective, and sometimes counter-productive, companies continue to set objectives and plans that emphasize profit and make social, environmental and moral issues peripheral or even disposable. The lesson from Sumitomo and other scandals is that the strategic and ethical must be intertwined. It is not enough to do a strategic plan with a parallel ethics policy. It is not enough to do a strategic plan with ethical implications. What is now needed is what I call a Strat-Ethic approach that completely integrates the commercial with the social and the business with the moral. A Strat-Ethic plan starts with a fundamental acknowledgment of interdependence. The company cannot function without the infrastructure and custom of the society in which it operates, without the knowledge, participation and creativity of its employees and without the contributions of suppliers, associations and competitors. Thus, business goals cannot be isolated from the impacts on the communities beyond the company. Strat-Ethic objectives automatically include corporate and community goals. Strat-Ethic plans and tactics are inseparably both commercial and ethical. And Strat-Ethic results are targeted and monitored only simultaneously and in balance with obligations.

Do we really need another word and another concept? Is not this merging of commercial and moral more appropriately done in mission or vision statements? Strat-Ethic is perhaps not the most creative expression of the concept, but it is precisely and functionally what companies need. It communicates that strategy is incomplete without ethics, and that the ethical is intrinsic rather than discretionary to strategy. It also challenges the ingrained assumption that the two thought patterns—that for business success and that for moral development—can proceed sequentially or separately. Strat-Ethic works because the process for a global ethic is itself a hybrid.

Missions and credos and core principles work for some companies, but mostly for those, like J&J and Kyocera, that have had a long practice integrating values into business decisions and behavior. For most corporations, missions were something undertaken in imitation of other, more successful organizations. Missions, like many total quality programs, were add-ons to behaviors and cultures. Often, rather than the company being transformed by the mission, the mission was transformed into the already set style and culture of the company. Many of these statements have become generic and ring hollow. Many mission statements have failed to penetrate operations and strategies. And the ruthlessness of the last seven years of reengineering has largely wiped away any of their value, credibility and moral authority. Whereas a mission or vision stands above a company, the Strat-Ethic process brings principles to the real, everyday work of making plans and decisions. It takes the sensibility of the mission statement down from the plaque in the lobby and works it into the jobs, meetings and projects that are the life activity of a company.

Those managers that regard an ethical orientation as a distraction fail, like at Sumitomo, to see how much bigger the distraction becomes without one. Gellerman points out that "contrary to popular mythology, managers are not paid to take risks; they are paid to know which risks are worth taking. Also, maximizing profits is a company's second priority, not its first. The first is ensuring its survival."[18] A Strat-Ethic planning model unifies the assessment of risk, recognizing that failure and fall-out are equally the result of bad management and bad practices. For Barings, Drexel Lambert, Manville, Dow Corning and Robins, ethical risks, not business ones, brought down the company.

A Strat-Ethic orientation is not developed overnight. It requires years of work—training people, hiring and supporting those whose values match the organization's, having senior managers lead by example and allowing actions to give authority and dimension to the words. It requires developing the skills and mental creativity for responding to a whole new set of business questions: What are the company's goals and what are the ethical obligations inherent in those goals? How are the symmetries managed between the company and its human, intellectual, natural and societal resources? Andrew Campbell and Kiran Tawadey of the Ashridge Strategic Management Centre in the U.K. studied business and strategic planning at such companies as BP, BOC, Courtaulds, ICI, Lloyds Bank and United Biscuits. They concluded that strong plans exist "when these four elements are closely knitted together: when strategy and values are supportive and reinforcing; when behaviour standards are clear and justified by both the commercial strategy and company's value."[19] This leads to other questions. How do ethical values and strategic variables align? How do they work to reinforce and complement each other? What are the behaviors reflecting Strat-Ethic direction and sensibility? Which behaviors must be modified or eliminated? Which must be amplified or introduced? How is the long-term commitment to the Strat-Ethic direction communicated and manifest? How well is this direction understood by individuals throughout the organization?

Strat-Ethic Implementation

Many smart and worthwhile programs for change never have much influence beyond the introductory workshop or seminar. One reason is that people return to work to find that the problems they face have not changed, and neither have the systems and supports for dealing with them. Even those enthused about the new find themselves inexorably pulled back into old habits just to keep from falling behind the ever quickening flow of work. Habits are hard to break and hard to change. For managers, this means not supposing that something will happen just because it makes sense, or because crisis has prompted realization. Habits require a discipline, both to shed those that are diminishing to the character of the individual or company as well as to encourage those that contribute to maturing and assumption of greater responsibility. The task is to change not just comprehension but the organization and the individual comprehensively. Many models have been introduced to achieve this pervasive change, including Deming and Juran's for quality, Senge's for learning, Bennis and Covey's for leadership, Porter and Mintzberg's for strategy, Moore and Hurst's for an ecologically based organic change, and RSA's for "Tomorrow's Company." Most models share essential characteristics. One is alignment—bringing together strategy and action, vision and values, managers and employees, systems and structures, into a cohesive, reinforcing unity. My structure of alignment for ethics, explained in the previous chapter, involves the commitment of the board, the example of the CEO, the direction for strategy, the support of culture, the trust of groups and the growth and commitment of individuals.

Another element common to programs of change is communication—the continuous dialogue between people, especially between senior management and employees, that clarifies and deepens the commitment to the new principles desired by the company. The RSA report stresses that such communication include the new language of inclusion to help overcome entrenched belief structures. This is important to create new meaning and understanding, but my experience has also been the opposite. People and companies usually master the vocabulary of change much more readily than change itself. As a result, words like *excellence, empowerment* and *respect* lose their salience. Communication is essential, but it is not enough. Communication must finally have the authority of example and action.

Most models begin with some expression (communication) of the vision for the shape and outcome of change. In *Working Wisdom,* I argued that the process starts at a level of pre-change. Companies generally train by adding new learning and skills. These new capabilities are often sabotaged by the attitudes and skills already in place. Before learning, we must prepare ourselves for the new by "unlearning" the old. For example, quality requires a high degree of collaboration and personal accountability. Quality teams, quality circles and quality management hinge on quality relationships between designers, engineers, managers, manufacturers, distributors, and sales and after-sales support. In the auto industry, the learning about quality was usually applied without unlearning the adversarial, confrontational operating style between management and employees. Crisis finally forced a rapprochement, first for Chrysler, then for Ford and recently for GM. The change took much longer because management failed to own up to the behaviors that contributed to the problem and failed to identify the traditions, style and attitude that needed to be unlearned before effective new skills could be brought onstream. Ethics, as values, particularly require this critical examination.

Table 15. Implementation Plan for an Ethical Orientation

Process	Involving
Unlearning	What are the biases impeding an ethical orientation?
	Which behaviors risk or undermine ethical virtue?
	What systems, traditions or assumptions support these?
	What is the critical ethical inadequacy? Or risk?
Management	How have the board and CEO signaled ethical expectations?
Responsibility	Which behaviors by example reinforce or undermine that ethic?
	How has an ethical orientation been integrated with strategy?
	How is senior management accountable for ethical performance?
	How are shareholders engaged in the issues and decisions regarding an ethical orientation?
Employee	In what ways is an ethical orientation included in performance appraisals and labor agreements?
Contract	How is ethical orientation expressed in recruiting and hiring?
	Which reciprocities does the company use to model ethical behavior for employees?
	Do all individuals in the company understand the ethical orientation and their responsibility for compliance?
	Would all employees similarly and accurately reflect back the values, expectations and processes for an ethical orientation?

Strat-Ethic Plan	How has the company expressed its commitment to a global ethic?
	What are the temptations and critical ethical factors to be focused on?
	What are the company's critical virtues to develop and exercise?
	What is the shape and scope of the company's ethical orientation model?
	• What are the process steps for understanding ethical implications and acting ethically?
	• What are the internal and external guides for ethical interaction?
	• What are the steps for engaging team members and management in ethical deliberation and decisions?
	• What resources are available for ethical understanding, disagreements and resolutions?
	• What is the process for managing ethical breakdowns?
	—For problem acknowledgment?
	—For addressing the issue?
	—For absorbing the learning?
	—For sharing and institutionalizing the lesson?
	—For rewarding those who acted ethically?
Ethical Orientation Audits	What are the internal measures of success for an ethical orientation? What are the external measures?
	How are these benchmarked and continuously improved?
	Are these formalized in the company's annual report?
	How are lessons and results shared with employees?
	How are behaviors reinforced or discouraged?

	In what ways does the reward and compensation structure encourage an ethical orientation? What are the steps for encoding new learning?
Updating	• How are all employees stretched and strengthened in their ethical orientation? • What new issues require a deepening ethical maturity?

Senior managers repeatedly ask me for the "silver bullet" or the "one thing"—that ingredient, activity or insight that makes change automatic and easy. Of course there is none, and one of the most destructive aspects of recent management practice has been the pursuit of the great "one thing." People change slowly and irregularly. And they grow to maturity only through experience. Organizations are the same. They are malleable, but they must be managed to change and guided to the lessons of growth. Leaders and managers do a disservice to their companies in expecting complex people to undertake complicated change with only simple bromides to inform them. The first obligation, before assuming other obligations, is self-understanding and self-knowledge. For companies as well as for persons, an honest appraisal of who we are, an honest assessment of strengths and weaknesses, must precede that which we wish to become. To have mature relations with employees, customers, suppliers, shareholders and others requires of a company an introspective sense of worth. An ethical orientation is intended not to sacrifice the company's interests for others but to undertake the obligations that go with self-interest and that are imperative within a system of interdependence.

Companies will become ethical and deepen their ethical orientation by practicing ethical behavior. Each by necessity will do this in different ways, to varying degrees and with their own unique set of successes and failures. It will take time to gain the experience to become truly wise about ethical issues. This should not be discouraging, but rather should be another reason for getting started right away. Maturing, growing and developing deeper relationships are not exactly optional.

Success in business and the survival of the global community both depend on attending to relationships. The practice of ethics, the lessons and mistakes, is therefore part of the maturing that in the end is an indispensable corporate asset.

Table 16. Operating Myths

Dilemma	Delusions
• **"If I don't, someone else will."** Business is tough, often ruthless. Sometimes, to not pay a bribe risks losing the project. Losing the project means losing jobs and firing people. The bribe thus can be justified as the lesser of two evils.	• **Corruption functions like an addiction.** If resources and profits are maintained through an illegal or immoral act, chances are more such cut corners will be required in the future. As with an addiction, businesses dependent on impropriety require more impropriety to sustain themselves. This dependency on ill-gotten business thus represents management's greatest failure.
• **"When in Rome, do as the Romans do."** Different countries have different traditions and expectations about how to do business. In some situations, what seem like unethical ptactices to Westerners are just "the cost of doing business" abroad.	• **A wired world is increasingly seamless.** The institutions of global development (OECD, IMF, World Bank) are increasingly adding their pressure to criminalize corruption. Even the most primitive economies understand that they cannot afford the drag of illegality and immorality. The tide of history, as well as the scrutiny of the informed global community, demands that companies do their part to contribute to this ethical productivity.
• **"We did it to hit our targets."** Many people who succumb to impropriety believe that they had no choice but to take the action that would ensure the sale and add to the results the company expected of them. In this sense, the decision is not theirs but surrendered to the demands of the objective.	• **Results are valid only if sustainable.** Neither shareholders nor stakeholders are served by such fleeting results. Not only is the company subject to penalties but its viability becomes dependent on non-value-contributing practices. In the knowledge economy, value increasingly depends not on the surrender of judgment but on its personal practice throughout the company.

• **"The team seemed to approve. It was not my job to object."** When many people are involved in a decision, individuals tend to focus on their specialty or expertise. The larger, moral consequences are delegated to the assumption that someone else has scrutinized them.	• **There is no "virtual" accountability for ethics.** As in the global economy, we as individuals participate in only a part of the action yet profoundly effect the whole. Ethical responsibility within cross-functional and virtual teams is shared and personal. The task of management is to make ethical discourse a valued part of the business process.
• **"No one will ever know."** Many decisions seemed to be made in the shadows, in the corners of operations that will never be exposed. Occasional infractions thus seem to boost results for the company and achievement for careers, but carry little risk of being caught.	• **Everyone knows everything.** The one constant in the information age is that facts and truth will eventually see the light of day. Ethics programs have asked participants to act with the caution of having their decision reported in the news. With the Internet and globalization of media, this hypothetical caution is now a reality.

CHAPTER TEN

EXAMPLES

*Times in which the ethical has become, and has had to become, a
theme for discussion must be followed by times when the moral
course goes without saying, times when a man's activity lies not
merely on the periphery but in the centre and in the fullness of
everyday life. That is true of the life of the
individual no less than of the community.*

Dietrich Bonhoeffer, *"Warrant for Ethical Discourse," in* Ethics

The consensus around a global ethic is still very fresh and forming.
A movement is now underway to have organizations like the
United Nations encode a Charter of Responsibility based on a global
ethic, to formalize obligations in parallel with already formalized rights.
But other than issuing declarations and embarking on grassroots adoption, few of the initiatives for promoting a global ethic have gained
awareness or currency in the mainstream. Every group and association,
every institution and discipline, has its own work to do toward realizing the aims and implementation of a global ethic. The purpose of this
book has been to build on the ethical issues already affecting business,
thereby heightening the sensitivity for the need and potential of a

global ethic. I have already made the point that no two companies will have the identical model or priorities for their ethical orientation. In this preliminary phase of adoption, companies, managers and individuals will need to be especially experimental, seeking those issues of particular moral relevance to their specific circumstances, and defining the appropriate principles for action.

Given the newness of a global ethic, and the challenge of dealing with its ambiguities, I thought it important to build on the practical framework for implementation outlined in the previous chapter, and provide some concrete examples for implementation. To that end I have taken four distinct business situations and applied the Ethical Orientation Model to show how business and ethical demands can be managed simultaneously and effectively. For the purpose of breadth, the examples are varied. The first is one of crisis—in this case the ethical quagmire of the Swiss banks as they attempt to deal with Holocaust-era accounts. The second attempts to be true to ethical principles while implementing an unavoidable series of cutbacks—an example I call "Downsizing with Dignity." The third seeks to show how the alignment of ethical values can be achieved in companies of average success, with few scandals under their belts, and with only average problems confronting them. And the fourth—what I have presumed to be the scenario of Microsoft and Nike—explores the obligations that attend great success and power in the marketplace. These examples are not meant to reflect any special insider expertise about the companies suggested, but are only attempts to apply the common sense of an ethical orientation to recognized problems. While the examples will share some structural aspects, I have varied the content and emphasis, customizing the model in the way most appropriate to each situation.

EXAMPLE 1: Recovering from Denial and Deception

The Story

Swiss banks, providing four centuries of political neutrality, and two centuries of conforming to a strict code of banking secrecy, became an ideal refuge for capital fleeing from war-ravaged Europe. Thousands of Jews opened accounts in Switzerland to protect their threatened assets. And thousands of Nazis used Swiss banks to hide gold, money and property plundered from victims, particularly those of the Holocaust. Using the cloak of institutional secrecy, the Swiss steadfastly refused for over fifty years to reveal any information about these accounts. In the last two years, under intense and growing international pressure, the Swiss government has tentatively admitted the error of its policy, creating a multibillion-dollar restitution fund for victims of the Holocaust and other persecutions. The Swiss banks held on longer, but finally capitulated only on the issue of supplying names of Jewish account holders from the Nazi era so that survivors and heirs would have access to their own accounts. Resistant and recalcitrant, the Swiss banks have lost much of their credibility and authority. A policy of secrecy is now seen as a facade for cover-up. And a code designed to protect customers is now understood to have been used for fifty years to benefit the banks at the expense of some of those very customers.

Ethical epiphanies happen more often in hindsight. The agonizingly slow submission of Swiss banks to the pressures of Jewish groups and the international community in making available information about lost accounts and stolen property, has been too late for most victims, and too late to salvage the once unassailable reputations of the banks. It is an injustice in which the victims have lost much more than the assailants, but still, both are losers. And in a wider sense, the Swiss community and the world community are poorer, emotionally and in terms of self-worth, from the prolonged denial and duplicity. The high-minded neutrality and secrecy of the Swiss banks has become a black hole that conceals some of the darkest secrets of human history, and the darkest capacities of the human heart.

To be fair, the bank managers now dealing with this tragic nightmare are one or two generations removed from those who knowingly cooperated with the Nazis. This does not absolve current managers for the denials and evasions made during their own tenure, but it does demonstrate how the ethical time frame varies from the business one. Results in business are quantified every quarter, while ethical consequences can reverberate, with costs to individuals, society and capital, for generations. It is this misalignment of results that often allows managers to choose the expedient over the ethically prudent. The Swiss banking scandal holds another lesson. Ironically, to save face the banks broke the centuries-old code of secrecy on an issue that, in the end, has proven that they themselves were guilty of gross wrongdoing. The sobering point is that unethical, immoral and unjust behavior rarely goes unaddressed. Admittedly, the information explosion provides a shroud for some wrongdoing. But it also leaks the truth. If the Swiss banks can no longer keep a secret, then no institutional crime can be committed with an expectation of being protected or invisible forever.

This tortuous situation, still unfolding, provides an acid test for the global ethic. In general terms, how would the implementation of a global ethic affect the business management of the Swiss banks involved in the Holocaust-looting scandal? And, in specific terms, how would the models presented in this book provide guidance for Swiss bank managers and employees?

Applying the Global Ethic

Ethical Assessment. The Swiss banking industry, and the individual institutions that it comprises, share an overall accountability. Some banks have likely been more at fault than others, but the system itself institutionalized the policies and practices that resulted in this ignominy. The first step then is to recognize how policies, even positive ones like neutrality and secrecy, are dangerous when they are applied so rigidly as to disengage any moral judgment. Bonhoeffer, himself a victim of the fear and exploitation that are still playing themselves out in Swiss banks, observed that people confronting moral uncertainty often retreat to duty. He wrote: "It looks as though the way out from behind the confusing multiplicity of possible decisions is the path of *duty*. What is commanded is seized upon as being surest. Responsibility for the command rests upon the man who gives it and not upon him who executes it. But in this confinement within the limits of duty there can never come the bold stroke of the deed which is done on one's own free responsibility, the only kind of deed which can strike at the heart of evil and overcome it."[1]

In the case of the Swiss government and Swiss banks, the commitment to the duties of neutrality and secrecy were so complete that moral judgment was subverted. That the codes were unbreakable relieved individuals and institutions of any responsibility for deciding. Duty is one of the disciplines that can develop virtue, but to be ethically virtuous duty must be dynamic, involving continuous questioning and recommitment to moral principle. The most pronounced temptation facing the Swiss banks is to be rigidly duty-bound to a code, in this case unilateral secrecy, that no longer completely satisfies the moral and social needs of the global community. In the last decade, cracks in secrecy were caused by pressures of exploited populations to account for plunder taken by dictators like Ferdinand Marcos of the Philippines, Baby-Doc Duvalier of Haiti and Idi Amin of Uganda. The drive to account for Holocaust assets has added more fissures. But while making some accommodations, the commitment to the code has not been formally addressed. Without the connection to conscience, without the affirmation that comes from personal questioning, the danger persists that duty will be a principle for future exploitations.

Critical Ethical Factors. Drawing on the moral guidance provided by the global ethic, the Swiss banks have two inescapable obligations: to see justice done; and to see it done in ways that honor the dignity of victims and affected individuals. Justice calls for an accounting, for an admission of mistakes, a return of stolen property, and restitution for damages. Dignity demands that this not be done generically through public funds for general purposes, but as much as possible to benefit the individuals and families and communities that suffered such grievous exploitation. The process of learning to implement justice with dignity would also prepare the Swiss bank industry for rearranging its professional codes and practices for the moral and strategic realities of the modern world.

Key Virtues. A lesson the industry has resisted learning but that is now being imposed on it is that the professional virtue of secrecy is untenable without a corresponding moral virtue of honesty. In other words, credibility is no longer simply a function of what is concealed, but of what is revealed. The Swiss have acknowledged as much by cooperating with law enforcement officials from other countries investigating illicit activity. But this is a concession rather than an ethos. Honesty must be cultivated with the same intensity and commitment as secrecy to prevent another such block-headed set of denials and evasions as has occurred in relation to Holocaust assets. Indeed, justice and dignity can only be extended to victims if Swiss banks commit themselves and behave with an honesty as unadulterated as their secrecy.

Honesty and secrecy seem paradoxical. They are admittedly more complicated to live with together; it would always be easier in terms of individual decisions to simply resort to a tradition or blind belief. However, tradition and belief have value only if they prove their relevance in the real world. Life is messy, with often unclear choices and variable implications. Ambiguity requires persons and institutions to test and remold tradition and beliefs to meet those less than clinical modern situations. Honesty and secrecy work as a symmetry, and it is the interplay between them that pulls the ideal into the practical and pushes the practical into the ideal. Tarnished by its flat-footed and self-serving dodges, the Swiss banking industry also needs honesty to recover its business credibility, and recover the confidence of its customers. Without trust, it is commercial success, not just public relations, that is at risk.

The Strat-Ethic Plan. Business as usual is impossible for the Swiss banks until the cloud of doubt over past practices is cleared. From a strategic perspective, the management time and fiscal investment involved in managing world-wide scrutiny over Holocaust funds is also diminishing the focus on other issues. The restructuring of regulations and organizations, and the investment in new skills and technologies, proceeding at full pace in other world financial capitals like Tokyo, New York, Frankfurt, Toronto and London, are hamstrung in Geneva, Bern and Basle. The business priority is then for a fast resolution to a long-drawn-out problem.

Justice done in the abstract is only partially satisfying. The ethical priority is to return to the individuals who were victimized the property and restitution owing to them. Many of the victims are dead, but those still living are in their seventies and eighties. As well, families and communities have been waiting for over two generations to have an accounting. There is then great urgency to see justice served immediately.

In this case, the strategic and ethical priorities align. A Strat–Ethic objective deduced from an analysis of business needs and ethical obligations would be to *make available all relevant documents and resolve all outstanding claims within three years.*

Table 17. Implementation Plan: Swiss Banks and Holocaust Accounting

Process	Involving
Unlearning	Owning up to the ethical failures of the policies and systems that were institutionalized over centuries. Recognizing that the modern, wired and interconnected world requires deconstructing old policies and creating the service structure and information accessibility. Acknowledgment that duty alone does not absolve institutions and individuals from moral accountability.
Management Responsibility	Although not the generation responsible for the improprieties committed during the Second World War, current management is accountable for delays and cover-ups, and is complicit by adhering to the institutional structures that caused the injustice. Professional codes and structures for the entire industry require reconstruction to implement the lessons of injustice. As a global banking power, the ethically renewed Swiss industry can also lead a worldwide effort to reform and standardize practices, and to pressure other jurisdictions like the Cayman Islands to conform to an industry ethic. If all banks are ethical, there is no advantage to those who break or shun laws or morals. The interdependence of banks, and their centrality in the global economy, makes them particularly powerful agents of moral change.

Employee Contract	As we have seen in other examples of evildoing, individuals often silence their own conscience to go along with institutional policy or objectives. Banking involves great sensitivity to customer needs, and a highly developed sensibility for trust building. Training and reward structures that complemented the old duties must be refocused on developing the virtues now needed to recover credibility and rebuild customer confidence.
EO Model	By a commitment to a global ethic, the Swiss banks can create a framework for accounting for past mistakes, as well as for leading a worldwide restatement of professional standards that better serves the moral needs of the global economy and global community.
	The *Principal Temptation* is to revert to duty without conscience, to hide behind a code of secrecy without accepting its obligations for honest disclosure.
	The *Critical Ethical Factors* are **Justice** and **Dignity**: making amends as dictated by universal social and moral norms; and making amends specifically and individually to the people affected.
	The *Critical Virtue* is **Honesty**, both to satisfy the information and accountability needs of victims, and to provide an ethical symmetry for the code of secrecy.
	The *EO Model* reflects the rebuilding by detailing the steps and stages for a deepening and demonstrable commitment.

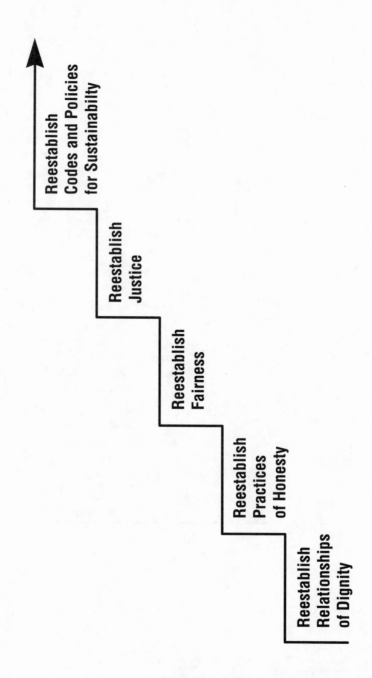

EO Model: Reestablishing Long-Term Trust

Reestablish
Codes and Policies
for Sustainabilty

Reestablish
Justice

Reestablish
Fairness

Reestablish
Practices
of Honesty

Reestablish
Relationships
of Dignity

Dignity
- Apologize for immorality of the delay.
- Extend personal restitution to victims.

Honesty
- Stop the spiral of denials.
- Implement full and immediate disclosure.
- Facilitate access and respond openly to all queries.

Fairness
- Ensure compensation is commensurate with loss.
- Accelerate reconciliations to serve as many as possible as quickly as possible.
- Encode and practice lessons to benefit future transactions.

Justice
- Put an equal effort into finding and addressing victims as went into avoiding and evading responsibility.
- Institutionalize industry regulations for fulfilling obligations.

Sustainability
- Use the humiliation of this experience to lead a worldwide effort to standardize global ethical banking practices.

EO Audits
- Establish formal frameworks for monitoring ethical orientation.
- Report ethical progress alongside financial progress.
- Organize an independent Banking Ethics Group, comprising individuals from various professions, interest groups and religions to supervise compliance and suggest ways to strengthen orientation.

Updating
- Begin planning for ethical mandate beyond resolution of the Holocaust issues.
- Report progress and plans to the world community, employees and industry associations.

EXAMPLE 2: Downsizing with Dignity

The Story

Telephone companies have been called "the railways of the information age" for good reason. Without the infrastructure of wires, fiber optics and switches, voice, data and even cellular communication would be barely more advanced than at the pigeon-courier stage, and the Internet would not exist at all. Telephony is indispensable to the commerce of our age just as trains were for the late nineteenth and early twentieth centuries. But the rail metaphor is apt for a less positive reason as well. Telephone companies have an infrastructure designed to meet a largely pre-digital, pre-competitive set of customer needs. New technologies and new competitors are doing to AT&T, Bell Canada, Nippon Telephone & Telegraph, Sip in Italy, and other established telecommunications giants exactly what airlines did to rail companies. In addition to MCI and Sprint and a host of other telephony-based competitors, the big phone companies are losing chunks of business to outsiders, to cable TV providers and, perhaps the biggest threat of all, to the phantasmic Internet.

Companies like AT&T, British Telecom and Bell Canada have a particular set of pressures that in combination can only mean that each will end up as much smaller companies. Much has been made of Robert Allen's ill-starred stewardship of AT&T. Bad management and poor strategies have certainly compounded an already difficult situation. And Allen's preposterous multimillion-dollar compensation, year after year, in the face of business gaffes has cast a cynical light on that company's actions. The inescapable reality of this business, as it was for railroads, is that changing technology, changing regulatory structures and changing needs of customers will not allow these companies to retain the business, and therefore the size of their monopoly beginnings. All the major telecom companies around the world are faced with this eventuality. These companies, even in the heightened competitive reality of full deregulation, retain considerable assets and huge pools of intellectual capital. The challenge, strategic and ethical, is in shrinking the companies to perhaps a half or even a third of their current size, while at the same time building the commitment, enthusiasm and trust among the remaining employees without which competitiveness is impossible.

Applying the Global Ethic

Ethical Assessment. Undergoing traumatic change puts in jeopardy the trust and goodwill of employees. Management theory holds that cuts and bad news be dished out once. Protracted change for organizations is likened to "death by a thousand cuts." The reality in this industry is that shrinking to the right size, developing the right strategy, or confirming the right mix of job skills, is an art no one has yet practiced successfully. Continuous cuts tend to shred organizational stability. Good people tend to find more secure and forward-moving jobs. And morale tends to become sick with an infection of never-lifting fear. Companies in this situation desperately need the intellectual and emotional contribution of their people to weather the storm, serve customers with the intensity required to secure them from competitors, and bring forth the innovations that are needed to renew business and restore growth. The key temptations, however, are to follow only the rationale of the numbers: to do first and foremost what makes fiscal sense for the company and compensation sense for the management.

Critical Ethical Factors. The business priority is to become radically smaller yet radically more trusting and collaborative. The ethical priority is, therefore, to be *fair* to employees in what is essentially a grossly unfair situation. All of the values of the global ethic affect the realization of that fairness. The dignity of engagement, the honesty of communication, justice in outcome, and sustainability—all are important to this process, but the critical ethical focal point is to be fair.

Key Virtues. For management, and for the organization as a whole, the endemic uncertainty of the business and the inherent unfairness of the situation require the virtues of *courage* and *selflessness.* Courage is needed, but not only for taking the difficult decisions attending down-

sizing. Courage is also vitally important for fulfilling the moral obligation to deal justly with all employees. Finally, courage must express
itself in the companies' strategic choices, and in the risks and new
creations of employees. Bureaucratic companies must find the heart, to
suffer with those who will be lost, to seek a new course with purpose
as well as profit potential, and to forgive the mistakes without which
innovation cannot happen.

One of the new and emerging global competitors to the traditional
telecom companies is premised exactly on this moral courage. Kazuo
Inamori, founder and Chairman of the fabled Japanese high-tech
ceramics company Kyocera, believes simply and profoundly that the
role of a corporation in society "is to engage in activities that please its
customers and the general public."[2] In the mid-1980s, when the Japanese telecommunications industry was still tightly regulated, and when
the monopolistic Nippon Telegraph and Telephone Corporation
enjoyed a market capitalization that surpassed the bulk of value on the
New York Stock Exchange, Inamori launched Daini Denden Inc., or,
"The Second Telegraph and Telephone Company." Against the odds,
DDI increased sales to $4.7 billion in 1996, with operating profits of
$576 million. Inamori explains: "The success of a company that
provides only a small reduction in long-distance telephone charges was
due entirely to the fact that the venture was based from the start on an
ideal: to do something good for the general public."[3] When companies
are put at risk, managers often see ideals as expendable, and put singular priority on "business" issues like cost-reduction or mergers. But as
Inamori shows, to sacrifice ideals is itself a business risk. Tough times
thus call for courage of conviction, as well as courage in action.

Companies often treat cast-off employees like pariahs. Horror stories
abound of tactics that are meant to protect company security but end in
totally dehumanizing both the people fired and those who are retained.
One major oil company cut off the phone system, asked employees to
wait in their cubicles, and had security guards visit each work station,
deliver notice of termination, and then escort individuals out of the
building. Imagine the feelings of fear, anger, resentment that everyone
experienced as they heard the security team move up and down the
hallways for the day-long purge. Another multi-national emptied its

offices, sent all its staff into parking lots, and then invited back only those who had survived the hit list. Organizations must take sensible precautions to protect corporate property, but to disregard courtesy and decency only means that commitment is downsized along with costs. Selflessness is the only antidote, the only human mechanism for achieving some fairness in a circumstance that is, by definition, imbalanced.

On the most functional level, selflessness involves creating severance packages that reflect contribution and past performance and are equitable by the moral standards of the community. Selflessness is also a cultural virtue, providing an emotional framework for relations between company and employees, between employees at risk and those secure, between those caught up in difficult change and those with the skills for finding ready advancement. This is not suggesting some utopian, hyper-cooperative, and unrealizable operating style. People inside companies have many relations. Sometimes these are cooperative, sometimes competitive, sometimes both at the same time. This reality of downsizing, however, creates a situation of prolonged imbalance, so selflessness is that relational attitude that restores some dignity to those at the losing end of the disequilibrium. Selflessness also means that some of the sacrifices of change are shared by all.

Strat-Ethic Plan. Doubtless, there are thousands of business decisions to be made in the management and turn-around of such complex companies. From a strategic perspective, there is an urgent need to reconfigure operations to be more efficient, rooting out the last vestiges of monopoly behavior and systems. With Microsoft and others entering the traditional domain of telecoms, there is as urgent a need to fire up innovation, create new applications and added-value services for customers. Two management skill-sets, usually not very compatible must, therefore, be mastered simultaneously: cutting and growing; conserving and risking; maximizing efficiency and maximizing innovation. Since the business is now global in scope, no single company can survive alone. Companies that were once the most vertically integrated of all must learn the statecraft of joint ventures, and the grass-roots sensitivity to connect and partner with the street-savvy entrepreneurs who are creating the real software revolution.

These strategic priorities cannot be separated from their ethical consequences. How moral obligations are served in relation to departing
employees will set the tempo for how the companies go forward. Badly
bruised and resentful employees will not provide the selflessness that is
needed to build deeper ties with customers. Nor will they take the risks
and display the courage for creating a dynamic new operating style and
services. A company that is unsure and divided from within will hardly
make an attractive or effective strategic partner. A company that mistreats
its own people will never have the sensitivity and patience to collaborate
with entrepreneurs and bring to market their inventions and innovations.
And a depressed, self-suspicious company cannot hope to win against the
exuberance and confidence of a Microsoft or DDI. In this context, the
strategic and the ethical are inseparable. A Strat-Ethic objective for the
short-term would thus be to *downsize with dignity.*

Table 18. Implementation Plan: Telecom Companies Derailed

Process	Involving
Unlearning	Loyalty from employees was easy to earn in paternal organizations that offered virtual lifetime job security. For the attitudes and expectations of employees to change, paternalism, particularly in the privileges it offers the most senior management, needs to be dismantled. Operations and decisions made with the capital investments and time horizons of monopoly must be transformed to operate at the new speed and creative level that bursts from the pages of *Wired*.
Management Responsibility	The board must set the tone, and manifest the patience, to allow managers and employees to transform these monolithic companies into competitors. The board also needs its own *courage* and *selflessness*, to consider strategic and ethical decisions (such as a radical deconstruction) that would diminish their own stature and privileges. Since there is little strategic clarity, senior executives will need to lead more by moral authority than by a clever delineation of direction. More than in any other managerial situation, this requires setting an example, for skills as well as attitude, for performance as well as values. In situations where strategies are irrelevant or unclear, people follow the leader more than the mission.

Employee Contract	Change is hard, but in this instance it is unavoidable. Any entitlement has evaporated. The key for the company and for its individual employees is to honestly confront the full implications of their new reality. The more open and forward the flow of information, the better people can prepare themselves to adjust to the new reality. Rather than wallow in resistance and denial, both corporate and individual interests are better met in realistic dialogue. Future employee contracts will be based not on security, but on learning, not on promotions, but on advancing the personal skills that yield the most marketplace flexibility. Dealing honestly with difficult downsizing issues is critical for building the foundation for this new contractual relation between people and the companies they work for.
EO Model	By adopting the principles and practices of a global ethic, telecom companies will have a framework for managing the intertwined priorities of people and company, obligations and profits. These have usually been handled separately, with varying degrees of importance, but now, any one without the other risks the ultimate productivity and success of these companies. The *Principal Temptation* is in holding onto and using the paternalistic style of these long-established companies to engender change that is totally inconsistent with, and undermined by, patriarchy. The *Critical Ethical Factor* is **Fairness**: ensuring that no one benefits disproportionately and that all have a context and understanding for what has happened, or may be about to happen to them. The *Critical Virtues* are **Courage** and **Selflessness,** to take the necessary strategic and ethical decisions, and to initiate institutionally the reciprocity of sacrifice. The *EO Model* in this case demonstrates that forward progress and momentum depend less on what people do and more on how they treat one another.

EO Model: Downsizing with Dignity

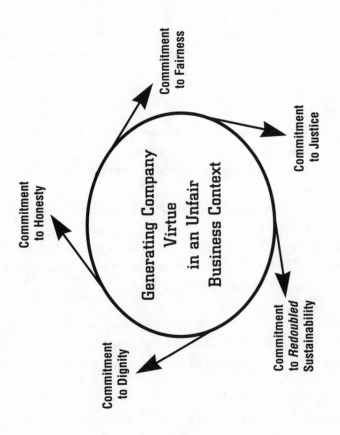

Dignity

- Treat and communicate with each employee as an individual deserving respect.
- Establish and meet criteria for disemployment and reemployment.

Honesty

- Provide full and honest context and appraisal of current business situation, with detailed and specific implications and options for employees.
- Do not "spin doctor."
- Give people as much advance notice as possible for changes.
- Provide access and respond openly to all queries.

Fairness

- See to it that the sacrifices and dislocations of downsizing are distributed evenly and without prejudice.
- Work with employees to extend compassion and support to those affected.
- Manage departing employees with the consideration due them as future customers.
- Uncouple compensation from job cuts (or related market results) and instead link rewards to measures of internal (employee) trust and external (customer) confidence.

Justice

- Since the "what" is unavoidable, only the "how" can serve justice.
- Make "unjust" behaviors as anathema as "unprofitable" ones.

Sustainability

- Aggressively seek to reduce waste and environmental damage, with the redoubled intensity of not only protecting the natural ecology, but using the cost savings to protect jobs and invest in training.

EO Audits

- Measure and evaluate the dignity with which employees who were terminated were dealt.

- Report ethical results to board of directors.
- Establish benchmarks against best practices among companies with the strongest employee relations.

Updating
- Learn, from applying an ethical orientation to downsizing, how to infuse growth strategies and future corporate initiatives with Strat-Ethic focus.

EXAMPLE 3: Building Equity Through Consistency

The Story

Financial services are at the core of the global economy, but, as we have seen in Italy, Britain, Japan, Korea and the U.S., this centrality has also attracted a disproportionate share of fraudulent behavior. Most companies in this sector—including banks, insurance and securities—operate in that ill-defined middle, never sanctioning anything but legal behavior, nor promoting any moral purpose beyond meeting business targets. For these companies, ethics become an issue only when they become an issue. While impropriety begets a response, the prevention of impropriety is not yet a defined or advanced process. Sometimes a crisis that befalls one company sends a sufficient chill through other companies occupying this not-moral-but-not-immoral middle to cause further reflection and action on ethical issues. When Bankers Trust lost the suit filed by Procter & Gamble over hundreds of millions in derivatives trading, most banks with similar operations revised client contracts and introduced, or dusted off, ethical codes for employees. P&G argued, successfully, that derivatives were so complicated that the bank had an obligation to use its expertise in a way that did not take advantage of less knowledgeable clients. Most derivative agreements now have legal disclaimers about this, and most traders and derivative marketers are expected to read and sign codes that commit them to a professional conformance. The action of Bankers Trust's $175-million liability prompted the reaction of an industry-wide rediscovery and implementation of professional, ethical standards.

There is a question about the depth of such ethical commitment, particularly since the culture of trading requires an attitude of aggressive exploitation. Banks, although they do not like the legal and reputational risks of such aggressive tactics, are also addicted to the highly profitable results. It was exactly this "having their cake and eating it too" dichotomy that led to the fall of Barings Brothers & Co. John Gapper, banking editor of the *Financial Times,* and Nicholas Denton, the *Times's* correspondent for investment banking, reveal that although Barings's management had reasons for wondering about Nick Leeson, although discrepancies should have sounded warning bells of fraud well before the collapse, those responsible swallowed their own cautions for the profits being generated. "The firm appeared to have stumbled upon a most extraordinary bubble of profit. Leeson had produced this cash, and it would be damaging if he left."[4] The collapse of Barings was indeed the result of a rogue trader. Leeson forged signatures, bought futures and options beyond the policy levels of the bank, and parked his trades in secretive accounts. But the culture and naivete of the company also created the conditions for Leeson's deception. Gapper and Denton note that the chairmen and CEOs of the British banks who had been asked by the Bank of England to contribute to a private sector bailout of Barings were appalled not only by the lack of managerial supervision, but by the seeming denial of culpability on the part of those managers. "They were being asked to risk their shareholders' money to rescue a bank which had paid inflated bonuses to directors who were so ignorant of what was going on under their noses that they had handed £700,000 over to a crooked trader to help him defraud them."[5]

Eventually, recognizing the wider accountability, the Securities and Futures Authority in the U.K. took action against nine of Barings' former managers, imposing "bans of up to three years from the City and costs of £10,000."[6] This, however, did not really address the central issues of vulnerability and accountability. With Bankers, executives faced one of the new risks of the global information economy: products so complex, so sophisticated, that only people with Ph.D.s in mathematics could create, explain and safeguard them. With Barings, executives faced an even more ominous second risk: virtually any persons of responsibility within a multinational enterprise, left to their own scruples and devices, could damage or mortally wound the company.

As with criminal fraud, corporate fraud is always one step ahead of the systems and monitors for catching it out. Leeson was more audacious than smart, using distance, time differences, and the arcane slang of swashbuckling derivatives traders to obscure what he was really up to. That he got away with it enough to have received a multimillion-dollar bonus just months before the whole Barings mess unraveled is an amazing managerial cock-up. But, as Gapper and Denton report, the bank's managers not only missed the clues of questionable business practices, they also overlooked the questionable personal conduct that suggested Leeson's flawed ethics. Like many others in his business, Leeson drank a lot. After one particularly raucous adventure, Leeson and another worker got involved in a tussle that led to a criminal conviction in Singapore. The Barings board was advised of this, and although there were some questions about the appropriateness of having Leeson as "an ambassador for Barings," this concern for principle was soon dissolved by the reality of the profits Leeson made for the bank.

Banks and financial services companies are in the business of risk, but risks of character require very different questions and skills than those for loans, trades and investments. A few companies have started coming to terms with this limitation, seeking to protect the business through the moral dependability of the persons within the company. "A prophylactic for crises"[7] is exactly the contraceptive many executives want as they introduce ethical codes and more dynamic programs of ethical development.

Applying the Global Ethic

Ethical Assessment. Without the motivation of a crisis or scandal, finding the rationale or engendering the focus for ethical renewal is often very difficult. Under the enormous pressure for results, managers are reluctant to take on the extra work and thinking required by an ethical renewal. Resistance to change is bolstered by the absence of a clear, single, catastrophic danger. One set of temptations for many companies is to "let sleeping dogs lie," or "not fix what isn't broken," or "not change horses in mid-stream." Another temptation is to deduce from Barings, Sumitomo, Kidder-Peabody and other scandals that the whole problem of ethics is exceptional—involving the misdeeds and misjudgments of a single, atypical individual. Defining the problem as one of abnormality frees managers and companies from considering the culpability or moral adequacy of normal operations.

Critical Ethical Factors. Although every business faces ethical issues, for companies not in the throes of scandal, or not on the horns of a company-risking moral dilemma, the *Critical Ethical Factor* is the basic one of creating the impetus for an ethical orientation. This involves bringing into alignment the business and managerial variables defined in previous chapters.

EO Model: Alignment

Board Guidance	**Cultural Supports**
CEO Example	**Group Dynamics**
Strategic Commitment	**Personal Commitment**

Implementation Plan: Achieving Ethical Alignment

Boards must lead the way, ensuring that the central desire to increase worth for shareholders is fulfilled only in ways that respect the spirit of the law and the moral expectations of the community. As we have seen so often, this commitment to ethics is not only beneficial to stakeholders, but also critical for protecting the assets and values of the corporation for its owners. Management hiring and personnel choices are critical for extending the Strat-Ethic guidance into day-to-day plans and operations. Board-level questions include:

- What are the world-leading benchmarks for ethical management?
- How can association standards be made more ethically comprehensive?
- In what ways do the organization's audits and annual reports reflect the commitment to an ethical orientation?
- What is the board's awareness and familiarity with ethical lapses, issues, and key temptations?
- How are ethical priorities rewarded at the executive level?
- What are the "character" components in evaluations for CEO succession?
- What structures (committees/membership composition/policy papers) are in place for furthering the board's own ethical orientation?
- How are employee and stakeholder issues represented?
- In what way have the lessons of Barings, Sumitomo, Bankers Trust, BCCI, Credit Lyonnaise, Prudential, Kidder-Peabody, Solomon been studied and institutionalized to avoid repetition?
- What plans and procedures are in place for dealing with illegal or immoral behavior?
- What contributions or activities are directed by the board to help support justice in the larger community?

For **CEOs,** the task is to protect the company's integrity and reputation while providing strategic vision and guidance. Again, these are symmetrical. Without trust, financial service companies become devalued. Trust is a result of experience in relations. And without trust, it is not just the relationship but the business performance which suffers. CEOs are the mirror that a company's employees and customers look to for discerning the interests, values and integrity of the organization. CEO questions include:

- What are the ethical considerations in the company's current reputation?
- How are ethical considerations measured and assessed within scores of customer satisfaction? (Quarterly reports? "Recovery" results? Training and attitude shifts among managers and employees?)

- In what ways are ethical norms expressed to staff and stakeholders?
- How often and to what depth are ethical issues brought in to operations meetings and decisions?
- How are the CEO's own ethical values reflected?
- How is the CEO "maturing" his or her ethical orientation?
- What learning or training is needed so that the CEO and senior management become as proficient in ethical problem solving as they are in business?
- How can the organization use its clout to strengthen industry ethical standards and improve behavior?
- What are the key ethical concerns confronting customers in their relation to the company? (Privacy? Technological inter-mediation? Cross-selling?)
- Which ethical accomplishments represent the CEO's legacy?

Strategy represents the plan for achieving short-term targets, and for building a long-term platform for value. The ethical is not only *not* a hindrance to strategy, but increasingly it provides the implications-context for facilitating stronger relationships with customers, and is insurance against the penalties and costs of impropriety that so often undermine strategy. The questions here include:

- How are the board's and CEO's ethical commitments reflected in strategic business plans?
- How does the implementation of the strategy encourage ethi-cal practice?
- How is the focus on fiscal results within the plan balanced to avoid the situation of complicity between management and errant employees like Nick Leeson?
- What are the particulars within the strategic plan that contribute to the community?
    - How is justice extended to small business or to single parents with low credit ratings?
    - Which initiatives, such as microcredit loans, represent the strategy's social commitments and re-earn the company's charter within its community?

Culture involves both the conscious contribution to an ethical orientation and the emotional and associative bonds that reinforce it. Questions include:

- What are the characteristics of the company's culture?
- How do these reflect a deepening commitment to an ethical orientation?
- Which behaviors are rewarded and reinforced?
- How is the company's own internal community nurtured and managed?
- Which behaviors are suppressed or assigned only secondary or tertiary priority?
- How are the company's policies and plans communicated to staff?
- How transparent are objectives, strategies and ethical policies?
- From the employee's perspective:
  — How honest is the company/management?
  — How fair are its policies and practices?
  — Which ethical policies are perceived as cosmetic versus real?
- What larger purpose unites staff in their pursuit of business success?

Performance, as well as ethical development, rely on all the above inputs, but finally only come together in the behavior of individuals in relation to each other. Understanding *group dynamics* is key to creating high-performance and highly ethical teams. Questions include:

- What are the critical inputs for building, rewarding, and renewing trust?
  — Among employees?
  — Between employees and management?
  — Between the company and its customers/suppliers/strategic partners?
- How do strategic business decisions affect that trust?
- Which actions or decisions represent the models for trust-building?
- How fair are practices, rewards and communications to employees?

- How fair are practices, policies and initiatives to customers and the larger community?

Ethics are a community expectation, whether that community be a city, country or company. But ethics finally are practiced by individuals. In its fulfillment of ethical principles any company is only as strong as the least ethical of its employees. Again and again we have seen strong, multibillion-dollar, multinational companies brought to their knees by the unethical escapades of single individuals. Sometimes these traumas of impropriety have been brought on by a rogue employee in a distant office. Less acknowledged, but probably even more significant, ethical damage is often caused by a "rogue CEO"—someone who does not commit the actual infraction, but by their personality, priority or pressure implicitly invites immorality. The questions in this regard are therefore meant to apply not to "other" individuals, but to oneself:

- What are my ethical priorities?
- How do my ethical norms affect my decisions and behaviors?
- How developed and mature is my sensibility and regard for others?
- What kind of company do I want to work for? And how am I personally contributing to the formation of that company?
- What do I expect from other employees? How is this mirrored in what they expect from me?
- What is my reputation?
- How would peers, subordinates and customers perceive me on a spectrum of:
  — Respectful to disrespectful?
  — Honest to dishonest?
  — Fair to unfair?
  — Just to unjust?
  — Committed to the environment to disrespectful of it?

Most financial services companies have at least attended to the optics of responsibility, recognizing that such a reputation is essential to trustworthiness. Much of this focus has been on symbols of solidity and success to reinforce their security and standing with customers. But trust in the interconnected reality of the global economy requires something much more intimate than stolid institutions have mostly been able to give. In a business increasingly dependent on relational equity, trust is a function not of image but of care. A caring culture will reflect itself in different ways, but there are some specifics that relate to this example.

Customer service is generally a strategic priority for banks and financial institutions, but most management policies work to undermine the relationships that are the medium for caring. First, managers are often rotated quickly through different assignments or branches. This broadens their experience, but at the price of their ability to "care" since they continually have to forge and break and reestablish relations with customers. Second, tellers and sales agents are usually low-paid, resulting in a yearly turnover that has in some cases been reported at 100 percent. Familiarity and understanding of specific customer needs are lost with every such employee swipe. Third, the technology, like ATMs, PCs and phone banking, that makes operations easier and more cost-efficient at the same time standardizes banking and removes customers from the personal experiences upon which satisfaction finally rests. And, finally, efforts at reengineering and cost-cutting have emphasized efficiency, often to the exclusion of the training and new products that are geared to enhance customer service.

Frederick Reichheld, a director of Bain & Company, and leader of its worldwide loyalty practice, provides a specific example: "In a major bank with several hundred branches, branch managers who had been in the system an average of twelve years stayed at a given branch for only two years. Only one branch manager had remained in place and, not surprisingly, his office had the highest customer-retention rate in the whole system."[8] To extend care to customers is not rocket science. It involves first extending care to employees, and deliberately nurturing company culture so that a caring attitude informs the other accountabilities of performance. As more learning and confidence accumulate in the individual employee, they naturally develop a deeper understanding of customers, and a more involved interaction with them. It is easy to care for high-value-adding employees, and easy to care for highly profitable customers or clients. But this is not how care grows in cultures. Care becomes a cultural asset when it is commonplace, directed to the least contributing worker and manifest to the least important customer. This does not mean caring equally for all, but at a minimum, caring genuinely for all and appropriately customizing expressions of that care to individuals and individual circumstances. Caring is contagious, but so is its opposite, so the task involves both consistency and constancy.

For the very powerful and capable companies in financial services, caring also means incorporating specific programs of justice that will demonstrate the mature exercise of their privilege. Initiatives such as the microcredit loans of several hundred dollars that have been made available with great success to those so poor as to be without collateral, have been pioneered and managed by non-financial institutions. This is shameful, but banks have the power to greatly extend microcredit implementation and its impact. The question, simply, is what other low-risk programs can be tested and developed to best use the competencies and resources of the company, to address the imbalances in local, national and global communities?

Ethical Orientation Model: Alignment Cube

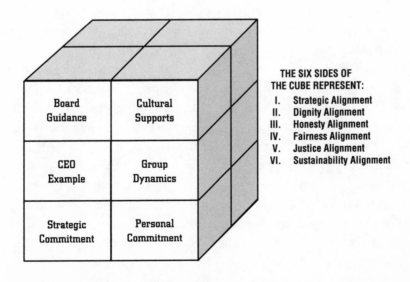

Board Guidance	Cultural Supports
CEO Example	Group Dynamics
Strategic Commitment	Personal Commitment

THE SIX SIDES OF THE CUBE REPRESENT:

I.	Strategic Alignment
II.	Dignity Alignment
III.	Honesty Alignment
IV.	Fairness Alignment
V.	Justice Alignment
VI.	Sustainability Alignment

EXAMPLE 4: The Obligations of Power

The Story

Microsoft and Nike are among the most potent companies on the planet, and while their products are worlds apart in style, attitude and usage, they also share some very important characteristics. Both are upstarts, recent arrivals that took on the established industry giants like IBM and Adidas and not only won but became dominant. Both companies are also still led by their highly competitive founders, Bill Gates and Phil Knight. These men have shown great vision and passion, and both have also seemingly become much more fiercely competitive even as their personal fortunes have skyrocketed into the stratosphere. Microsoft and Nike hire smart, young people, and operate with what some analysts call charisma and others deride as cult-like single-mindedness. Hugely successful, both companies have also slipped on an ethical floor mat—in Microsoft's case for brutalizing much smaller competitors; in Nike's case for accepting the brutalization of workers in the sweatshops of its subcontractors. Even as Microsoft and Nike have tried to be imaginative in addressing the moral pressures now exerting themselves on their companies, both have struggled and stumbled in repairing the ethical damage. Undoubted pros in the business of building market share and innovation, Microsoft and Nike are still adolescents in the larger world of moral responsibility.

Is this an overstatement? Let me explore two examples of this adolescence, starting with Microsoft. A publishing-industry trade journal recently included several lists of books, and among its top thirty computer bestsellers it listed eight variations of the "Dummies" books for various Microsoft programs. Of those books listed that were not "Dummies" editions, 90 percent had words in their title like "mastering," "quick reference" and "made easy." At first blush, this list seems like yet another example of Microsoft's strength. So dominant is this company that customers would pay extra money—and stoop to admitting their own techno-stupidity—in order to participate in the Microsoft juggernaut. A more considered impression, however, is that the "dummy" is not the buyer. Any company that creates products so complex and unintuitive is obviously not creating value with the customer in mind. The brilliance of Bill Gates is legendary. And Microsoft is famous for hiring the best of the best from tech schools like Waterloo University. But this compression of high-wattage intelligence at the Microsoft campus in Redmond, Washington, seems to have created a form of intellectual incest in which the only people who can fully use Microsoft's products are the people technologically skilled enough to work there. Multimedia is not supposed to mean that the only way to use a computer is with a book. So it seems obvious that the brat pack at Microsoft just know more about programming than about people.

Nike too has in some situations become a victim of its own arrogance. With my background in marketing, I was amazed at how fast Nike moved to secure Tiger Woods, and my first reaction was one of enthusiasm. As I watched Woods in the interview announcing his participation in his first pro tournament, I was impressed with his cool demeanor. Woods was wearing a Nike baseball cap and it was clear from his banter with reporters that he was going to be the Michael Jordan of golf. My enthusiasm turned cold, however, when Woods turned his head to reveal a second swoosh logo stitched on the side of his baseball cap. And I experienced a further sense of disconnection when Woods turned around to reveal that both his cap and golf shirt also had Nike's logo on the back. Somehow, all this brand momentum had turned into crass overexposure. What seemed at first like another brilliant sponsorship suddenly became a type of corporate ownership in which the celebrity athlete was reduced to chattel.

I cheered for Woods in his subsequent play, and Nike no doubt received more exposure in his first three weeks as a pro than the $40 million they paid him. But my sense of Nike diminished even as its brand exposure continued to grow. Nike has become a big brand but it is practicing small marketing. In assuming such huge proportions, it may be losing the street-level credibility on which much of its equity rests. As a fairly adolescent marketer, Nike may have to learn a lesson that has also been humbling to other great growth companies, like Intel and Starbucks. Getting big brings new responsibilities. And one of those responsibilities is maintaining a sense of proportion so that the viewpoint of the customer does not get trampled.

For these companies, the ethical challenge goes beyond the typical temptations encountered by other organizations. With their great power, Microsoft and Nike have to assume a commensurate obligation. Again, this does not require surrendering any of their competitive instincts, but it does require developing an appreciation for and commitment to ethics, to ensure that their competitive practices do not unfairly affect their larger communities. Still operating with the hunger of start-ups, Nike and Microsoft are so far largely ignoring the opportunities and responsibilities of their global reach and global impact. Ryuzaburo Kaku, Canon's chairman, observes that, "Because multibillion-dollar corporations control vast resources around the globe, employ millions of people, and create and own incredible wealth, they hold the future of their planet in their own hands. Although governments and individuals must do their part, they do not possess the same degree of wealth and power."[9]

Applying the Global Ethic

Strat-Ethic Plan. The opportunity for Microsoft and Nike to exercise their power with the wisdom demanded by their stature requires consciously embedding an ethical orientation into the core of their strategies. This involves not a duality of objectives, nor a duplication of planning, but a synthesis that acknowledges that business performance and moral obligation are to be interwoven and interdependent.

Table 19. Implementation Plan : Microsoft and Nike Growing Up

Process	Involving
Unlearning	Having mastered the fundamentals of competitiveness, Microsoft and Nike must progress to a level of business and ethical maturity that better reflects their global standing and importance. Part of this growth requires leaving behind the insecurities and justifications for ethical insouciance that suited the companies as start-ups.
Management Responsibility	The board has the obligation to guide these companies into strategies and actions in keeping with their new global roles, and prepare structures and systems for the breadth of interactions that come with success and market domination. The founders have an opportunity to influence the community in terms far greater than the operations of their companies. This is not a call for philan-thropy, but for acknowledging that privi-lege carries with it obligations. Both companies' products have had important social consequences, and warrant special attention for the underprivileged and economically disconnected. In other words, these products of success can also be products of hope.
Employee Contract	Employees in both companies have great opportunities, but also operate under great pressures. The maturing of these companies will involve maturing of the cultures, not by discrediting the youth that is integral to their success, but by engaging the idealism of that youth more constructively. For employees, this requires extending the ethos of privilege and respect that operates within the company to the various communities outside of it.

EO Model	By adopting the principles and practices of a global ethic, Microsoft and Nike can have as revolutionary an impact on the world community as they have had on their respective industries. First, the power and potential that inheres in these companies would alone have enormous benefits for the global community. Second, that these brands are recognized globally means that their association with a global ethic would provide this moral initiative with credibility as well as momentum. Third, as two of the companies most admired and studied by businesspeople, by their example Nike and Microsoft would convert countless others to the cause of a global ethic.
	The *Principal Temptation* for each is in holding onto adolescent impulses and behaviors long after their business has matured into a position of global leadership and influence.
	The *Critical Ethical Factor* in maturing is to grow a recognition of the needs and legitimacy of individuals other than oneself. For companies with great resources and potential the CEF reflecting this other-orientation is encapsulated in the concept of *Justice*.
	The *Critical Virtues* would include **Vision** and **Responsibility**: to see roles in new ways and appreciate the strategic and ethical responsibilities that necessarily come with success, reputation and wealth.
	The *EO Model* in this case reflects that strategic and ethical principles are inseparable and that growth in one sphere requires and is helped by growth in the other.

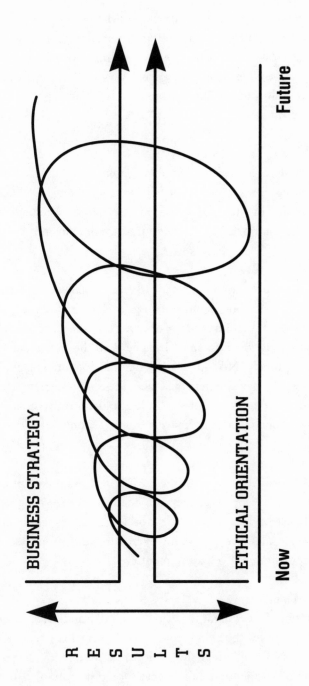

An EO Model for Simultaneously
Planning Strategy and Ethics

Dignity

Extend respect to all customers. In Microsoft's case this means not talking down to them or assuming an unrealistic technical competence. In Nike's case this means acknowledging responsibility for encouraging dreams among many underprivileged kids that are largely unrealizable and only distract them from the real choices to be made in their circumstances.

Honesty

Provide open access and full accountability. In Nike's case this means making worker conditions in subcontractors' facilities available for scrutiny. In Microsoft's case, honesty requires better value for money, particularly in ease of use and intuitive intelligence.

Fairness

This involves a commitment to treat employees not as automatons of productivity, but as human beings deserving of respect. Companies that profit so much from the market must ensure that the value they withdraw as profits is in some balance with the individual and social good they provide. Nike's P.L.A.Y. program, encouraging adult participation in youth development and activities, represents a start, but fairness requires that Nike not just advocate this involvement, but lead it and work much more aggressively toward its outcome.

Justice

As international powerhouses, Microsoft and Nike can have a profound impact on labor practices, wages and educational opportunities virtually everywhere around the world. These valuable brands can earn an even more revered stature by representing hope as well as success, opportunity as well as momentum.

Sustainability

Setting the standards for marketing, Nike and Microsoft can also set the standards for the enlightened environmental practices of the new economy. Nike and other shoe companies sometimes offer refunds for used running shoes and collect these for distribution to homeless shelters and other charities. This again is a start in minimizing waste and extending the life of products.

EO Audits

Having redefined their industries, Microsoft and Nike can now help redefine auditing and accounting practices to include the variables and performance of ethical principles. As beneficiaries of this new economy, both companies can help set the benchmarks for measuring its relational dynamics.

Updating

Learn from applying a Strat-Ethic focus to their incredible success how to infuse products, services and future corporate initiatives with a deepening ethical orientation.

I recognize that the examples detailed above represent only the most surface of insights. My reasons for exploring them have been threefold: to demonstrate the workability of the model for *ethical orientation;* to show its flexibility so that each company can customize an approach suited to its particular circumstances; and to prove, by the range of examples, that no company or individual can legitimately exempt themselves from moral performance. Again, my priority has been not to diminish in any way the objective or disciplines of profit, but to advance appreciation within companies for the objective and disciplines of ethical conduct. To be ethical is never a substitute for competitive competence, but increasingly, competitive competence hinges on ethical excellence.

CHAPTER ELEVEN

CONVERSION

Responsibility is always a relation between persons.

Dietrich Bonhoeffer, "The World of Things," in Ethics

We know only too well that change is difficult for human beings. Corporate downsizing and social welfare roll-backs have been accepted less for reasons of strategy and intelligence than in response to the brute force of crisis. And we have also learned from problems with cigarettes, drugs and alcohol how difficult it is to overcome addiction. Even when our minds know that something can hurt us, even when we have rallied all the emotion and conviction within ourselves to break from something that can kill us, we struggle mightily to do for ourselves what we know categorically is for our own good. Overhauling something as broad and unstable as the global economy will not be at all easy. As with the Kyoto conference, attempts to limit emissions of greenhouse gases, facts will be contested and statistics used to support competing agendas. In a society of declining civility, persuading consumers to consume less requires great vision and moral authority. In a corporate environment that rewards the short-term, reprogramming companies to consider the long-term consequences of their activities requires brave management. In a world of growing fragmentation, the credibility for asking the billions who seek an industrialized lifestyle to revise their dreams requires that those of us who already have so much be willing to lead by example.

In her introduction to a report from the United Nations Research Institute for Social Development, Cynthia Hewitt de Alcantara explains that: "The particular form of 'globalization' currently shaping our lives—with its overriding emphasis on competition and its degrading lack of concern with human security—is not immutable. It is the product of adherence to an ideology that interprets life as a vicious struggle to be won by the strongest. Such a world view requires modification. Human beings are motivated by solidarity and hope, as well as by selfishness."[1] There are three insights encoded in this. First is the recognition that the current form of global economic activity is not fixed or rigid, but dynamic and flexible. A free-market economy is not so much an achievement as a work in progress. Second, this particular type of economy represents an ideology. Based on certain principles, and now providing a record of successes and failings, this ideology, like all other human constructs, is neither absolute, nor unchangeable, nor is it morally complete. Indeed, history has shown that ideologies that claim to be absolute, and that are practiced to their extreme—from Communism on the left to Fascism on the right—are dangerous, intolerant and ultimately self-defeating. Third, Hewitt de Alcantara reminds us that human motivation and meaning are complex. Along with our selfishness, we also have a great capacity for generosity. We withdraw and seek to protect ourselves from threats, but we also reach out to help others to solve common problems.

This thesis is explored further by financier, mogul and market idol George Soros in a much-publicized article for *The Atlantic Monthly*. Under the headline "The Capitalist Threat," Soros set the context that "market values [have] served to undermine traditional values." Where once the economy bore the imprint of its society, it is now so dominant that it is imposing its values on the global community. The most disturbing implication of this reversal is that the ruthless competitiveness of the market is spilling over into the social and national institutions that were, until not very long ago, considered essential for the common good. Soros, a billionaire who made billions more for his investors, makes the indictment that "there is something wrong with making the survival of the fittest a guiding principle of civilized society."[2]

The business press, which had previously lionized Soros, harshly criticized him for his foray into philosophy. *Forbes* even ran an investigative piece suggesting that Soros's huge philanthropy to Eastern Europe—once widely applauded and considered a factor in the fall of Communism—was actually spurious and counter-productive. Once again, human ideals are made the enemy of the economy, and people are forced to confront a false dichotomy between conscience and comfort. The antipathy Soros aroused in the business community shows the depth to which the market ideology has penetrated our belief system. Ideologies have in the past caused wars, and ideologies have in the past been proven faulty or worthy, usually on a field of battle. As Soros showed, to take on any ideology is difficult for the initiator and threatening to the believer. To take on an ideology like the market economy, one which has so recently defeated its nemesis, is almost sacrilegious. Ideology will not be shaken by mere logic. It will not be transformed by facts. Ideology, except for when we regress to violence, can only be changed by conversion.

The Meaning of Conversion

The word "conversion" is important because it involves more than intellect and more than a change of heart. Conversion takes the totality of an individual—reason, emotion, body and spirit—and redirects fully that person's beliefs and behaviors. With conversion, there are no halfway measures. Life pivots to such a degree that discontinuity with the past is not an issue because the past no longer makes sense. Marketers talk of "converting consumers," but this refers merely to brand-switching. Genuine conversion shifts the very meaning of life. In this case, conversion demands that the economy, consumption and materialism be resituated where they properly belong within, but not exclusive to, human purpose. Some socially responsible business commentators have said that profit is like oxygen—essential for survival, but not the only dynamic for surviving and flourishing. For society and individuals, the economy is exactly like profit—absolutely necessary, but not the absolute end of human life.

Given the momentum of the global economy, how is any such conversion to be undertaken? Bernard Lonergan worked very hard during the mid–twentieth century to bring the discipline of scientific methodology to the practice of theology. One of his contributions was to develop a formal structure for describing how we grow in knowledge and achieve conversion. The process is dynamic and continuous, but essentially involves four stages that he expresses declaratively as "Be attentive, Be intelligent, Be reasonable, Be responsible."[3] With *attentiveness*, we open ourselves to the possibility of learning something new and being moved by it. Most information targeted to us today is unwanted—trying to sell, or spin or convince us—so we have all developed a degree of cynicism as protection against being taken in. Attentiveness is the personal choice to listen and observe, to suspend the filters. Although it sounds passive, attentiveness is an active receptivity. And it requires discipline, both to calm the restlessness of expecting sound-bite solutions, and to prevent the sense that we already know better from sabotaging our efforts to learn.

The stage of *intelligence* in Lonergan's methodology is when we question what we have attended to. Do the facts measure up? Is the story or argument compelling? How does it relate to our own experience and learning? Does it ring true? Through continuous questioning, testing and probing, the knowledge grows deeper and more convincing. We are now not just receiving, but interacting with the learning, so we are also beginning to be changed by it. This change multiplies during the third stage, which Lonergan calls *reasonableness*. From input and questioning, we now draw out the conclusions and implications that make sense to us as thinking and sentient beings. It is in reasonable analysis that the interconnection and interdependence of issues are creatively linked. By discerning implications we are really recognizing the underlying cause and effect. We see the whole picture, and while recognizing that it is moving and incomplete, we also understand the choices available to us. Reasonableness for Lonergan is more than rationality. As the highest capacity of human beings, reasonableness equates to wisdom.

The final stage of development in conversion is *responsibility*. Here, the interconnection of issues is so thorough and comprehensive that it involves the self. The interaction between knower and knowledge grows more complex with each of Lonergan's stages, and now that interactivity is all-encompassing. To understand fully, to appreciate fully the consequences, compels one to act. Aristotle taught that wisdom is only wisdom in action. Responsibility is therefore expressed, not as an intellectual achievement, but in day-to-day behavior. What we know is only a prelude for what we do. And it is what we do, finally, that is most important.

In the context of the deceits around us and the challenge of this book, conversion asks us first to be *attentive* to what is really happening: What is happening at work and at home? What is happening in society and in nature? How is life unfolding? What are the pressures and disappointments? What provides joy and satisfaction? This is like a personal audit—taking stock of our own personal balance sheet to recognize the factors that give and drain meaning from our life. To be *intelligent* takes us into a more evaluative questioning: Is life only work? Do consumption and possession represent life's most precious accomplishments? Is it balance or imbalance that is growing as we grow older? What are the stresses in our lives and what is behind them? Are we living a life we are proud of?

To be *reasonable* connects foresight with insight, and lessons about the past with implications for the future. To be reasonable is to understand clearly the real "why?" Why is the economy harsher and society less generous even though the first is more successful and the latter wealthier than ever? Why do we invest so much more in technology than in people? Why is there a split between humans and nature? And why is nature reduced to being simply a platform for economic exchange? Why do we work so hard and neglect our own creativity and our own families? Why do we go along with destructive corporate, social, and environmental behaviors when we know in our bones that these are unsustainable and personally diminishing? Finally, as the "why?" reveals its reasons, we are left no choice but to be *responsible*. Now that we know, what should we do? Now that we know, what *must* we do?

EO Adaptation of Lonergan's Conversion

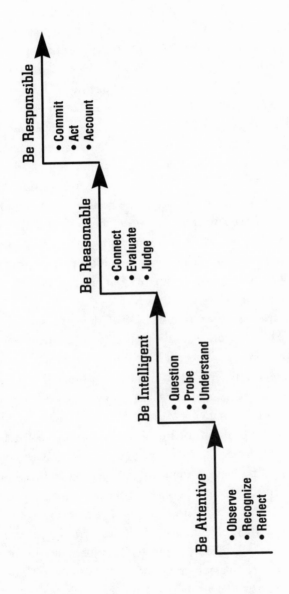

Conversion invites fundamental change in behavior and beliefs, but it does not deny the sensible or the practical. For individuals, conversion does not mean the end of consumption, only the end of consumption that is gratuitous, unconscious, wasteful and unfulfilling. With conversion, each purchase is an affirmation of belief as well as the satisfaction of a need. Rather than being under the control of our compulsions and fears, decisions are made from the understanding earned in "being attentive" and "questioning intelligently." This, to a degree, and only very superficially, is already happening. Robert Haas, chairman and CEO of Levi Strauss & Co., refers to a survey that showed that a vast majority (84 percent) of American consumers agree that "a company's reputation can well be the deciding factor in terms of what product or service they buy." Another survey by MarketVision in Canada found that an astounding 25 percent of the respondents had boycotted a product or service in the previous year (1994) because of concern over ethics and values.[4] Understanding that purchases matter, that they affect other people and the environment, is a recognition of the power inherent in choice. With that power, with that knowledge of cause and effect, comes the responsibility to act justly.

For companies, conversion involves all the complexity and difficulty of change, but in many ways also only represents having behavior catch up with promises and objectives. If there is one great failing of management in the last fifteen years it is the inconsistency and incompetence with which it has applied even the most essential and obvious of performance improvements. As noted earlier, more than 80 percent of companies that took on total quality management failed to make the reforms stick. More than 80 percent of those that chose merger or acquisition as the route to improving efficiencies and synergies failed to reach the objectives that rationalized the investment or restructuring. And by their own admission, the pioneers of reengineering, James Champy and Michael Hammer, admit that up to 70 percent of companies implementing this most imitated of structural reforms have failed to make their companies stronger for the long term.[5] All this wheel-spinning suggests that in their impatience to change, companies have forfeited the deliberation, reflection and questioning that are essential for a shift from one set of beliefs and practices to another.

Conversion

Facts motivating change are presented as a force unto themselves, but we all need more than data to transform attitudes and behaviors. To be attentive, we must be included. To be intelligent, we must be able to probe, pry and resolve our own doubts. To be reasonable we must be respected as individuals who are capable of discerning right from wrong, correct from incorrect. And to be responsible we must see the action that invites our own action of change. Our environmental crisis and growing social problems are calling out for a conversion. Although we cannot escape the issues, we can by our beliefs and actions delay dealing with the consequences. To do so—to fail to reform in the light of the evidence, and to ignore the call to conversion despite knowing the consequences—is the equivalent of conscious sin.

Table 20. EO Conversion Overview

	Personal	Corporate
Attentive	• What is really happening in life? • What is the role of work? • What are the joys/pressures? • What is the balance between them? • What is happening in society? • What is happening in nature?	• What is the purpose of the company? • What role does it play in human life? • What are its family policies? • What place does it have in society? • What are its culture and prospects? • What is the value of nature?
Intelligent	• Is life only work? • Is life's meaning only in production? • Is personal growth only in career? • Is consumption alone fulfilling? • What achievements really matter? • What makes morality worth it?	• Is there a purpose beyond profit? • Is there pride among employees? • Is there loyalty from customers? • Are activities sustainable? • What is the long-term vision? • How is the strategy inspiring?
Reasonable	• Why does work pre-empt life? • Why is success so important? • Why is everything competitive? • Why do people matter less than results? • Why do we accept the status quo? • Why do we not pursue our dreams?	• Why are profits disconnected from moral responsibilities? • Why are sacrifices inconsistent? • Why are rewards inconsistent? • Why does productivity focus on fewer people rather than less resource waste?
Responsible	• How are actions/beliefs congruent? • What improves life for the future? • How can nature be preserved? • What legacy is to be left behind? • How will benefits be reciprocated? • What contributes to social justice?	• How are results life-affirming? • How are resources maximized? • What contributions warrant society's charter and nature's resources? • How is corporate/social/natural well-being and sustainability enhanced?

Lonergan's model of conversion is especially relevant for the information age because it links responsibility to knowledge and understanding. Knowing that many are excluded from participating in the economy, that many are injured, abused, underpaid or disrespected, compels us to seek to infuse human dignity into the workings of the free market. Seeing the disparity between executives and workers, and between companies and communities, demands that we ask for, and work toward, fairness. Understanding the direct connection between gains in First World wealth and growing impoverishment in the Third World means that we can no longer operate under the delusions of personal autonomy and corporate independence. Recognizing that current free-market practices have concentrated ever-greater wealth in the hands of an ever-smaller group means that we can no longer escape responsibility for the system's injustices. And knowing with certainty that the economy is destroying the natural ecosystem imposes an obligation on those who benefit from this exploitation. Personal beliefs continue to play an obvious role in defining morality, but the authority and urgency for a global ethic are not a matter of individual faith but of common knowledge. Indeed, the moral crisis of our time is not the fragmentation of ethical principle, but rather the insouciance, apathy and disregard with which we seek personal and corporate advantage while being fully aware and fully cognizant of the consequences.

Emile Durkheim wrote that: "A society is not simply the mass of individuals that comprises it, nor the territory it occupies, nor the things it uses, nor the movements it carries out, *but above all it is the idea that it has of itself.*"[6] If an audit were done on the idea that society has of itself, we would find a reflection that is primarily, and almost exclusively, economic. The value of a person is largely determined by possessions and wealth. The value of the community is largely that of supporting the infrastructure for business growth and job creation. The value of education is mostly in the job or career that it possibly secures. The value of science is in the R&D of new products. And the very value of human life is reduced to an equation of productivity, consumption, and contribution to gross national product. It is impossible to extricate ourselves from the world's present economic reality. Nor should we want to, given that the free-market system provides so many of the basic services and opportunities without which human life would now be impossible. What is required, however, is context: recognizing that the economy provides many advantages to humans but paradoxically destroys humanity when it operates as the defining idea (and ideal) of human activity.

A global ethic for the global economy will be resisted by many as an imposition, but, in reality, it is the practice of business without an ethic that is the aberration. "Whether we like it or not," wrote John Macmurray, "we are all enmeshed in that network of relation that binds us to make up human society. We are parts of one great process—the process of human history."[7] Identity is thus something we develop and that has value only in interaction with other people. Who we are, and the family, community and society we belong to, are therefore inextricable. This means our essence is social, not isolated; that it is interdependent and not independent. By contrast, the ruthless individualism of business is a distortion of the fundamental sociability of humans. Adam Smith instinctively knew this. Before he conceived of the "invisible hand," Smith introduced the notion of "moral imagination." Patricia H. Werhane, professor of philosophy at the University of Virginia, explains that for Smith, "sympathy and imagination are necessary for moral judgment, since one must first understand what another feels or engage in imaginative self-evaluation in order to experience a sentiment of approval or disapproval, a sentiment that is the basis for judgment." This moral imagination, with its sense of others, reflects the inherent social character of human nature, while the invisible hand, with its accurate insight about self-interest, reflects the inherent individuality of human nature. Both are essential to humanity. In Werhane's view, Smith "saw human beings as egoists and altruists in equal measure."[8]

Martin Buber expresses this duality more poetically, writing that "through the *Thou* a man becomes *I*. That which confronts him comes and disappears, relational events condense, then are scattered, and in the change, consciousness of the unchanging partner, of the *I*, grows clear and each time stronger."[9] The primary premise for ethics is that no human individual can function or grow or prosper alone. Yes, we are responsible for our own initiative, actions and outcomes. And certainly, we must accept responsibility for our individual lives and circumstances.

But to operate in an exclusively competitive mode is to mistake other people and the community as being apart from and unessential to ourselves. For Buber, "personal individuality is not an original given fact. It is achieved through the progressive differentiation of the original unity of the 'You and I'."[10] In other words, who I am only has dimension in relation to other people. And what I believe only has meaning in relation to the human community to which I belong.

The modern economy involves exactly this intimacy and relation. When the previously buoyant Asian economies ran into difficulties late in 1997, one factor economists recognized as compounding the problem was the overdevelopment of plant capacity versus the underdevelopment of consumer confidence. In other words, by holding back the wages of employees and continually disturbing job security with restructuring, business has undermined the very source of its future returns. Hoarding impoverishes all, whether it is attempted by countries through protectionism, by companies through excessive profiteering or by shareholders through greed.

Dilemmas abound as we rush headlong into constructing a global economy without first solidifying the basis for a global community. The logic of trade has built a momentum and near-global consensus about wealth creation without a corresponding development in the values and infrastructure of a global society. We are therefore in the dangerous position of having rules in place for how to compete on a global basis, but not for coordinating the larger, globally shared outcomes relating to social justice, environmental management and human resource deployment. We know how to sell globally but not how to resolve the conflicting agendas and cultural priorities of the still divided and tentative global community. Such facility for competition does not automatically translate into the necessary facility for cooperation. Martin Albrow notes: "We cannot derive either globality or culture from capitalism. They each have their own autonomy in influencing the other."[11]

For some, this is all too heady and way too impractical for business people. But is it? Underplaying the intellectual and philosophical capabilities of investors, executives, and managers simply perpetuates the outdated charade of business depending on brute force to survive in the competitive jungle. The knowledge economy, involving the creation of value through intellectual capital, requires much more nuance and sensitivity. Since, as most business people readily acknowledge, worth increasingly comes from people and not machines, the dynamics of relation that are encoded in a global ethic are now simply the fundamentals for good business. If it is hard to work with a global ethic, and to think through all its implications, it is not because morality is a burden but because the knowledge economy is itself fraught with uncertainty and unpredictability. If doing business with a global ethic is hard, much harder is the prospect of doing business without one.

Applying a global ethic to the global economy involves issues of great complexity and scale, but the process actually starts in that most humble context of the individual. A global ethic will work only if it is my ethic and your ethic, our ethic and their ethic. Diversity will not end, nor will disagreements about values, priorities and culture. But it will be the fundamental mutuality of a global ethic that will allow us to solve common, inescapable problems. And it will be its essential reciprocity that allows us to be enriched rather than divided by diversity, and protective rather than exclusive of our individuality. As Küng and Swidler have both noted, a global ethic does not impose uniformity but represents the minimum we have in common. From this base we can complete the trajectory of history and overcome the no-longer-workable divisions and territoriality. From this base we can answer the call of the future and finally work toward that ever-evasive and never complete harmony of interdependence.

From personal commitment flows action, affecting our communities as well as our companies. Since we are talking about a transformation that may take many generations to realize, we must begin now to introduce the principles of a global ethic into school curricula. Rather than proselytizing any specific theology, this will provide an expansive sense of how we share some basic values while experiencing life in such richly different ways. Community, cultural and political institutions can be brought into endorsing, reflecting and reinforcing a global ethic. Universities can be deployed to provide the interdisciplinary insights that add weight and credibility to common ethical principles. Where science and philosophy, biology and theology, evolution and religion have been split, a global ethic provides a synthesis that overcomes the limitations of each. A unifying theory in physics will go only part way to explaining creation and our place within it. The rest will come from a unifying theory of humanity, of relationships, and through creative resolution of currently impenetrable differences. Local groups working with international counterparts provides one leverage for a global ethic. Another comes from participating with human rights groups, environmental activists, or interfaith organizations like the Parliament of the World's Religions. No one of us alone can achieve success, but no success can be achieved without each of us. The degrees of separation from personal to global are so much fewer than we think.

Ethical orientation on a corporate level involves the alignments and practices detailed earlier, but again this represents only a starting point. As a company develops its ethical muscles, it has the opportunity (and credibility) to begin engaging its other stakeholders. As shown, reciprocity is a risk in that it must be extended, but it is also a risk with returns of goodwill, commitment, loyalty and profits. A corporate commitment to a global ethic does not diminish the importance of profit, but only enhances the importance of relationships and their attendant responsibilities. Using their power, companies can expand the influence and adoption of a global ethic through its industry associations and international standards. ISO, for example, is one of several associations that certify compliance to specialized and specific environmental norms. These are geared to efficiency and minimizing waste, and not directly to sustainability. Nevertheless, they show the potential for setting ever-steeper environmental and social standards, corresponding to our ever-steeper ecological problems and social dislocations. Shell has led the way in one regard, inviting environmental activists to participate as "insiders" in the company planning and policy making. Where issues were once either business-enhancing or business-limiting, Shell's move acknowledges that business and its effects are on a continuum. Working with people and groups outside conventional business structures is the only way to shift relations between company and community, from confrontation to cooperation. Ultimately, with the input of many groups, including governments, business, activists, theologians and others, there will be an opportunity to create an international body to administer the specific norms and performance requirements of a global ethic certification.

Other persons and groups will have their own imaginative ideas for implementing and extending a global ethic. This is indeed a project for our times, and one to which everyone can contribute uniquely for themselves. The key is to see this as an orientation, as a progressive deepening that will never achieve a fixed conclusion but is nevertheless important and beneficial.

A Global Ethic: Implementation Steps

ACTIVITIES

CORPORATE CHANGE PROJECTS

- Working toward a global ethical certification process
  - With activists representing other constituencies
  - With other business and government bodies
  - With international standards councils
- Within industry associations
- With all stakeholders
- Within the company

PERSONAL COMMITMENT REQUIRING PARTICIPATION
- Within the education system
- With communities
- With universities and cross-cultural study programs
  - With groups like the Parliament of the World's Religions
  - With international activists
- In global ethic standardization initiatives

GRASSROOTS CHANGE PROJECTS

For managers, the adoption of a global ethic requires its own disciplines. At its core, such an orientation involves activating a sense of purpose as well as an awareness of punishments for non-compliance. The latter is important, but it is the possibility of doing something unique and meaningful, beyond the usual parameters of business, that is truly motivating. Importantly, ethical success hinges on sharing accountability, and making accessible to all many of the information pieces and strategic perspectives that most often are the exclusive domain of managers. In order to operate with integrity, every employee must have as total as possible a perspective on reasons, motives and objectives.

Ethical change, like any corporate renewal, is premised on four "C words." The program for ethical orientation must first of all be *coherent*, making sense of big-picture long-term strategy as well as the tiny snap-shot of immediate results. Any change must also be *comprehensive*, applied equally to the most senior executive and most junior employee, across the spectrum of company operations and activities. This obviously involves training and teaching, but also requires managerial skills for reinforcing, rewarding and building upon desired attitudes and behaviors. For credibility and success, an ethical orientation needs *consistency*. Words like "respect," "honesty," "fairness," "justice" and "sustainability" can easily become generic: only specific actions and specific examples will imbue these principles with the meaning appropriate to a particular organization. The final C word is *communication*. Any great project, any task involving change, only comes to life with dialogue and exchange. Answers will give impetus to new questions. And real life in the business trenches will present new dilemmas. Constant communication keeps the sense of an ethical orientation. By speaking and listening, people learn the lessons of implementation, and pass on the stories and examples that will become paradigmatic for the next conflict or ambiguity. And by such communication, companies can recalibrate their objectives and norms to keep refining the orientation as well as the ethical.

As shown throughout this book, there are numerous advantages for ethically oriented companies. Customers are more loyal. Employees are more committed. Partners and suppliers are more engaged and likely to contribute. There are also, inevitably, some disadvantages in behaving according to principle. Some opportunities may indeed be lost to a competitor with fewer scruples. While all of these considerations are important, the motivation for an ethical orientation is finally one that goes beyond any cost/benefit analysis. The reason for ethical behavior is not that it ensures personal advantage, but that the human community within which we as individuals and companies function would be impossible without such reciprocity. Rather than seek to justify ethics as legitimate to business practice, we must demand justification and recompense from those companies and managers who dismiss and neglect their inescapable moral obligations to the human community and natural environment. It is the ethical abusers who must be called to task. It is those practicing "profit without principle" who must defend their distortion. It is those separating personal belief from business action who must be exposed for their hypocrisy. Although its principles will need to be continually refined, a global ethic is, in fact, the only natural construct for engaging in a global economy. It is imperative because the world's natural and social problems will remain intractable as long as the world's economics are unprincipled. And it is imperative because only when each and every manager and company operates with ethical principles will no single individual or business be at any disadvantage.

None of this is easy, nor is much of it optional. While the objective is difficult, and the problems urgent, a global ethic is more than just an imposition created out of crisis. A global ethic is, most of all, a standard born of hope. History has shown that the human spirit is restless for progress and security, but also for justice and equitable improvement. A global ethic reflects this optimistic wisdom, springing from the hearts and minds of thousands, representing the values and aspirations of millions more. Scholars from many disciplines, individuals from many cultures and businesspeople of every stripe from every continent are adding their voices and ideas to its expression. It took the horrendous wars of this century for the global community to begin the process of encoding the human rights of individuals. The globalization of the economy, with its opportunities and excesses, is now the impetus for defining the obligations that go with those rights. No one can have the final word on a global ethic, but we all have an undeniable stake in its impact, and an unavoidable effect on its practice. So, while it involves the policies of nations and strategies of companies, a global ethic is in the end only realizable as an individual ethic. While it requires planetary codes and norms, a global ethic is only practicable as a personal commitment. For people in business, this does not mean valuing profit less, but instead valuing people more. It means recognizing that the right thing for business and the right thing ethically have become one and the same.

NOTES

INTRODUCTION

1. Hans Küng, *Global Responsibility: In Search of a New World Ethic* (London: SCM Press, 1991), 15.
2. Marilynne Robinson, "Dietrich Bonhoeffer," in *Martyrs*, ed. Susan Bergman (San Francisco: HarperCollins, 1996), 155.

CHAPTER ONE

1. Gary Gardner, "Global Trade Continues Upward," in *Vital Signs* (London: Earthscan, 1997), 74, 77.
2. Ibid., 76.
3. Erik R. Petersen, "Looming Collision of Capitalisms?" in *New Forces in the World Economy* (Cambridge: MIT Press, 1996), 5.
4. "Different Outlooks," *The Economist*, 7 September 1997, 7.
5. Paul Krugman, *Pop International* (Cambridge: MIT Press, 1997), 9.
6. Anthony Giddens, "Affluence, Poverty and the Idea of a Post-Scarcity Society," in *Social Futures: Global Visions*, ed. Cynthia Hewitt de Alcantara (Oxford: Blackwell, 1997), 153.
7. Amitai Etzioni, "Positive Aspects of Community and the Dangers of Fragmentation," in *Social Futures*, ed. Cynthia Hewitt de Alcantara, 28.
8. Martin Albrow, *The Global Age* (Stanford: Stanford University Press, 1997), 23.
9. Samuel Huntington, *The Clash of Civilizations and the Remaking of World Order* (New York: Simon & Schuster, 1996), 218.
10. Lester Thurow, *The Future of Capitalism* (New York: Penguin, 1996), 194.
11. Cynthia Hewitt de Alcantara, ed., *Social Futures: Global Visions* (Oxford: Blackwell, 1997), 3.

12. Johan Galtung, "On the Social Costs of Modernization," in *Social Futures,* ed. Hewitt de Alcantara, 191.

13. Peter Senge, "Rethinking Control and Complexity," in *Rethinking the Future,* ed. Rowan Gibson (London: Nicholas Brealey, 1997), 126.

14. Huntington, *The Clash of Civilizations,* 68.

15. David C. Korten, *When Corporations Rule the World* (Hartford: Berrett-Koehler, 1996), 152–53.

16. Albrow, *The Global Age,* 91, 95.

17. Ralf Dahrendorf, "Economic Opportunity, Civil Society and Political Liberty," in *Social Futures,* ed. Hewitt de Alcantara, 31.

18. Albrow, *The Global Age,* 85.

19. Lester Thurow, "Rethinking the World," in *Rethinking the Future,* ed. Gibson, 239.

20. John Plender, *A Stake in the Future: The Stakeholding Solution* (London: Nicholas Brealey, 1997), 106.

21. "Aid Donors Vow War on Graft," *Globe and Mail,* 20 September 1997.

22. Richard von Weizsacker, "Towards a Shared Global Ethic," in *Yes to a Global Ethic,* ed. Hans Küng (New York: Continuum, 1996), 31.

23. Joseph L. Badaracco, *Business Ethics: Roles and Responsibilities* (Chicago: Richard D. Irwin, 1995), 5.

24. Thomas Donaldson, "The Business Ethics of Social and Organizational Processes," in *Codes of Conduct: Behavioral Research into Business Ethics,* ed. David M. Messick and Ann E. Tenbrunsel (New York: Russell Sage Foundation, 1996), 187.

25. Jonathan Baron, "Do No Harm," in *Codes of Conduct,* ed. Messick and Tenbrunsel, 198.

26. Baron, "Do No Harm," 199.

27. Badaracco, *Business Ethics,* 5.

28. Huntington, *The Clash of Civilizations,* 97.

29. Hans Küng, ed., *Yes to a Global Ethic* (New York: Continuum, 1996), 1.

30. E.J. Hobsbawm, "The Future of the State," in *Social Futures,* ed. Hewitt de Alcantara, 62.

31. Robert Heilbroner, *Twenty-First Century Capitalism* (Toronto: House of Anansi, 1992), 112–13.

32. Robert Lawrence, Albert Bressand and Takatoshi Ito, *A Vision for the World Economy: Openness, Diversity and Cohesion* (Washington, D.C.: The Brookings Institution, 1996), 33.

33. Ibid., 30.

34. Ibid., 33.

35. Ibid., 59, 60.

36. Hans Küng, *Global Responsibility: In Search of a New World Ethic* (London: SCM Press, 1991), 31.

37. Lawrence, Bressand and Ito, *A Vision for the World Economy,* 60.

38. Dietrich Bonhoeffer, *Ethics* (London: SCM Press, 1955), 205.

39. Pauline Graham, *Integrative Management: Creating Unity from Diversity* (Oxford: Blackwell, 1991), 28.
40. "Rights and Wrongs," *Financial Times,* 18 March 1997, 18.
41. "A Green Piece of the Action," *Management Today,* May 1997, p. 86.
42. "Rights and Wrongs," 18.
43. Galtung, "Social Costs of Modernization," 166–67.
44. Krugman, *Pop International,* 120.
45. Ibid., 208.

CHAPTER TWO

1. "Less Overtime Won't Create Jobs," *Globe and Mail,* 11 December 1997.
2. Peter Senge, "Rethinking Control and Complexity" in *Rethinking the Future,* ed. Rowan Gibson (London: Nicholas Brealey, 1997), 127.
3. John Maynard Keynes, "Essays in Persuasion," in *The Great Thoughts,* ed. George Seldes (New York: Ballantine Books, 1985), 226.
4. Philip Selznick, *The Moral Commonwealth: Social Theory and the Promise of Community* (Berkeley: University of California Press, 1992), 321.
5. Herman E. Daly and John B. Cobb, *For the Common Good,* rev. ed. (Boston: Beacon Press, 1994), 5.
6. "Handy Homily," *The Economist,* 6 September 1997, 16.
7. "Work and Family," *Business Week,* 15 September 1997, 96.
8. Ibid.
9. Amitai Etzioni, *The Moral Dimension: Towards a New Economics* (New York: The Free Press, 1988), 107.
10. Lester Thurow, *The Future of Capitalism* (New York: Penguin, 1996), 307–8.
11. Edward O. Wilson, *The Diversity of Life* (New York: Norton, 1996), 51–2.
12. Motoko Yasuda Lee and Charles L. Mulford, "Reasons Why Japanese Small Businesses Form Cooperatives," *Journal of Small Business Management* 28, no. 3 (1990): 63.
13. David Gordon, *Fat and Mean: The Corporate Squeeze of Working Americans and the Myth of Managerial Downsizing* (New York: The Free Press, 1996), 101–2.
14. Thurow, *Future of Capitalism,* 35–9.
15. "Are These America's 'Good Old Days'? Not So Fast," *International Herald Tribune,* 19 June 1997.
16. Gordon, *Fat and Mean,* 100–1.
17. Thurow, *Future of Capitalism,* 29–30.
18. "Seeing Things As They Really Are," *Forbes,* 10 March 1997, 124.
19. "Green Piece of the Action," *Management Today,* May 1997, 88.
20. "Take Warming Seriously," *International Herald Tribune,* 18 June 1997.

21. Anjali Acharya, "Forest Loss Continues," in *Vital Signs* (London: Earthscan, 1997), 122.
22. Odil Tunali, "Global Temperature Sets New Record," *Vital Signs,* 66.
23. E. Von Weizsacker, A.B. Lovins and L.H. Lovins, *Factor Four: Doubling Wealth and Halving Resource Use* (London: Earthscan, 1997), xx.
24. Senge, "Rethinking Control," 126.
25. Kenneth R. Andrews, *Ethics in Practice* (Cambridge: Harvard Business Press, 1989), 88.
26. Mehrene Larudee, "Trade Policy: Who Wins, Who Loses?" in *Creating A New World Economy,* ed. Gerald Epstein, Julie Graham and Jessica Nembhard (Philadelphia: Temple University Press, 1993), 55.
27. Senge, "Rethinking Control," 126.
28. George Reisman, "Economy," *Fortune,* 28 April 1997, 68.
29. Weizsacker, Lovins and Lovins, *Factor Four,* 189.
30. Ibid., xxvii.
31. *Business Week,* 21 April 1997, 59–62.
32. John Plender, *A Stake in the Future: The Stakeholding Solution* (London: Nicholas Brealey, 1997), 23, 22.
33. Herman E. Daly and John B. Cobb Jr., *For the Common Good,* rev. ed. (Boston: Beacon Press, 1994), 373.
34. Charles Handy, "Rethinking Principles," in *Rethinking the Future,* ed. Rowan Gibson (London: Nicholas Brealey, 1997), 28.
35. Samuel P. Huntington, *The Clash of Civilizations and the Remaking of the World Order* (New York: Simon & Schuster, 1996).
36. Johan Galtung, "On the Social Costs of Modernization," in *Social Futures: Global Visions,* ed. Cynthia Hewitt de Alcantara (Oxford: Blackwell, 1996).
37. Selznick, *The Moral Commonwealth,* 494.
38. Hans Küng, *Global Responsibility: In Search of a New World Ethic* (London: SCM Press, 1991), 31.
39. *Globe and Mail,* 16 October 1997.
40. "Verbatim," *Time,* 6 October 1997, 13.
41. Lester Thurow, "Surging Inequality and Falling Real Wages" in *The American Corporation Today,* ed. Carl Kaysen (New York: Oxford University Press, 1996), 386–8.
42. Freeman Dyson, *Imagined Worlds* (Cambridge: Harvard University Press, 1997), 198–9.

CHAPTER THREE

1. Dawn-Marie Driscoll, Michael W. Hoffman and Edward S. Petry, *The Ethical Edge* (New York: Master Media, 1995), 233, 74.
2. Robert B. Cialdini, "Social Influence and the Triple Tumor Structure of Organizational Dishonesty," in *Codes of Conduct: Behavioral Research into*

Business Ethics, ed. David M. Messick and Ann E. Tenbrunsel (New York: Russell Sage Foundation, 1996), 58.

3. Saul W. Gellerman, "Why 'Good' Managers Make Bad Ethical Choices," in *Ethics in Practice,* ed. Kenneth R. Andrews (Cambridge: Harvard Business School Press, 1989), 18.

4. "The Mob on Wall Street," *Business Week,* 16 December 1996, 94.

5. Peter Senge, *Rethinking the Future,* ed. Rowan Gibson (London: Nicholas Brealey, 1997), 138.

6. "The Bank Scandal That Keeps Growing," *Fortune,* 7 July 1997, 36.

7. "Three More Japan Firms Linked to Payoffs," *International Herald Tribune,* 1 July 1997.

8. "Familiar Sins," *The Economist,* 15 March 1997, 74.

9. "Stuck in Their Ways," *Newsweek,* 9 June 1997, 48.

10. "Hanbo Chief Gets Prison Term," *International Herald Tribune,* 3 June 1997, 15.

11. "The Hidden Hand," *Newsweek,* 7 July 1997, 19.

12. "A Charter to Cheat," *The Economist,* 15 February 1997, 61.

13. "Scandal Tarnishes Hong Kong Market," *Globe and Mail,* 9 September 1996.

14. "The Mob on Wall Street," *Business Week,* 95.

15. Deborah Thompson, *Greed: Investment Fraud in Canada and Around the Globe* (Toronto: Viking, 1997), 45–6.

16. Ibid., 17.

17. Ibid., 8.

18. Ibid., 9.

19. John M. Darley, "How Organizations Socialize Individuals into Evildoing," in *Codes of Conduct,* ed. Messick and Tenbrunsel, 15.

20. Ibid.

21. Francis J. Aguilar, *Managing Corporate Ethics* (New York: Oxford University Press, 1994), 20.

22. Darley, "How Organizations Socialize Individuals," 23.

23. Ibid.

24. Aguilar, *Managing Corporate Ethics,* 35.

25. Darley, "How Organizations Socialize Individuals," 19.

26. William Wolman and Anne Colamosca, *The Judas Economy: The Triumph of Capital and the Betrayal of Work* (Reading: Addison-Wesley, 1997), 61.

27. Darley, "How Organizations Socialize Individuals," 24.

28. Dietrich Bonhoeffer, *Ethics* (London: SCM Press, 1955), 57.

29. "The Black Market vs. the Ozone," *Business Week,* 30 June 1997, 82–3.

30. "Taiwan the Wasteland," *The Economist,* 31 May 1997, 71.

31. Darley, "How Organizations Socialize Individuals," 16.

32. E. von Weizsacker, A.B. Lovins and L.H. Lovins, *Factor Four: Doubling Wealth and Halving Resource Use* (London: Earthscan, 1997), xxvii.

33. "Blind Ambition," *Business Week,* 23 October 1995, 79–80.

34. "Japanese Finance Survey," *The Economist*, 28 June 1997, 9.
35. Wolman and Colamosca, *The Judas Economy*, 70.
36. "Second Thoughts About Globalisation," *The Economist*, 21 June 1997, 86.
37. David Gordon, *Fat and Mean: The Corporate Squeeze of Working Americans and the Myth of Managerial Downsizing* (New York: The Free Press, 1996), 101–2.
38. Joseph W. Weiss, *Organizational Behavior and Change* (Minneapolis/St. Paul: West Publishing, 1996), 90.
39. Ibid., 302–3.
40. Mary Midgley, *Heart and Mind* (New York: St. Martin's Press, 1981), 72, 75, quoted in Kenneth E. Goodpaster, "Ethical Imperatives and Corporate Leadership," in *Ethics in Practice*, ed. Kenneth R. Andrews (Cambridge: Harvard Business School Press, 1989), 213.
41. "Butterflies Aren't Free," *Newsweek*, 26 May 1997, 73.
42. "Even Executives Are Wincing at Executive Pay," *Business Week*, 12 May 1997, 40.

CHAPTER FOUR

1. Texaco Press Release, 15 November 1996, 1.
2. "1-800-22-ETHIC," *Financial World*, 16 August 1994, 27, Internet site.
3. Ibid.
4. Ibid.
5. Kenneth E. Goodpaster, "Ethical Imperatives and Corporate Leadership," in *Ethics in Practice*, ed. Kenneth R. Andrews (Cambridge: Harvard Business School Press, 1989), 217.
6. "Texaco's High Octane Racism Problems," *Time*, 2, November 1996, 33.
7. Sharon Daloz Parks, "Young Adults and the Formation of Professional Ethics," in *Can Ethics Be Taught*, Thomas R. Piper, Mary C. Gentile and Sharon Daloz Parks (Cambridge: Harvard Business Press, 1993), 39.
8. Ibid., 31–2.
9. Dietrich Bonhoeffer, *Ethics* (London: SCM Press, 1955), 57.
10. John Costello, "Lecture at Regis College," 4 March 1997.
11. Charles Handy, "Rethinking Principles," in *Rethinking the Future*, ed. Rowan Gibson (London: Nicholas Brealey, 1997), 28–9.
12. "Forum," *Harpers*, May 1996, 37.
13. Ibid., 40.
14. Robert B. Cialdini, "Social Influence and the Triple Tumor Structure of Organizational Dishonesty," in *Codes of Conduct: Behavioral Research into Business Ethics*, ed. David M. Messick and Ann E. Tenbrunsel (New York: Russell Sage Foundation, 1996), 53–6.

15. Lynn Sharp Paine, "Moral Thinking in Management: An Essential Capability," in *Business Ethics Quarterly* 6, no. 4 (1996): 477.
16. Hans Küng, *Global Responsibility: In Search of a New World Ethic* (London: SCM Press, 1991), 31.
17. John Macmurray, *Reason and Emotion* (New Jersey: Humanities Press International, 1992), 69.
18. Amitai Etzioni, *The Moral Dimension: Toward a New Economics* (New York: The Free Press), 5.
19. Lynn Sharp Paine, "Moral Thinking in Management," 488.
20. George Soros, "The Capitalist Threat," *The Atlantic Monthly,* February 1997, 53.
21. Hector Saez, "The Latin American Environment," in *Creating a New World Economy,* ed. Gerald Epstein, Julie Graham and Jessica Nembhard (Philadelphia: Temple University Press, 1993), 355.
22. Ibid., 335.
23. "Good Enough?" *Industry Week,* 20 February 1995, 63.
24. "Kicking the Kickbacks," *The Economist,* 31 May 1997, 82.
25. "OECD Sets Date for Law on Bribery," *The Financial Times,* 24–25 May 1997, 3.
26. John M. Darley, "How Organizations Socialize Individuals into Evildoing," in *Codes of Conduct,* ed. Messick and Tenbrunsel, 34.
27. Philip Selznick, *The Moral Commonwealth: Social Theory and the Promise of Community* (Berkeley: University of California Press, 1992), 451.
28. Ibid., 479.
29. Macmurray, *Reason and Emotion,* 56.
30. Robert D. Haas, "Ethics—A Global Business Challenge: Character and Courage" (speech to the Conference Board of New York, 1 June 1994), 4.
31. Bonhoeffer, *Ethics,* 9.
32. "Good Grief," *The Economist,* 8 April 1995, 58.
33. Bonhoeffer, *Ethics,* 232.
34. Sharp Paine, "Moral Thinking in Management," 486.
35. Howard Gardner, *Creating Minds* (New York: Basic Books, 1993).
36. Kenneth E. Goodpaster and Joanne B. Ciulla, "Note on the Corporation as a Moral Environment," in *Ethics in Practice,* ed. Kenneth R. Andrews (Cambridge: Harvard Business Press, 1989), 91–2.
37. Nicholas Rescher, *Ethical Idealism: An Inquiry into the Nature and Function of Ideals* (Berkeley: University of California Press, 1992), 112.
38. Ibid., 110.

CHAPTER FIVE

1. John Kekes, *Moral Wisdom and Good Lives* (Ithaca: Cornell University Press, 1995), 7.

2. Robert Wright, *The Moral Animal: Why We Are the Way We Are* (New York: Vintage Books, 1995), 190.

3. Mary Midgley, "The Origin of Ethics," in *A Companion to Ethics,* ed. Peter Singer (Cambridge: Blackwell, 1993), 5.

4. Hans Küng, *Global Responsibility: In Search of a New World Ethic* (London: SCM Press, 1991), xvi.

5. Martin Albrow, *The Global Age* (Stanford: Stanford University Press, 1997), 121.

6. Ibid., 135.

7. Philip Selznick, *The Moral Commonwealth: Social Theory and the Promise of Community* (Berkeley: University of California Press, 1992), 33.

8. Kekes, *Moral Wisdom and Good Lives,* (Ithaca: Cornell University Press, 1995), 5.

9. Emile Durkheim, *Elementary Forms of Religious Life* (New York: The Free Press, 1965), 21.

10. John Macmurray, *Reason and Emotion* (New Jersey: Humanities Press International, 1992), 144.

11. Hans Küng, ed., *Yes to a Global Ethic* (New York: Continuum, 1996), 15.

12. Swidler, Leonard, "Notes on the Global Ethic Workshop," Philadelphia; 22 August 1995, 2.

13. Hans Küng and Karl-Josef Kuschel, *A Global Ethic: The Declaration of the Parliament of the World's Religions* (London: SCM Press, 1993), 8.

14. Ibid.

15. Ibid., 13–36.

16. Simon Webley, "The Interfaith Declaration: Constructing a Code of Ethics for International Business," in *Business Ethics,* January 1996, 53.

17. David C. Korten, *When Corporations Rule the World* (Hartford: Berrett-Koehler, 1996), 146.

18. Ad Hoc Interfaith Working Group on Canada's Future, *Mutual Responsibility: The Tie That Binds,* 29 October 1991, 4.

19. Ryuzaburo Kaku, "A Call for Global Business Principles," Canon Inc. Documents, January 1997, Internet site.

20. Fons Trompenaars, *Riding the Waves of Culture: Understanding Diversity in Global Business* (Chicago: Irwin Professional, 1993 and 1994), 180.

CHAPTER SIX

1. "Generals and Politics," *The Economist,* 19 July 1997, 21.

2. Richard P. Feynman, *Six Not So Easy Pieces: Einstein's Relativity, Symmetry and Space* (Reading: Addison-Wesley, 1997), 23–4.

3. John H. Holland, *Hidden Order: How Adaptation Builds Complexity* (Reading: Addison Wesley, 1995), 3.

4. Russell Hardin, "The Psychology of Business Ethics," in *Codes of Conduct: Behavioral Research into Business Ethics,* ed. David M. Messick and Ann E. Tenbrunsel (New York: Russell Sage Foundation, 1996), 349.

5. James Collins and Jerry Porras, *Built to Last* (New York: Harper Business, 1994), 228.

6. John Kekes, *Moral Wisdom and Good Lives* (Ithaca: Cornell University Press, 1995), 12.

7. Ronald M. Green, "Sears Auto Shock," in *Case Studies in Business Ethics,* ed. Thomas Donaldson and Al Gini (Upper Saddle River, New Jersey: Prentice Hall, 1996), 231.

8. Dawn-Marie Driscoll, Michael W. Hoffman and Edward. S. Petry, *The Ethical Edge* (New York: Master Media, 1995), 135.

9. Sydney H. Schanberg and Marie Dorigny, "Six Cents an Hour," *Life,* June 1996, 39.

10. David Schilling, "Sneakers and Sweatshops: Holding Corporations Accountable," *The Christian Century,* 9 October 1996, 932.

11. Ibid., 934.

12. Robert Reich, "Sky and Ground," *The New Yorker,* 1 September 1997, 8.

13. Jeffrey Wattles, *The Golden Rule* (Oxford: Oxford University Press, 1996), 188.

14. Schilling, "Sneakers and Sweatshops," 937.

15. William Wolman and Anne Colamosca, *The Judas Economy: The Triumph of Capital and the Betrayal of Work* (Reading: Addison-Wesley, 1997), 71.

16. Schanberg and Dorigny, "Six Cents an Hour," 45.

17. "Microsoft to Pirates: Pretty Please?" *Business Week,* 22 September 1997, 4.

18. Ibid.

19. Gabriel Moran, *A Grammar of Responsibility* (New York: The Crossroad Publishing Company, 1996), 55.

20. Will Kymlicka, "The Social Contract Tradition," in *Companion to Ethics,* ed. Peter Singer (Oxford: Blackwell, 1993), 187.

21. Jeffrey Olin and Vincent Barry, *Applying Ethics* (Belmont, California: Wadsworth, 1992), 15.

22. Schilling, "Sneakers and Sweatshops," 943.

23. Lester Thurow, *Head to Head* (New York: William Morrow and Company, 1992), 220.

24. "The In-Your-Face Economist," *Business Week,* 30 June 1997, 76.

25. J. Baird Callicott, "Benevolent Symbiosis: The Philosophy of Conservation Reconstructed," *Earth Summit Ethics,* ed. J. Baird Callicott and Fernando. J. R. da Rocha (Albany: State University of New York Press, 1996), 142.

26. Ibid., 144.

27. Ibid., 151.

28. Thurow, *Head To Head,* 226.

29. Nanette Byrnes, "The Smoke at General Electric," in *Case Studies in Business Ethics,* ed. Donaldson and Gini, 333.

CHAPTER SEVEN

1. Robert Cialdini. "Six Principles of Influence" in *Codes of Conduct: Behavioral Research into Business Ethics,* ed. David M. Messick and Ann E. Tenbrunsel (New York: Russell Sage Foundation, 1996), 52.
2. Edward J. Waitzer, "Model Behaviour," *CA Magazine,* August 1997, 29.
3. Ibid., 30.
4. William Wolman and Anne Colamosca, *The Judas Economy: The Triumph of Capital and the Betrayal of Work* (Reading: Addison-Wesley,1997), 169.
5. Thomas O. Jones and W. Earl Sasser Jr., "Why Satisfied Customers Defect," in *The Quest for Loyalty,* ed. Frederick Reichfeld (Cambridge: Harvard Business Press, 1996), 146.
6. Ibid., 150.
7. Gael M. McDonald, "Common Myths About Business Ethics: Perspectives from Hong Kong," *Business Ethics* 4, no. 2 (1995): 67.
8. Steven E. Prokesch, "Competing on Customer Service: An Interview with British Airways' Sir Colin Marshall," in *The Quest for Loyalty,* ed. Reichfeld, 168.
9. "And Now, Motorola Junior High," *Business Week,* 28 March 1994, 160.
10. Letter to Stakeholders, 1995.
11. Ibid., 146.
12. Linda K. Stroh and Anne H. Reilly, "Loyalty in the Age of Downsizing," *Sloan Management Review* (Summer 1997): 86.
13. Ibid., 83.
14. Arie de Geus, "The Living Company," *Harvard Business Review,* March-April 1997, 57.
15. "Quick-Change Artists," *Business Week,* 1 September 1997, 47.
16. Ikujiro Nonaka and Hirotaka Takeuchi, *The Knowledge-Creating Company* (New York: Oxford University Press, 1995), 17.
17. Ibid., 31.
18. Ibid., 85.
19. de Geus, "The Living Company," 57.
20. Warren Bennis and Patricia Ward Biederman, *Organizing Genius* (Reading: Addison Wesley, 1997), 206.
21. James Collins and Jerry Porras, *Built to Last* (New York: Harper Business, 1994), 191.
22. Gerald Nadler and Shozo Hibino, *Breakthrough Thinking: The Seven Principles of Creative Problem Solving* (Rocklin, CA: Prima Publishing, 1994), 391.
23. John P. Kotter, *Matsushita Leadership* (New York: The Free Press, 1997), 2.
24. Ibid., 249.
25. "3M Receives Environmental Award from the White House," 7 March 1996, Internet site.

26. Collins and Porras, *Built to Last,* 85.
27. David G. Knott, "Vertical Integration," *Strategy & Business,* Third Quarter 1997, 53.
28. Adam M. Brandenburger and Barry J. Nalebuff, *Co-opetition* (New York: Currency Doubleday, 1996), 21–2.
29. Knott, "Vertical Integration," 54.
30. James F. Moore, *The Death of Competition: Leadership and Strategy in the Age of Business Ecosystems* (New York: Harper Business, 1995), 53.
31. Ibid., 53.
32. Charles Handy, "Rethinking Principles," in *Rethinking the Future,* ed. Rowan Gibson (London: Nicholas Brealey, 1997), 36
33. de Geus, "The Living Company, 52.
34. Waitzer, "Model Behaviour," 30.
35. Eric Young, interview by author, 14 August 1997.

CHAPTER EIGHT

1. Philip Selznick, *The Moral Commonwealth: Social Theory and the Promise of Community* (Berkeley: University of California Press, 1992).
2. Peter Senge, *Rethinking the Future,* ed. Rowan Gibson (London: Nicholas Brealey, 1997).
3. Lynn Sharp Paine, "Moral Thinking in Management: An Essential Capability," *Business Ethics Quarterly* 6, no. 4 (1996): 483
4. Robert Waterman, quoted in "Tomorrow's Company: The Role of Business in a Changing World," in *Frontiers of Excellence* (London: RSA, 1995), 7.
5. Amitai Etzioni, *The Moral Dimension: Towards a New Economics* (New York: The Free Press), 69.
6. "Rights and Wrongs," *Financial Times,* 18 March 1997, 18.
7. "The Best and the Worst Boards," *Business Week,* 8 December 1997, 90.
8. Lynn Sharp Paine, "Managing for Organizational Integrity," *Harvard Business Review,* March-April 1994, 111.
9. James Gillies, *Boardroom Renaissance: Power, Morality and Performance in the Modern Corporation* (Toronto: McGraw-Hill Ryerson, 1992), 24.
10. Edmund P. Learned, Arch R. Dooley and Robert L. Katz, "Personal Values and Business Decisions," in *Ethics in Practice,* ed. Kenneth R. Andrews (Cambridge: Harvard Business School Press, 1989), 55.
11. Benyamin M. Lichtenstein, Beverly A. Smith and William R. Torbert, "Leadership and Ethical Development: Balancing Light and Shadow," *Business Ethics Quarterly* 5, no. 1 (1995): 100.
12. Ibid., 99.
13. Ibid., 106.
14. Ibid., 100.

15. Warren Bennis and Burt Nanus, *Leaders: Strategies for Taking Charge,* rev. ed. (New York: Harper Business, 1997), 98.
16. Henry Mintzberg, *The Rise and Fall of Strategic Planning* (Toronto: The Free Press, 1994), 175.
17. Gael M. McDonald, "Common Myths About Business Ethics: Perspectives from Hong Kong," *Business Ethics* 4, no. 2 (1995): 65.
18. "Tomorrow's Company," 9.
19. Ryuzaburo Kaku, "The Path of *Kyosei,*" *Harvard Business Review,* July-August 1997, 55.
20. Ibid., 56.
21. Ibid., 63.
22. Sharp Paine, "Managing for Organizational Integrity," 107.
23. Selznick, *The Moral Commonwealth,* 233.
24. As quoted in Leonard Boff, *Church Charisma and Power* (New York: Cross-roads, 1985), 41.
25. Rosabeth Moss Kanter, "How to Turn Firms into Good Corporations," in *Corporate Conduct Quarterly* 4, no. 4, Internet site.
26. "Business Fax," CITY-TV, Toronto, 20 August 1997.
27. Gerald F. Cavanagh, Dennis J. Moberg and Manuel Velasquez, "Making Business Ethics Practical," *Business Ethics Quarterly* 5, no. 3 (1995): 402.
28. Ibid., 403.
29. Ibid., 403.
30. Arie de Geus, "The Living Company," *Harvard Business Review,* March–April 1997, 52.
31. Ibid., 54.
32. Charles Handy, "Trust and the Virtual Organization," in *The Quest for Loyalty,* ed. Frederick Reichfeld (Cambridge: Harvard Business Press, 1996), 35.
33. Ibid., 36.
34. Joseph Des Jardins, "Virtues and Corporate Responsibility," in *Corporate Governance and Institutionalizing Ethics,* ed. Michael Hoffman, Jennifer Mills Moore and David A. Fedo (Lexington: Lexington Books, 1984), 138.
35. Selznick, *The Moral Commonwealth,* 322.
36. John Macmurray, *Reason and Emotion* (New Jersey: Humanities Press International, 1992), 58.
37. Hal Michaelson and May Anne Easley, interview by author, Hewlett-Packard, April 1997.

CHAPTER NINE

1. Hans Küng, ed., *Yes to a Global Ethic* (New York: Continuum, 1996), 3.
2. Nick Gilbert, *Financial World* 163, 16 August 1996, 21.
3. Saul W. Gellerman, "Why 'Good' Managers Make Bad Ethical Choices,"

in *Ethics in Practice,* ed. Kenneth R. Andrews (Cambridge: Harvard Business Press, 1989), 22.

4. "Seeing Things As They Really Are," *Forbes,* 10 March 1997, 128.
5. Ibid., 24.
6. Jane Collier, "The Virtuous Organization," *Business Ethics Quarterly* 4, no. 3, 144.
7. Dietrich Bonhoeffer, *Ethics* (London: SCM Press, 1955), 48.
8. Collier, "The Virtuous Organization," 144.
9. Ibid., 145.
10. Ibid., 146.
11. Lynn Sharp Paine, "Moral Thinking in Management: An Essential Capability," *Business Ethics Quarterly* 6, no. 4 (1996): 486.
12. Ian Maitland, "Virtuous Markets: The Market as School of the Virtues," *Business Ethics Quarterly* 7, no. 1 (1997): 22.
13. Ibid., 23.
14. Bill Shaw, "Sources of Virtue: The Market and the Community," *Business Ethics Quarterly* 7, no. 1 (1997): 33.
15. "Tomorrow's Company," RSA Report, 1995, 1.
16. "Denting Copper: How Far Will Japan's Massive Trading Scandal Spread?" *Maclean's,* 1 July 1996, 28.
17. James Collins and Jerry Porras, *Built to Last* (New York: Harper Business, 1994), 73.
18. Gellerman, "Why 'Good' Managers Make Bad Ethical Choices," 23.
19. Andrew Campbell and Kiran Tawadey, *Mission and Business Philosophy* (Oxford: Butterworth-Heinemann, 1990), 5.

CHAPTER TEN

1. Dietrich Bonhoeffer, *Ethics* (London: SCM Press, 1955), 48.
2. Kazuo Inamori, *For People—and for Profit: A Business Philosophy for the 21st Century* (Tokyo: Kodansha International, 1997), 72.
3. Ibid., 73.
4. John Gapper and Nicholas Denton, *All That Glitters: The Fall of Barings* (London: Hamish Hamilton, 1996), 255.
5. Ibid., 51.
6. Ibid., 341.
7. Hans Küng, *Global Responsibility: In Search of a New World Ethic* (London: SCM Press, 1991), 15.
8. Frederick F. Reichheld, "Loyalty-Based Management," in *The Quest for Loyalty: Creating Value Through Partnership,* ed. Frederick F. Reichheld (Cambridge: Harvard Business Press, 1996).
9. Ryuzaburo Kaku, "The Path of *Kyosei,*" *Harvard Business Review,* July–August (1997): 63.

CHAPTER ELEVEN

1. Cynthia Hewitt de Alcantara, ed., *Social Structures: Global Vision* (Oxford: Blackwell, and United Nations Research Institute for Social Development, 1996), 17.
2. George Soros, "The Capitalist Threat," *The Atlantic Monthly,* February 1997, 52–3.
3. Bernard Lonergan, *Method in Theology* (Toronto: University of Toronto Press, 1971), 302.
4. MarketVision Survey, 1994.
5. "Reengineering," *Financial Post Magazine,* June 1996.
6. Emile Durkheim, quoted in John E. Costello, S.J., "From Laity to the People of God," 10.
7. John Macmurray, *Reason and Emotion* (New Jersey: Humanities Press International, 1992), 3–4.
8. Patricia H. Werhane, "The Business Ethics of Risk, Reasoning and Decision Making," in *Codes of Conduct: Behavioral Research into Business Ethics,* ed. David M. Messick and Ann E. Tenbrunsel (New York: Russell Sage Foundation, 1996), 339, 331.
9. Martin Buber, *I and Thou* (New York: Charles Scribner's Sons, 1958), 28.
10. John Macmurray, *Persons in Relation* (New Jersey: Humanities Press, 1993), 91.
11. Martin Albrow, *The Global Age* (Stanford: Stanford University Press, 1997), 148.

BIBLIOGRAPHY

Ad Hoc Interfaith Working Group on Canada's Future. *Mutual Responsibility: The Tie That Binds.* 1991.

Aguilar, Francis J. *Managing Corporate Ethics.* New York: Oxford University Press, 1994.

"Aid Donors Vow War on Graft." *Globe and Mail,* 20 September 1997.

Albrow, Martin. *The Global Age.* Stanford: Stanford University Press, 1997.

"The Americans Strike Back." *The Economist,* 18 October 1997.

"And Now, Motorola Junior High." *Business Week,* 28 March 1994.

"Are These America's 'Good Old Days'? Not So Fast." *International Herald Tribune,* 19 June 1997.

Badaracco, Joseph L. *Business Ethics: Roles and Responsibilities.* Chicago: Richard D. Irwin, 1995.

"The Bank Scandal That Keeps Growing." *Fortune,* 7 July 1997.

Baron, Jonathan. "Do No Harm." In *Codes of Conduct: Behavioral Research into Business Ethics,* ed. David M. Messick and Ann E. Tenbrunsel. New York: Russell Sage Foundation, 1996.

Bennis, Warren, and Burt Nanus. *Leaders: Strategies for Taking Charge.* New York: Harper Business, 1997.

Bennis, Warren, and Patricia Ward Biederman. *Organizing Genius.* Reading: Addison-Wesley, 1997.

"The Black Market vs. the Ozone." *Business Week,* 30 June 1997.

"Blind Ambition." *Business Week,* 23 October 1995.

Boff, Leonard. *Church Charisma and Power.* New York: Crossroads, 1985.

Bibliography

Bonhoeffer, Dietrich. *Ethics*. 1955. Reprint, London: SCM Press, 1993.

Bonk, Eugene T. "The Information Revolution and Its Impact on SME Strategy." *Journal of Small Business Management* 34, no. 1 (1996).

Bouwsma, William J. "Christian Adulthood." *Daedalus,* spring 1976.

Brandenburger, Adam M., and Barry J. Nalebuff. *Co-opetition*. New York: Currency Doubleday, 1996.

Buber, Martin. *I and Thou*. New York: Charles Scribner's Sons, 1958.

"Butterflies Aren't Free." *Newsweek,* 26 May 1997.

Byrnes, Nanette. "The Smoke at General Electric." In *Post-Capitalist Society,* by Peter F. Drucker. New York: Harper Business, 1993.

Callicott, J. Baird. "Benevolent Symbiosis: The Philosophy of Conservation Reconstructed." In *Earth Summit Ethics,* by J. Baird Callicott and Fernando J.R. da Rocha. Albany: State University of New York Press, 1996.

Campbell, Andrew, and Kiran Tawadey. *Mission and Business Philosophy*. Oxford: Butterworth-Heinemann, 1990.

Carroll, Stephen J., and Martin J. Gannon. *Ethical Dimensions of International Management*. London: Sage Publications, 1997.

Cavanagh, Gerald F., Dennis J. Moberg and Manuel Velasquez. "Making Business Ethics Practical." *Business Ethics Quarterly* 5, no. 3 (1995).

Charkham, Jonathan. *Keeping Good Company*. Oxford: Oxford University Press, 1995.

"A Charter to Cheat." *The Economist,* 15 February 1997.

Cialdini, Robert. "Six Principles of Influence." In *Codes of Conduct: Behavioral Research into Business Ethics,* ed. David M. Messick and Ann E. Tenbrunsel. New York: Russell Sage Foundation, 1996.

Cialdini, Robert B. "Social Influence and the Triple Tumor Structure of Organizational Dishonesty." In *Codes of Conduct: Behavioral Research into Business Ethics,* ed. David M. Messick and Ann E. Tenbrunsel. New York: Russell Sage Foundation, 1996.

Collier, Jane. "The Virtuous Organization." *Business Ethics Quarterly* 4, no. 3.

Collins, James, and Jerry Porras. *Built to Last*. New York: Harper Business, 1994.

Costello, John. Lecture at Regis College, 4 March 1997.

Dalla Costa, John. "Managing the Profit Stream." *Financial Post Magazine,* June 1997.

Daloz Parks, Sharon. "Young Adults and the Formation of Professional Ethics." In *Can Ethics Be Taught,* ed. Thomas R. Piper, Mary C. Gentile and Sharon Daloz Parks. Cambridge: Harvard Business Press, 1993.

Daly, Herman E., and John B. Cobb. *For the Common Good.* Updated edition, Boston: Beacon Press, 1994.

Darley, John M. "How Organizations Socialize Individuals into Evildoing." In *Codes of Conduct: Behavioral Research into Business Ethics,* ed. David M. Messick and Ann E. Tenbrunsel. New York: Russell Sage Foundation, 1996.

De George, Richard T. *Competing with Integrity in International Business.* Oxford: Oxford University Press, 1993.

de Geus, Arie. *The Living Company.* London: Nicholas Brealey, 1997.

de Geus, Arie. "The Living Company." *Harvard Business Review,* March–April 1997.

"Denting Copper: How Far Will Japan's Massive Trading Scandal Spread?" *Maclean's,* 1 July 1996.

Des Jardins, Joseph. "Virtues and Corporate Responsibility." In *Corporate Governance and Institutionalizing Ethics,* ed. Michael W. Hoffman, Jennifer Mills and David A. Fedo. Lexington: Lexington Books, 1984.

"Different Outlooks." *The Economist,* 6 September 1997.

Donaldson, Thomas. "The Business Ethics of Social and Organizational Processes." In *Codes of Conduct: Behavioral Research into Business Ethics,* ed. David M. Messick and Ann E. Tenbrunsel. New York: Russell Sage Foundation, 1996.

Donaldson, Thomas, and Al Gini. *Case Studies in Business Ethics.* Upper Saddle River, N.J.: Prentice-Hall, 1996.

Driscoll, Dawn-Marie, Michael W. Hoffman and Edward S. Petry. *The Ethical Edge.* New York: Master Media, 1995.

Drucker, Peter F. *Post-Capitalist Society.* New York: Harper Business, 1993.

Dunant, Sarak, and Roy Porter. *The Age of Anxiety.* London: Virago, 1996.

Durkheim, Emile. *Elementary Forms of the Religious Life.* New York: The Free Press, 1965.

Dyson, Freeman. *Imagined Worlds.* Cambridge: Harvard University Press, 1997.

"The End of the Frontier." *The Economist,* 31 May 1997.

Etzioni, Amitai. *The Moral Dimension: Towards a New Economics.* New York: The Free Press, 1988.

Etzioni, Amitai. "Positive Aspects of Community and the Dangers of Fragmentation." In *Social Futures: Global Visions,* ed. Cynthia Hewitt de Alcantara. Oxford: Blackwell, 1997.

"Even Executives Are Wincing at Executive Pay." *Business Week,* 12 May 1997.

Bibliography

"Familiar Sins." *The Economist,* 15 March 1997.

Feynman, Richard P. *Six Not So Easy Pieces: Einstein's Relativity, Symmetry and Space.* Reading: Addison-Wesley, 1997.

Fitz-Enz, Jac. *The Eight Practices of Exceptional Companies.* New York: AMACOM, 1997.

"The 500 Largest U.S. Corporations." *Fortune Magazine,* 28 April 1997.

Flavin, Christopher. "Oil Production Rises." In *Vital Signs 1996–1997,* ed. Linda Starke. London: Earthscan, 1997.

"Forum." *Harper's,* May 1996.

"French Boardrooms Besieged." *International Herald Tribune,* 16 July 1996.

Galtung, Johan. "On the Social Costs of Modernization." In *Social Futures: Global Visions,* ed. Cynthia Hewitt de Alcantara. Oxford: Blackwell, 1997.

Gapper, John, and Nicholas Denton. *All That Glitters: The Fall of Barings.* London: Hamish Hamilton, 1996.

Gardner, Gary. "Global Trade Continues Upward." In *Vital Signs 1996–1997,* ed. Linda Starke. London: Earthscan, 1997.

Gardner, Howard. *Creating Minds.* New York: Basic Books, 1993.

Gellerman, Saul W. "Why 'Good' Managers Make Bad Ethical Choices." In *Ethics in Practice,* ed. Kenneth R. Andrews. Cambridge: Harvard Business Press, 1989.

"Generals and Politics." *The Economist,* 19 July 1997.

"The Ghost in the Machine." *Financial Post Magazine,* May 1996.

Giddens, Anthony. "Affluence, Poverty and the Idea of a Post-Scarcity Society." In *Social Futures: Global Visions,* ed. Cynthia Hewitt de Alcantara. Oxford: Blackwell, 1997.

Gillies, James. *Boardroom Renaissance: Power, Morality and Performance in the Modern Corporation.* Toronto: McGraw-Hill Ryerson, 1992.

Gini, Al, and Terry Sullivan. "A.H. Robbins: The Dalkon Shield." In *Post-Capitalist Society,* by Peter F. Drucker. New York: Harper Business, 1993.

"Global Warming: The Heat's on Bill (Clinton)." *Business Week,* 7 July 1997.

"Good Enough?" *Industry Week,* 20 February 1995.

"Good Grief." *The Economist,* 8 April 1995.

Goodin, Robert E. "Utility and the Good." In *A Companion to Ethics,* ed. Peter Singer. Cambridge: Blackwell, 1993.

Goodpaster, Kenneth E. "Ethical Imperatives and Corporate Leadership." In *Ethics in Practice,* ed. Kenneth R. Andrews. Cambridge: Harvard Business Press, 1989.

Goodpaster, Kenneth E., and Joanne B. Ciulla. "Note on the Corporation as a Moral Environment." In *Ethics in Practice,* ed. Kenneth R. Andrews. Cambridge: Harvard Business Press, 1989.

Gordon, David M. *Fat and Mean: The Corporate Squeeze of Working Americans and the Myth of Managerial Downsizing.* New York: The Free Press, 1996.

Graham, Pauline. *Integrative Management: Creating Unity from Diversity.* Oxford: Blackwell, 1991.

Green, Ronald M. "Sears Auto Shock." In *Post-Capitalist Society,* by Peter F. Drucker. New York: Harper Business, 1993.

"A Green Piece of the Action." *Management Today,* May 1997.

Haas, Robert D. "Ethics—A Global Business Challenge: Character and Courage." Speech to the Conference Board of New York, 1 June 1994.

Haldane, John. "Mediaeval and Renaissance Ethics." In *A Companion to Ethics,* ed. Peter Singer. Cambridge: Blackwell, 1993.

Hampden-Turner, Charles, and Fons Trompenaars. *Mastering the Infinite Game.* Oxford: Capstone, 1997.

"Hanbo Chief Gets Prison Term." *International Herald Tribune,* 3 June 1997.

Handy, Charles. "Rethinking Principles." In *Rethinking the Future,* ed. Rowan Gibson. London: Nicholas Brealey, 1997.

Handy, Charles. "Trust and the Virtual Organization." In *The Quest for Loyalty,* ed. Frederick Reichfeld. Cambridge: Harvard Business Press, 1996.

"Handy Homily." *The Economist Review,* 6 September 1997.

"Hard Graft in Asia: Business Ethics." *The Economist,* 25 May 1995.

Hardin, Russell. "The Psychology of Business Ethics." In *Codes of Conduct: Behavioral Research into Business Ethics,* ed. David M. Messick and Ann E. Tenbrunsel. New York: Russell Sage Foundation, 1996.

Heilbroner, Robert. *Teachings from the Worldly Philosophy.* New York: Norton, 1996.

Heilbroner, Robert. *Twenty-First Century Capitalism.* Toronto: House of Anansi, 1992.

"The Hidden Hand." *Newsweek,* 7 July 1997.

Hobbes, Thomas. *Leviathan.* London: Pelican Books, 1968.

Hobsbawm, E.J. "The Future of the State." In *Social Futures: Global Visions,* ed. Cynthia Hewitt de Alcantara. Oxford: Blackwell, 1997.

Hoffman, Michael W., Judith Brown Kamm, Robert E. Frederick and Edward S. Petry Jr. *Emerging Global Business Ethics.* Westport, Conn.: Quorum Books, 1994.

Holland, John H. *Hidden Order: How Adaptation Builds Complexity*. Reading: Addison-Wesley, 1995.

Huntington, Samuel. *The Clash of Civilizations and the Remaking of World Order*. New York: Simon & Schuster, 1996.

Inamori, Kazuo. *For People—And for Profit: A Business Philosophy for the 21st Century*. Tokyo: Kodansha International, 1997.

"Insiders, Watch Your Back." *Business Week*, 7 July 1997.

International Monetary Fund. *World Economic Outlook*. September 1997.

"In This Drug War, Consumers Are the Casualties." *Business Week*, 25 August 1997.

"The In-Your-Face Economist." *Business Week*, 30 June 1997.

"Japanese Finance Survey." *The Economist*, 28 June 1997.

Jones, Thomas O., and W. Earl Sasser Jr. "Why Satisfied Customers Defect." In *The Quest for Loyalty*, ed. Frederick Reichfeld. Cambridge: Harvard Business Press, 1996.

Kaku, Ryuzaburo. "A Call for Global Business Principles." Canon Inc. documents. Internet site, January 1997.

Kaku, Ryuzaburo. "The Path of *Kyosei*." *Harvard Business Review*, July-August 1997.

Kanter, Rosabeth Moss. "How to Turn Firms into Good Corporations." *Corporate Conduct Quarterly* 4, no. 4 (Internet site).

Kekes, John. *Moral Wisdom and Good Lives*. Ithaca: Cornell University Press, 1995.

"Kicking the Kickbacks." *The Economist*, 31 May 1997.

Knott, David G. "Vertical Integration." *Strategy and Business*, third quarter 1997.

Korten, David C. *When Corporations Rule the World*. Hartford: Berrett-Koehler, 1996.

Kotter, John P. *Matsushita Leadership*. New York: The Free Press, 1997.

Krugman, Paul. *Pop International*. Cambridge: MIT Press, 1997.

Küng, Hans. *Global Responsibility: In Search of a New Global Ethic*. London: SCM Press, 1991.

Küng, Hans, ed. *Yes to a Global Ethic*. New York: Continuum, 1996.

Küng, Hans, and Karl-Josef Kuschel. *A Global Ethic: The Declaration of the Parliament of the World's Religions*. London: SCM Press, 1993.

Kuttner, Robert. *Everything for Sale*. New York: Alfred A. Knopf, 1997.

Bibliography

Kymlicka, Will. "The Social Contract Tradition." In *A Companion to Ethics*, ed. Peter Singer. Cambridge: Blackwell, 1993.

Larudee, Mehrene. "Trade Policy: Who Wins, Who Loses?" In *Creating a New World Economy*, ed. Gerald Epstein, Julie Graham, and Jessica Nembhard. Philadelphia: Temple University Press, 1993.

Lawrence, Robert, Albert Bressand, and Takatoshi Ito. *A Vision for the World Economy: Openness, Diversity and Cohesion*. Washington, D.C.: The Brookings Institution, 1996.

Learned, Edmund P., Arch R. Dooley and Robert L. Katz. "Personal Values and Business Decisions." In *Ethics in Practice*, ed. Kenneth R. Andrews. Cambridge: Harvard Business Press, 1989.

Lee, Motoko Yasuda, and Charles L. Mulford. "Reasons Why Japanese Small Businesses Form Cooperatives." *Journal of Small Business Management* 28, no. 3 (1990).

Leibholz, G. "Memoir." In the introduction to *The Cost of Discipleship*, by Dietrich Bonhoeffer. 1948. Reprint, London: SCM Press, 1996.

Leighton, David S.R., and Donald H. Thain. *Making Boards Work*. Toronto: McGraw-Hill Ryerson, 1997.

"Levi's Is Leaving China." *Business Horizons*, March–April 1995.

Lichtenstein, Benyamin M., Beverly A. Smith and William R. Torbert. "Leadership and Ethical Development: Balancing Light and Shadow." *Business Ethics Quarterly* 5, no. 1 (1995).

Lodge, George C., and Ezra F. Vogel. *Ideology and National Competitiveness*. Cambridge: Harvard Business School Press, 1987.

Lonergan, Bernard. *Method in Theology*. Toronto: University of Toronto Press, 1971.

McDonald, Gael M. "Common Myths About Business Ethics: Perspectives from Hong Kong." *Business Ethics* 4, no. 2 (1995).

MacIntyre, Alasdair. *A Short History of Ethics*. 1966. Reprint, New York: Touchstone, 1996.

Macmurray, John. *Persons in Relation*. New Jersey: Humanities Press, 1993.

Macmurray, John. *Reason and Emotion*. New Jersey: Humanities Press International, 1992.

Maitland, Ian. "Virtuous Markets: The Market as School of the Virtues." *Business Ethics Quarterly* 7, no. 1 (1997).

"March of the Roadhogs: Detroit Vies to Turn Out the Biggest and Baddest." *International Herald Tribune*, 18 June 1997.

Bibliography

Michaelson, Hal, and May Anne Easley, chief counsel, Hewlett-Packard, interview with author, April 1997.

"Microsoft to Pirates: Pretty Please?" *Business Week,* 22 September 1997.

Midgley, Mary. *Heart and Mind.* New York: St. Martin's Press, 1981.

Midgley, Mary. "The Origin of Ethics." In *A Companion to Ethics,* ed. Peter Singer. Cambridge: Blackwell, 1993.

Mintzberg, Henry. *The Rise and Fall of Strategic Planning.* Toronto: The Free Press, 1994.

"The Mob on Wall Street." *Business Week,* 16 December 1996.

Moggridge, D.E. *Maynard Keynes: An Economist's Biography.* London: Routledge, 1992.

Monseau, Mac. "Beware the Potential Client. He May Be a Spy." Internet file from *Independent Newspapers,* 1997.

Moore, James F. *The Death of Competition: Leadership and Strategy in the Age of Business Ecosystems.* New York: Harper Business, 1995.

Moran, Gabriel. *A Grammar of Responsibility.* New York: The Crossroad Publishing Company, 1996.

"Mountie Misery." *Maclean's,* 28 July 1997.

Nadler, Gerald, and Shozo Hibino. *Breakthrough Thinking: The Seven Principles of Creative Problem Solving.* Rocklin, Calif.: Prima Publishing, 1994.

"New Power." *The Economist,* 30 August 1997.

Nonaka, Ikujiro, and Hirotaka Takeuchi. *The Knowledge-Creating Company.* New York: Oxford University Press, 1995.

"OECD Sets Date for Law on Bribery." *Financial Times,* 24 and 25 May 1997.

Olin, Jeffrey, and Vincent Barry. *Applying Ethics.* Belmont, Calif.: Wadsworth, 1992.

"1-800-22-ETHIC." *Financial World,* 16 August 1994.

O'Neil, Onora. "Kantian Ethics." In *A Companion to Ethics,* ed. Peter Singer. Cambridge: Blackwell, 1993.

O'Shea, James, and Charles Madigan. *Dangerous Company: The Consulting Powerhouses and the Businesses They Save and Ruin.* New York: Times Business, 1997.

Paine, Lynn Sharp. "Managing for Organizational Integrity." *Harvard Business Review,* March–April 1994.

Paine, Lynn Sharp. "Moral Thinking in Management: An Essential Capability." *Business Ethics Quarterly* 6, no. 4 (1996).

Bibliography

Paret, Peter, ed. *Makers of Modern Strategy: From Machiavelli to the Nuclear Age.* Princeton: Princeton University Press, 1986.

Petersen, Erik R. "Looming Collision of Capitalisms?" In *New Forces in the World Economy.* Cambridge: MIT Press, 1996.

Plender, John. *A Stake in the Future: The Stakeholding Solution.* London: Nicholas Brealey, 1997.

"Prodi Trial Decision Delayed." *International Herald Tribune,* 1 July 1997.

Prokesch, Steven E. "Competing on Customer Service: An Interview with British Airways' Sir Colin Marshall." In *The Quest for Loyalty,* ed. Frederick Reichfeld. Cambridge: Harvard Business Press, 1996.

"Quick-Change Artists." *Business Week,* 1 September 1997.

Reich, Robert. "Sky and Ground." *The New Yorker,* 1 September 1997.

Reichfeld, Frederick F. "Loyalty-Based Management." In *The Quest for Loyalty.* Cambridge: Harvard Business Press, 1996.

Rescher, Nicholas. *Ethical Idealism: An Inquiry into the Nature and Function of Ideals.* Berkeley: University of California Press, 1992.

Rifkin, Jeremy. *Algeny.* New York: Penguin, 1984.

"Rights and Wrongs." *Financial Times,* 18 March 1997.

Robinson, Marilynne. "Dietrich Bonhoeffer." In *Martyrs,* ed. Susan Bergman. San Francisco: HarperCollins, 1996.

"Royal Tries New Insurance Path." *Financial Post,* 26 August 1997.

Saez, Hector. "The Latin American Environment." In *Creating a New World Economy,* ed. Gerald Epstein, Julie Graham and Jessica Nembhard. Philadelphia: Temple University Press, 1993.

Schanberg, Sydney H., and Marie Dorigny. "Six Cents an Hour." *Life,* June 1996.

Schilling, David. "Sneakers and Sweatshops: Holding Corporations Accountable." *The Christian Century,* 9 October 1996.

Schneewind, J.B. "Modern Moral Philosophy." In *A Companion to Ethics,* ed. Peter Singer. Cambridge: Blackwell, 1993.

Schor, Juliet B. "Global Equity and Environmental Crisis." In *Creating a New World Economy,* ed. Gerald Epstein, Julie Graham and Jessica Nembhard. Philadelphia: Temple University Press, 1993.

"Second Thoughts About Globalisation." *The Economist,* 21 June 1997.

"Seeing Things As They Really Are." *Forbes,* 10 March 1997.

Selznick, Philip. *The Moral Commonwealth: Social Theory and the Promise of Community.* Berkeley: University of California Press, 1992.

Senge, Peter. "Rethinking Control and Complexity." In *Rethinking the Future,* ed. Rowan Gibson. London: Nicholas Brealey, 1997.

Shaw, Bill. "Sources of Virtue: The Market and the Community." *Business Ethics Quarterly* 7, no. 1 (1997).

Singer, Peter, ed. *A Companion to Ethics.* Cambridge: Blackwell, 1993.

Soros, George. "The Capitalist Threat." *Atlantic Monthly,* February 1997.

"Spinning Paper from Straw." *Equinox,* September 1997.

Stewart, Thomas A. *Intellectual Capital.* New York: Currency Doubleday, 1997.

Stroh, Linda K., and Anne H. Reilly. "Loyalty in the Age of Downsizing." *Sloan Management Review,* summer 1997.

"Stuck in Their Ways." *Newsweek,* 9 June 1997.

"Taiwan the Wasteland." *The Economist,* 31 May 1997.

Taormina, Tom. *Virtual Leadership and the ISO 9000 Imperative.* Upper Saddle River, N.J.: Prentice-Hall, 1996.

Texaco. Press release. 15 November 1996.

"Texaco's High Octane Racism Problems." *Time,* 25 November 1996.

Thompson, Deborah. *Greed: Investment Fraud in Canada and Around the Globe.* Toronto: Viking, 1997.

"3 More Japan Firms Linked to Payoffs." *International Herald Tribune,* 1 July 1997.

Thurow, Lester. *The Future of Capitalism.* New York: Penguin, 1996.

Thurow, Lester. *Head to Head.* New York: William Morrow and Company, 1992.

Thurow, Lester. "Rethinking the World." In *Rethinking the Future,* ed. Rowan Gibson. London: Nicholas Brealey, 1997.

Thurow, Lester. "Surging Inequality and Falling Real Wages." In *The American Corporation Today,* ed. Carl Kaysen. New York: Oxford University Press, 1996.

Trompenaars, Fons. *Riding the Waves of Culture: Understanding Diversity in Global Business.* Chicago: Irwin Professional, 1993 and 1994.

Tunali, Odil. "Carbon Emissions Hit All-Time High." In *Vital Signs 1996–1997,* ed. Linda Starke. London: Earthscan, 1997.

Tunali, Odil. "Global Temperature Sets New Record." In *Vital Signs 1996–1997,* ed. Linda Starke. London: Earthscan, 1997.

"Unfinished Business." *Business Week,* 9 September 1996.

Bibliography

von Weizsacker, Richard. "Towards a Shared Global Ethic." In *Yes to a Global Ethic,* ed. Hans Küng. New York: Continuum, 1996.

von Weizsacker, R., A.B. Lovins and L.H. Lovins. *Factor Four: Doubling Wealth and Halving Resource Use.* London: Earthscan, 1997.

Waitzer, Edward J. "Model Behaviour." *CA Magazine,* August 1997.

Waterman, Robert. Quoted in "Tomorrow's Company: The Role of Business in a Changing World." In *Frontiers of Excellence.* London: RSA, 1995.

Wattles, Jeffrey. *The Golden Rule.* Oxford: Oxford University Press, 1996.

Webley, Simon. "The Interfaith Declaration: Constructing a Code of Ethics for International Business." *Business Ethics,* January 1996.

Weiss, Joseph W. *Organizational Behavior and Change.* Minneapolis/St. Paul: West Publishing, 1996.

Werhane, Patricia H. "The Business Ethics of Risk, Reasoning and Decision Making." In *Codes of Conduct: Behavioral Research into Business Ethics,* ed. David M. Messick and Ann E. Tenbrunsel. New York: Russell Sage Foundation, 1996.

"What's News." *Wall Street Journal,* 26 August 1997.

Wiesel, Elie. "Towards an Ethic Which Honours Humankind and the Creator." In *Yes to a Global Ethic,* ed. Hans Küng. New York: Continuum, 1996.

Wilson, Edward O. *The Diversity of Life.* New York: Norton, 1996.

Wolman, William, and Anne Colamosca. *The Judas Economy: The Triumph of Capital and the Betrayal of Work.* Reading: Addison-Wesley, 1997.

"Work and Family." *Business Week,* 15 September 1997.

"The World's Most Admired Companies." *Fortune,* 27 October 1997.

Wright, Lesley, and Marti Smye. *Corporate Abuse.* Toronto: Key Porter Books, 1996.

Wright, Robert. *The Moral Animal: Why We Are the Way We Are.* New York: Vintage Books, 1995.

INDEX

A

Abstraction of harm, 78–79
Ad Hoc Interfaith Working Group, 128–29, 133–34
Advertising expense, 19–20
Aguilar, Francis J., 78
A.H. Robins Co., 77–78, 80–81, 115
Ahtisaari, Martti, 31
Akiyama, Tomichi, 252–53
Albrow, Martin, 15, 20, 21, 120, 313
Alcantara, Cynthia Hewitt de, 18, 303
Alcoa, 158–59, 160
Alignment, ethical, 146, 148, 234–36, 256, 287–93
Allen, Robert, 274
Allied Chemical Company, 84
Andrews, Kenneth, 53
Anscombe, Elizabeth, 246
Applications of EO, *see* Strat-Ethic approach
Aquinas, Thomas, 24, 233
Archer Daniels Midland (ADM), 41–42, 102, 115, 209, 225, 248
Aristotle, 246, 251, 306
Asian economies, 313
Attentiveness, in conversion, 305, 306, 307, 310
Authority, acquiescence to, 82

B

Badaracco, Joseph L., Jr., 23, 24, 111
Ballard Energy Systems, 195
Bankers Trust, 283, 284
Banks, *see* Financial institutions; Swiss banks

and Holocaust
Barings Bank, 8, 21, 101, 209, 216, 284–85
Baron, Jonathan, 23
Barry, Vincent, 166–67
Bausch & Lomb, 85–86, 101, 115, 216
Beck, Ulrich, 121
Benefits from EO, 250–51, 301, 318–19
    cooperation with partners and suppliers, 195–203
    customer loyalty, 179–85, 208–9
    employee commitment, 185–95
    summary, 204
Bennis, Warren, 56, 191, 204, 214–15, 256
Berry, Thomas, 134
Bird, Frederick B., 79
Boards
    in EO model, 146, 147, 287–88
    ethical obligations, 207–10, 214
Bonhoeffer, Dietrich, 9–10
    on idolization of success, 82, 99, 211
    on limits of duty, 229, 246–47, 266
    living a belief, 12, 143, 237, 242, 263
    other comments, 34, 65, 92, 111–12, 205
    on responsibility, 117, 121, 247, 266
    self and community, 29, 175, 189, 302
Bouwsma, William J., 128
Boycotting by customers, 112, 181, 308
Brandenburger, Adam M., 197, 253
Bre-X scandal, 70, 72, 74
Bressand, Albert, 27, 28
British Airways, 181–82, 183, 202, 228
Buber, Martin, 312–13
Buchman, Frank, 134–35
Burke, James, 217
Business Week, 43, 56, 67, 74, 83–84, 85, 187, 209
Byrnes, Nanette, 172

C

Callicott, J. Baird, 169–70
Campbell, Andrew, 255
Canada
    Ad Hoc Interfaith Working Group, 128–29, 133–34
    corruption in business, 70, 73–75
Canon, 219
Car companies, 195–97
    see also Chrysler; Ford; General Motors
Caring, 139, 168, 228–29, 292–93
Caux Principles, 129, 134–37
Cavanagh, Gerald F., 228, 229
CEOs
    in EO model, 146, 288–89, 291
    vital for ethical orientation, 210–15

Index

Index

Gellerman, Saul W., 243, 246, 255
General Electric, 81, 225, 248
  ethical leadership opportunity, 172–74
General Motors, 79–80, 197
  confidential documents, 244–45
  export of defective cars, 106
  housing program in Mexico, 167–68
Geneva Convention, 31
Gerstner, Louis, 194
Giddens, Anthony, 14, 19
Gillette, 162
Gillies, James, 209–10
Glendon, Barbara, 167–68
Global community
  formation of a just community, 168–69
  human need for, 28, 120–21, 206–7, 313
  outpaced by global economy, 20–21, 313
Global economy
  assets and liabilities, 116
  costs index, 90–91
  dynamic nature, 303
  limits, 12–14, 36, 37
  needs ethical guidance, 55, 62, 97, 135–37, 313, 319
  obsession with economic concerns, 58–62, 311–12
  problems, 15–17, 26–28, 33, 157–58
Global ethic
  challenges exclusivity, 224, 226, 227
  corporate ethical virtues, 246–52
  critical ethical factors (CEFs), 242–46, 275, 286, 298
  EO model *see* Ethical orientation (EO) model
  evolution of relations, 229–32
  factors for success, 118–19, 238, 256–57, 320
  GE's leadership chance, 172–74
  implementing, 312–20
  mutuality *see* Mutuality
  self and community, 103–4, 118, 122–23, 126, 138, 149, 151, 232–34
  shared basic ideas, 127–42, 189
  variety in practice, 238–39, 260, 264
  see also Caux Principles; *Declaration Toward a Global Ethic*; Ethical orientation; Interfaith Declaration; *Tie That Binds, The*
Global ethic, applications
  financial services, 285–93
  Microsoft and Nike, 296–301
  Swiss banks, 266–73
  telecom companies, 275–83
Global warming, 49–50, 98
Golden Rule, 130, 132, 141–42, 150, 160
Goodpaster, Kenneth E., 95, 113, 214
Gordon, David, 46–47, 88

Governments
  intervention in economy, 26–27, 54
  standardization of laws, 107
Graham, Pauline, 31
Greed, 67–68, 75, 83
"Green," 4, 50
Green, Ronald, 154
Greenpeace, 16, 31, 84
Group dynamics, 146, 223–32, 290–91
Grove, Andy, 200
Growth, slowing, 15, 35–36, 46–47, 159, 179–80

H

Haas, Robert D., 109–10, 348
Habits, 247–48, 251–52
  breaking, 256–57
Hamanaka, Yasuo, 252–53
Hammer, Michael, 308
Handy, Charles, 43, 59, 99, 198, 230, 231
Hausman, Jerry, 169
Heilbroner, Robert, 26–27
Helsinki Process, 31
Herkstroter, Cornelius, 32
Hewlett-Packard, 191–92, 194, 200, 204, 227
  code of ethics, 234–36
Hobsbawm, E.J., 26
Hoffman, Michael W., 156
Holland, John H., 150
Holocaust, 82, 124, 157, 246
  accounts in Swiss banks, 91, 264–73
Homelessness, 47–48
Honda, advantages of teamwork, 187–88, 189
Honesty, 132, 139, 153, 183, 191, 200, 231, 300
  downsizing, 280, 282
  imperative explained, 163–66
  Swiss banks, 267–68, 271, 272, 273
Hong Kong, crime in, 70–71, 73
Human rights, 126, 130, 137, 158–60, 238, 319
  see also Dignity
Huntington, Samuel, 16–17, 19, 25, 60, 226
Hypocrisy, 43, 94–95, 217

I

Iacocca, Lee, 108
IBM, 56–57, 177, 194, 218–19, 220
Ideologies, 151–52, 304
Implementing ethics, *see* Strat-Ethic approach
Inamori, Kazuo, 276
Inclusion, 218–19, 251

Index

Income differences, 14, 15, 47, 86, 101, 161
Income growth, flat in America, 15, 46–47, 159, 179–80
Individual and community
  balance needed, 28, 103–5, 138, 151
  ethical framework, 104, 118, 122–23, 126, 149, 151, 232–34
  identity achieved in relation, 109, 312–13
Indonesia, fires in, 103
INSEAD business school, 129, 135
Institute for International Economics, 88
Institution and individual, 82, 118
Integrity, 139, 191–92, 209, 214, 221–22, 234–36
Intel, 200
Intelligence, in conversion, 305, 307, 309, 310
Interdependence, 28, 128, 148, 254
Interfaith Declaration, 128, 131–33
International Monetary Fund, 13, 22
Internet and privacy, 242
Intervention by governments, 26–27, 27–28, 54
"Invisible hand," 27, 28, 52, 312
Italy, political corruption, 67, 70
Ito, Takatoshi, 27, 28

J

Japan, corruption, *see* Nomura Securities
Jennings, John, 32, 208–9
Johnson & Johnson, 22, 81, 217–18
Johnston, Chalmers, xi–xii
Jones, Thomas O., 180, 185
Jung, Carl, 228
Justice, 89, 153, 183, 193, 201, 231, 282, 293, 298, 300, 311
  imperative explained, 166–69
  key interfaith concept, 132, 133, 139
  Swiss banks, 267, 268–69, 271, 273

K

Kaku, Ryuzaburo, 137, 218, 219, 220, 296
Kant, Immanuel, 130, 233
Kanter, Rosabeth Moss, 226–27
Katz, Robert, 211
Kekes, John, 119, 122, 152
Kellogg's, 180
Keynes, John Maynard, 37, 76
Knight, Phil, 294
Knott, David G., 196, 198
Korea, corruption in, 70, 73
Korten, David, 19–20, 132
Krugman, Paul, 14, 33

Kung, Hans
  on a global ethic, 6–8, 30, 120, 126, 128, 129–30, 239, 314
  on religious convictions, 7, 25, 239
  on self and community, 28, 62, 103
Kuschel, Karl-Josef, 128, 129–30
Kymlicka, Will, 166
Kyosei, 219–20

L

Labor abuse, 3, 6, 158–59, 294
Larudee, Mehrene, 53
Lawrence, Robert, 27, 28
Laws, inadequacy, 105–10, 125
Layoffs, *see* Downsizing
Leadership, 100, 210–15, 279
Learned, Edmund P., 211
Lee, Motoko Yasuda, 46
Leeson, Nick, 21, 216, 224, 284, 285
Leibholz, G., 9–10
Leopold, Aldo, 170, 171
Levi Strauss, 109–10, 162, 167, 183
Lichtenstein, Benyamin, 212–13
Lies, 39–64, 164
Lonergan, Bernard, 305–6, 307
Longevity of companies, 229–30
Lovins, Amory B., 50, 55, 85
Lovins, L. Hunter, 50, 55, 85
Luttwak, Edward, 101

M

McDonald, Gael M., 217
McDonald's, 108
MacIntyre, Alasdair, 233, 246, 247
Maclean's magazine, 67
McLuhan, Marshall, 5
Macmurray, John, 6, 103–4, 109, 124, 128, 233–34, 312
Madigan, Charles, 176
Maitland, Ian, 249–50, 251
Management and ethics, 146, 149, 244–45, 258, 287–92, 297
  communicating purpose, 318
  moral considerations avoided, 79, 308
  responsibility, 270, 279
  strategic clarity, 146, 154–57, 289
  see also Boards; CEOs; Fallacies of pessimism
Manville Corporation, 243
Marshall, Sir Colin, 181–82
Matsushita, Konosuke, 193
Maturity, 120–21, 124, 128, 129, 222–23, 260–61

Index

Tawadey, Kiran, 255
Teams at work, 44–45, 226, 290
  accomplishments at Honda, 187–89
Technology
  and corruption in business, 75
  increases wage gap, 64
  magnifies power for harm, 157
  reduces personal contact, 64, 292
Telephone companies and ethical downsizing, 274–83
Tenbrunsel, Ann E., 82
Texaco
  costs of poor ethics, 102, 112, 114
  race bias, 87–88, 101, 104, 105, 108, 110
  remorse not enough, 92–93, 96, 168, 240–41
Texas Instruments, 95
Thompson, Deborah, 74, 75, 76
3M, 192, 193–94
Thurow, Lester, 17, 21, 44–45, 47, 169, 171
Tie That Binds, The, 133–34, 171
Tobacco companies, 105, 114, 223, 224
Torbert, William, 212–13
Toyota, 201
Trade
  multilateral, 136
  world trade and world production, 33
Tradeoffs
  between global and local, 19
  wage increases for time off, 35–36
Trompenaars, Fons, 140
Trust, 113, 125, 135, 146, 189–90, 195, 198, 204, 230–32, 292
Trustworthiness, 230, 245, 249, 251, 291–92
Truthfulness, *see* Integrity
Turner, Charles Hampden, 247

U

Unethical business conduct, *see* Barings Bank; Corruption; Ford Pinto; Swiss banks and Holocaust; Texaco
United Nations, 16
  Charter of Responsibility, 263
  Charter of Rights, 238
  Conference on Trade and Development (UNCTAD), 13
  Research Institute for Social Development, 18
"Unlearning" old ways, 257, 258, 270, 279, 297
Updating EO, 260, 273, 283, 301

V

Values, 22–23, 123, 124, 151–52

in relationships, *see* Relational equity
religious, *see* Religion
sources of moral values, 24–25
Vardey, Lucinda, 6
Velasquez, Manuel, 228, 229
Virgin Islands, 73
Virtual organization, 230
Virtues, 246–52, 267–68, 275–77
Vision, 298
Von Weizsacker, Richard, 22, 32, 50, 55, 85

W

Wage gap, *see* Income differences
Waitzer, Edward J., 177, 178, 202
Wal-Mart, 123
Wars, global economy recovering from, 33
Waste, 50, 55
  see also Sustainability
Waterman, Robert, 208
Waters, James A., 79
Wattles, Jeffrey, 160
Webb, Allen, 111
Webley, Simon, 131
Weiss, Joseph W., 88–89
Welch, Jack, 172–74
Werhane, Patricia H., 312
Williams, George, 119
Wilson, Edward O., 45
Wolfensohn, James, 22
Wolman, William, 80, 86, 161, 179
Women
  feminization of business, 168, 227–29
  inequities in business, 38, 227
Woods, Tiger, 295
World Bank, 22
World Watch Institute, 13, 49
World Wildlife Fund, 16
Wurman, Robert, 164
Wyschogrod, Edith, 157

X

Xerox, 180, 184, 204

Y

Youth unemployment, 48